Recovery or Relapse in the Global Economy

Recovery or Relapse in the Global Economy

Comparative Perspectives on Restructuring in Central America

Edited by
Jolyne Melmed-Sanjak
Carlos E. Santiago
and
Alvin Magid

Westport, Connecticut
London

Library of Congress Cataloging-in-Publication Data

Recovery or relapse in the global economy : comparative perspectives
on restructuring in Central America / edited by Jolyne Melmed-
Sanjak, Carlos E. Santiago, and Alvin Magid.
    p. cm.
  Includes bibliographical references and index.
  ISBN 0-275-94605-3 (alk. paper)
  1. Central America–Economic conditions–1979- 2. Central
America–Economic policy. 3. Structural adjustment (Economic
policy)–Central America. I. Melmed-Sanjak, Jolyne. II. Santiago,
Carlos Enrique. III. Magid, Alvin.
HC141.R425 1994
338.9728–dc20   93-17117

British Library Cataloguing in Publication Data is available.

Library of Congress Catalog Card Number: 93-17117
ISBN: 0-275-94605-3

First published in 1993

Praeger Publishers, 88 Post Road West, Westport, CT 06881
An imprint of Greenwood Publishing Group, Inc.

Printed in the United States of America

∞™

The paper used in this book complies with the
Permanent Paper Standard issued by the National
Information Standards Organization (Z39.48-1984).

10 9 8 7 6 5 4 3 2 1

The editors and publisher gratefully acknowledge permission for use of the following material:

Reprinted from *Reindustrializing New York State: Strategies, Implications, Challenges* by Morton
Schoolman and Alvin Magid, eds., by permission of the State University of New York Press. © 1986
State University of New York Press.

Contents

Figures and Tables   ix

Acknowledgments   xi

I. Perspectives on Central American Development and Change   1

ONE: Economics and Politics in Central American
       Development: An Overview   3
       Jolyne Melmed-Sanjak, Alvin Magid, and
       Carlos E. Santiago

TWO: Costa Rica in the 1980s: A Balance of Social
       Development   13
       José Luis Vega Carballo

II. Themes in the Restructuring of the Political Economy   41

THREE: External Debt, Structural Adjustment, and
       the Labor Market   43
       Carlos E. Santiago

FOUR: The Dynamics of Agrarian Policy in United
        States History: Implications for Contemporary
        Central America   61
        Jolyne Melmed-Sanjak

FIVE: Structural Adjustment and Honduran Agriculture:
        Some Considerations   79
        Hugo Noé Pino

SIX: Industrial Democracy and Reindustrialization:
        Cross-Cultural Perspectives   103
        Alvin Magid

SEVEN: The Future of Cooperativism in Central
        America: Elements for Discussion   129
        Marielos Rojas Viquez

EIGHT: The Future Role of Multinational Enterprise
        and Foreign Direct Investment   143
        Walter Goldstein

NINE: Political Integration: A Central American Option   161
        Carlos A. Astiz

III. Recovery or Relapse: Reflections on Central
America in the New World Order   179

TEN: Central American External Debt in the
        Context of Economic Globalization   181
        Jorge González del Valle

ELEVEN: Central America in the Global Economy   191
        Alvaro de la Ossa

TWELVE: Understanding Economic Integration:
        Its Role and Reason in Central America   201
        Dante Ramírez

Contents vii

References 209

Index 225

Contributors 237

Figures and Tables

FIGURES

3.1 A Multisectoral Framework for the Analysis of Labor
    Market Change   54

TABLES

1.1 Selected Socioeconomic Indicators for Central America   5

2.1 Consumer Price Index and Nominal Average Salary for
    Costa Rica (June, 1976-1990)   25

2.2 Socio-Occupational Structure of the Employed and
    Unemployed Costa Rican Population (1980-1989)   27

3.1 Principal Economic Indicators for Latin America and
    the Caribbean, 1980-1990   45

7.1 Number of Cooperatives and Associated Members in
    Central America, by Country, 1952-1988   131

7.2 Number of Cooperatives by Economic Activity and
    Country, 1990   132

7.3 Number of Members of Cooperatives by Economic
    Activity and Country, 1990   135

7.4 Number of Cooperatives and Associated Members in
    Central America, by Country and Economic
    Sector, 1990   136

7.5 Percentage Contribution of Cooperatives to Total
    National Product, by Country and Principal Product   137

9.1 Public and Private International Debt in 1970 and
     1986 (in millions of U.S. dollars)   163
9.2 International Debt Service as a Percentage of the
     Gross Domestic Product and of Exports, 1970
     and 1986   164
9.3 Average Growth Rate of the Gross Domestic Product,
     1965-86, and Changes in the Terms of Trade,
     1984 and 1986 (1980=100)   165
9.4 Distribution of Income in Selected Countries Share
     of Gross Domestic Product: 1970-1986   166
9.5 Aggregate Indices of Political Participation, Culture
     and Welfare: 1980   173
9.6 Aggregate Indices of Education, Health, Defense,
     and Economic Performance: 1980   174
9.7 Aggregate Indices of Political Participation, Culture
     and Welfare: 1983   174
9.8 Aggregate Indices of Education, Health, Defense,
     and Economic Performance: 1983   175

Acknowledgments

Recovery or Relapse in the Global Economy: Comparative Perspectives on Restructuring in Central America represents the culmination of several years of intellectual exchange on two fronts, in the State University of New York at Albany and at the University of Costa Rica in San José. The idea of bringing together U.S. and Central American scholars from diverse disciplines to explore issues of political economy was first broached to the University at Albany's Department of Latin American and Caribbean Studies by Sergio Reuben Soto, a visiting scholar in late 1990 from the University of Costa Rica. For nearly a year thereafter, three social scientists in the University at Albany, Robert Carmack, Jolyne Melmed-Sanjak, and Alvin Magid, met frequently to plan a conference on "Reorganizing the Political Economy: U.S. and Central American Perspectives."

Financial and logistical support for the week-long conference, held at the University of Costa Rica in November 1991, was provided by the Consortium for Legislative Development, through the Center for Legislative Development in the State University of New York at Albany. We are grateful to Abdo Baaklini, director of the Center for Legislative Development, and his staff, including Charles Dawson, Clare Yates, Elizabeth Campisi, Jorge Bela, and Ana Fiorella Carvajal. At the University of Costa Rica, Sergio Reuben Soto and his colleagues worked tirelessly on local arrangements.

The conference was inaugurated by the rector of the University of Costa Rica, Luis Garita Bonilla. Papers were presented by twelve scholars, six from the State University of New York at Albany and an equal number from various countries in Central America. Also participating in the conference were Milton Henríquez, a member of the National Assembly of Panama, and Rosemarie Karpinsky, a scholar at the University of Costa Rica and former president of Costa Rica's National Assembly.

For assisting us to ready *Recovery or Relapse in the Global Economy* for publication, we are especially grateful to Karen Davis, Anne Kiefer, Cathryn Lee, and William Neenan, at Praeger Publishers; Edna Acosta-Belén, director, and Sandra Pullyblank, at the Center for Latin America and the Caribbean in the State University of New York at Albany; and Librada Pimentel-Brown and Donna LaHue, in the University at Albany's Department of Latin American and Caribbean Studies and Department of Economics, respectively. We are grateful, too, to Carol Inskip for preparing the index.

It is our hope that more intellectual exchanges between the State University of New York at Albany, the University of Costa Rica in San José, and the scholarly community throughout Central America will result

Albany, New York   Jolyne Melmed-Sanjak
July 1993   Carlos E. Santiago
                                                          Alvin Magid

I

Perspectives on Central American Development and Change

One

Economics and Politics in Central American Development: An Overview

Jolyne Melmed-Sanjak, Alvin Magid,
and Carlos E. Santiago

Political developments in Central America over the past decade have been profound. We have seen the end of civil war in Nicaragua and El Salvador, the U.S. invasion of Panama, and the general movement toward democratic reform, which holds out the prospect of economic advance. Yet, the region continues to exhibit sluggish economic growth in those countries with the most favorable economic prospects and virtual stagnation in the others—a condition which contrasts strikingly with that obtaining on a wider international economic front. In the international case, change has been dramatic and deep. For example, international capital flows, worldwide movements of production facilities, and the structure of internal markets have all been heavily influenced by transnational corporations. Moreover, trading blocs have begun to appear, an inevitable development perhaps, given economic restructuring and the globalization of production. It is likely that these international trends and events, among others, will play a key role in determining the paths that are chosen to promote economic growth and development within the Central American republics.

The processes for achieving economic recovery, political stability, and democratic reform in Central America are essentially interdependent and, at the moment, extremely precarious. To the extent that fundamental economic issues are not resolved and individuals and groups in society view their living standards as subject to long-term decline, pressure may build for authoritarian regimes with their imposed solutions. This is apt to be the case particularly where mechanisms for the intergenerational transmission of wealth remain blocked. It is one thing for adults to realize that their prospects for economic advance are limited; it is quite another for them to feel that their children will not be better off.

Within Central America, only Costa Rica has shown impressive resilience and impetus for economic recovery; most of its neighbors have continued to languish. But even in Costa Rica, per capita income is lower than it was ten years ago. Nevertheless, most analysts agree that the worst of the debt crisis confronting the Central American republics is over and that the low point of the region's economic depression has already been reached. In each country, institutional support mechanisms have been stretched to the limit to prevent the standard of living from deteriorating still further. Given the dramatic decline in the economic base of all the Central American countries, it is likely that even marginal improvements in productivity and infrastructure will yield economic gains. Although this is a real hope, the likelihood is that the recovery will continue at its present slow, but steady, pace.

The changes occurring in the international arena have already had a significant impact on Central America and its prospects for renewed economic development. What role is there for Central America in the global economic configurations that are emerging? How will the various national economies in the region balance the need for foreign capital, modern technology, and international liquidity with that of having to promote widespread economic development? A great paradox marked the economy and politics in Central America in the 1980s: economic stagnation and a declining standard of living throughout the region, accompanied by movement toward a democratic institutionalism. In that decade, the traditional way of responding to economic crisis, that is, resorting to political authoritarianism, was cast aside in favor of broadening the base of social participation in political life. Credit for that remarkable development goes partly to a U.S. administration which promoted the cause of democratic pluralism with increased privatization in the economic sphere, and partly to Central America's military elites who had the good sense to loosen the political fetters. Decisions taken in Central America to turn the political corner, as it were, testify to the impressive resilience and strength of the people in most countries of the region who supported a transition to democratic rule in the face of persistent domestic political and economic pressure to follow the well-worn authoritarian path.

But alas, there still remains the problem of the Central American economies lagging far behind politics in the race to reform. Table 1.1 presents some basic indicators that attest to the depth of the economic crisis in the region and the prospects for a painfully slow recovery

Table 1.1
Selected Socioeconomic Indicators for Central America

Countries	Population (millions) mid-1990s	GDP per capita (millions of 1988$) 1989	GDP per capita Growth Rate (1981-1990)	Gross Domestic Investment (% growth 1981-1989)
Costa Rica	2.8	1,659	-0.6	2.2
El Salvador	5.2	1,074	-2.3	-0.9
Guatemala	9.2	888	-2.2	0.6
Honduras	5.1	913	-1.2	2.3
Nicaragua	3.9	694	-5.0	-1.7
Panama	2.4	1,890	-2.1	0.0

Source: Inter-American Development Bank, *Economic and Social Progress in Latin America*. Baltimore: Johns Hopkins University Press, 1990.

over the long term. Not only does the gross domestic product (GDP) remain low; as of 1990, it continued to show a declining trend from its 1980 base for all countries in the region. Moreover, although some slight recuperation in the growth of domestic investment is evident in Costa Rica and Honduras, for the most part the base is low and the trend suggests considerable stagnation in net capital formation over the 1980s. These conditions, coupled with the limited size of domestic markets, suggest that cooperation, perhaps in the form of regional political and economic integration and/or the search for foreign markets, constitutes the limited choice set for an effective regional development strategy. This simultaneous promotion of inward- and outward-looking strategies is not mutually exclusive and could form the basis for a lasting economic renewal.

A number of recently published books on the state of the Central American economies attest to the strong academic and policy interests in the political economy of Central America. These books focus on, among other issues, the factors that contributed to the making of the economic crisis in Central America; the trade-offs between internally oriented and externally focused development strategies; the future role of the Central American Common Market; the promotion of an export policy based on non-traditional goods; the continuing external debt and dependence on foreign direct investment; the depletion of natural resources; and the political economy of policy reform. In a review dealing with these books, Zuvekas (1992) concludes by asking the key question confronting Central America: "Will...liberalizing policy reforms...reduce poverty, narrow income inequalities, and make the process of economic growth more sustainable? By 1995 [he conjectures], we may know some of the answers" (p. 150).

The present volume contributes directly to this important intellectual and policy debate but is distinguishable from many of the studies highlighted in Zuvekas's review. *Recovery or Relapse in the Global Economy: Comparative Perspectives on Restructuring in Central America* has its genesis in a process of review and discussion undertaken by policymakers together with academics representing a wide range of social science disciplines. Such cross-disciplinary interaction is largely absent from much of the scholarly literature on contemporary Central America. Our own experience has led us to conclude that, whatever their academic disciplines, scholars of political economy and public policy are likely to benefit along with practitioners of the policy art from sustained discourse on important issues of common concern.

Our experience has further underscored that dissonant voices can provide a special enrichment in the aforesaid enterprise. In a time of such dramatic change as the 1980s were and the 1990s are for Central America and for the world, it is increasingly difficult to examine and understand contemporary issues from the vantage point of any one academic discipline. Therefore, the analyses that inform some of the essays in this volume deal with important facets of political, economic, and social life in contemporary Central America from an explicitly multidisciplinary perspective.

Recovery or Relapse in the Global Economy brings together authors from the disciplines of economics, sociology, and political science. Perhaps more important, each author seeks to transcend the traditional limits of his or her discipline to arrive at a multidisciplinary perspective. None of the authors seeks to adopt an ideological stand or promote an ideological cause. Intellectual and political and ideological pluralism informs the chapters in the hope that their content will have some resonance in policy arenas in Central America. Finally, collectively the chapters span both the past and the present in Central America and seek to project toward its future—in light of experience within the region and beyond its borders, in the United States and elsewhere.

Recovery or relapse? These words in the title of this volume reflect the widely held view that today the Central American republics, among many countries in the world, find themselves straining toward a new and better future in the face of structural inequities which have long blocked development. In our essays, we try to give interpretation to the new global political economy and its implications for Central America. It is not our purpose to outline a strategy or the steps for Central America to follow as it faces the future in an undefined post-Cold War new international order. It is, rather, our objective to deal seriously with some of the key issues confronting Central America and other like countries as they continue to strain toward that future. In this way, we seek to enrich the dialogue between scholars of political economy and public policy and practitioners of the policy art—in Central American studies and in development studies generally.

This volume originated in a conference entitled "Reorganizing the Political Economy: U.S. and Central American Perspectives" held at the University of Costa Rica, San José, in November 1991. Principals in the conference included six faculty members from the State University of New York at Albany (an anthropologist, two economists, and three political scientists), six Central American social scientists (two economists, three sociologists, and a development specialist), and several incumbent and former national legislators from Costa Rica and Panama. The Central American social scientists were from Costa Rica, Guatemala, and Honduras. All told, twelve papers were presented at the conference; ten of those, revised, appear as chapters in this volume. In addition, the coeditors invited a Honduran agricultural economist to prepare a chapter for the volume.

Recovery or Relapse in the Global Economy: Comparative Perspectives on Restructuring in Central America contains three sections. Section I, whose focus is "Perspectives on Central American Development and Change," includes the coeditors' overview of "Economics and Politics in Central American Development" and José Luis Vega Carballo's chapter on "Costa Rica in the 1980s: A Balance of Social Development." Vega Carballo examines Costa Rica's socioeconomic evolution in the 1980s in order to deepen our understanding of how "Latin America's Switzerland," so-called, was able to retain that status despite its worst economic depression in this century. The chapter attends particularly to the institutionalized role of liberal-democratic forces in the country, which, in conjunction with external influences, allows Costa Rica to maintain political stability and social peace in a region scarred by political violence and civil war. Lessons drawn by Vega Carballo from the Costa Rican case take on special importance in light of continuing economic, social, and political distress throughout Central America.

Section II has seven chapters that address "Themes in the Restructuring of the Political Economy." Collectively, these chapters cover a wide range, both topically and geographically, dealing with countries in Central America and outside that region. Carlos E. Santiago, in his chapter on "External Debt, Structural Adjustment, and the Labor Market," draws the implication for Latin American and Caribbean labor markets of the general state of economic liberalization, external debt, and structural adjustment in those regions. The limits of a strategy of promoting non-traditional exports are also discussed by him. Santiago attributes the limitations upon export promotion partly to the inconsistencies between the pursuit of macroeconomic policies and underlying microeconomic behavior and constraints. His analysis is drawn from the cases of Jamaica, the Dominican Republic, Costa Rica, and Puerto Rico, within a comparative framework.

Two areas of inquiry are the foci for Jolyne Melmed-Sanjak's chapter on "The Dynamics of Agrarian Policy in United States History: Implications for Contemporary Central America." The first is the history of agrarian policy in the United States up to the early twentieth century, with special attention to how agrarian policy affected the process of economic growth and development in the United States. The second area of inquiry concerns the program of structural adjustment in Central America. Using the United States' experience as a basis for comparison, Melmed-Sanjak argues that the current policy of structural adjustment in Central America—and by extension throughout Latin America—provides a window of opportunity to successfully undertake "restructured" agrarian reform in the region. She bases this assertion primarily on evidence that there is a potentially symbiotic relationship between agrarian reform and some of the policies of structural adjustment. The chapter concludes, however, with a discussion of whether and to what extent such potential will be realized, raising a serious challenge to her optimism.

Hugo Noé Pino is less optimistic than Jolyne Melmed-Sanjak about the prospects for agrarian development in Central America. His outlook is heavily influenced by the case of Honduras. Noé Pino begins his chapter on "Structural Adjustment and Honduran Agriculture: Some Considerations" by reviewing the historical record of structural adjustment in that country's agricultural sector, with special attention to major reforms instituted since 1990. He contends that the language of current structural-adjustment proposals completely ignores the main feature of Honduran agriculture, that is, inequities in the distribution of land and, concomitantly, the need for agrarian reform. He underlines the crucial distinction between short-term macroeconomic policies and medium- and long-term restructuring policies. While all types of policies are seen by Noé Pino as having a profound impact on the agricultural sector, he prefers to concentrate on the effects of restructuring policies, despite the fact that it is still too early to fully evaluate them. Noé Pino concludes that restructuring in the agrarian sector is apt to worsen the lot of landless peasants and small-scale producers—principally because the financial institutions that serve them will likely remain underfunded and because access to credit to modernize agriculture will probably be dominated, if not outright controlled, by export agriculture, cattle ranching, and other large landholding interests. He notes further that price volatility and the elimination of grain stocks, all results of liberalization, will further weaken the peasant sector and exacerbate the problem of food security in Honduras. Noé Pino is seen to support current restructuring proposals that do away with the industrial bias that pervades policies of import-substituting industrialization, and to feel that efforts to modernize agriculture via structural adjustment will penalize the bulk of the agrarian sector wherein *minifundios* (very small, semi-subsistence farms) and inefficient agriculture still predominate. He has little confidence that policies to promote non-traditional exports will prove beneficial, largely because the U.S. market will not support them and because the major industrial countries in the world remain steadfastly protectionist toward Central America even as they continue to pressure countries in that region to promote openness in their export sectors.

The next two chapters in Section II deal with the organization of labor—the first by Alvin Magid, in the United States and selected European countries, the second, by Marielos Rojas Viquez, in Central America. Magid's concern is with democratization in the industrial labor sector over the past two centuries, and with how democratic innovations targeted to industrial labor may help vitalize a contemporary strategy of reindustrialization. He begins his chapter on "Industrial Democracy and Reindustrialization: Cross-Cultural Perspectives" by highlighting the philosophical roots of industrial democracy in the Industrial Revolution. He sees various factors as possibly giving impetus today to industrial democracy, specifically in the United States: plant closings and the loss of jobs; worker demoralization and declining industrial productivity; the United States in international trade; the trade deficit; borrowing and interest rates; and relations between the United States and Japan. Magid next undertakes an assessment of different schemes for promoting industrial democracy in the United States: worker ownership in the form of employee stock option plans (ESOPs)—an innovation that appears to have attracted interest in Costa Rica, Taiwan, and Zimbabwe, among other countries—and labor-management cooperation. Drawing upon cases from the United States, Sweden, Spain, and Socialist Yugoslavia, he underlines the distinction between worker participation in corporate ownership and worker participation in corporate management. Magid observes that opening up the ranks of corporate ownership to industrial workers via ESOPs, especially in the United States, has done little to empower those workers as decision makers at the upper echelons of corporate management, and that except for industrial cooperatives at Mondragón, a small city in Spain's Basque region, European attempts at empowering workers via schemes for industrial democracy have also met with only limited success. Magid discerns little evidence in the United States and Europe that industrial democracy based on the principle of genuine worker empowerment will soon help vitalize a strategy of national industrial renewal. His assessment in this regard is cautiously optimistic, based on the impressive achievements of the system of industrial cooperatives at Mondragón. Magid is quick to add that the Mondragón model may prove to be a special case. It remains to be seen whether it will have wide applicability outside the domain of Basque culture and social practice.

Marielos Rojas Viquez's chapter has as its central concern "The Future of Cooperativism in Central America: Elements for a Discussion." She places the region's cooperative movement in historical context as a basis for exploring various issues that she regards as having overriding importance for the movement's growth today. She pays special attention to the impact of economic austerity measures and stabilization policies on cooperativism in Central America. Finally, Rojas Viquez examines the prospects for strengthening the cooperative movement under current conditions, and the feasibility of utilizing the movement to further national and regional integration.

Water Goldstein, in his chapter on "The Future Role of Multinational Enterprise and Foreign Direct Investment," underlines the importance of multinational corporations (MNCs) and international investment flows in the economic-development process. Goldstein highlights the role of MNCs in the current process of economic restructuring and the globalization of production. And he examines why criticism of the MNC in the Third World has become muted. While conceding that the MNCs are not the only or even the best agent to alleviate the pressing human problems in the Third World, Goldstein decries the inefficiencies in non-market solutions and the reluctance to welcome foreign direct investment.

Carlos A. Astiz's chapter on "Political Integration: A Central American Option" focuses on the political factor in the long history of regional organization in Latin America. Astiz affirms that economic and political integration is the guiding principle in the globalization of production. But in Latin America, he notes, the many efforts to achieve regional integration based on shared interests and joint policies have failed. He ascribes these failures to the *political* nature of the integration process. Astiz's examination of the Latin American experience with integration leads him to conclude that the smaller countries in the region—and especially those in Central America—may find it necessary to join regional blocs in which power is evenly distributed in order to pursue their national interests *vis-à-vis* large semi-developed countries which are themselves moving toward regional integration.

Three chapters in Section III are broadly related to the theme "Recovery or Relapse: Reflections on Central America in the New World Order." The first chapter, by Jorge González del Valle, deals specifically with the issue of "Central American External Debt in the Context of Economic Globalization." González del Valle assesses the effectiveness of austerity measures currently employed to promote economic stabilization and growth in the region. Finding all such measures unsuccessful in combating the problem of external debt, he then proposes an alternative solution to correct the current imbalance. The proposed solution rests on a strategy of internationalizing external debt—a strategy which González del Valle sees as likely also to help alleviate the economic hardship that afflicts Central America.

The next chapter, by Alvaro de la Ossa, focuses on "Central America in the Global Economy." De la Ossa's principal concern is with how the region is affected by the globalization of production. Arguing that the process of globalization has led to the marginalization of vast sectors within Central America, de la Ossa then explores possible correctives. He warns that the countries in the region must cooperative with each other in defense of their interests or face the prospects of continued dependent development and stagnation.

Alvaro de la Ossa's warning that the countries of Central America can advance their interests only by a strategy of regional cooperation is one of several themes taken up by Dante Ramírez in his chapter on "Understanding Economic Integration: Its Role and Reason in Central America." He discusses the problem of Central American integration in the context of growing international interdependence and transnationalism and the emergence of trade blocs. Echoing Carlos Astiz's argument regarding the importance of the political factor in regional integration, Ramírez contends that economic integration is inextricably linked with political integration and that discussion of the two aspects of integration can be expected to raise social consciousness throughout Central America. Ramírez sees regional integration as likely to prove the most effective means by which small- and medium-sized countries can hope to influence economic and political forces in the global context. He proposes ways to enhance the prospects for achieving desired results. Like Jorge González del Valle, Ramírez stresses the need to forgive the external debt of the world's poorest countries, several of which are in Central America. And he urges that a reassessment be undertaken of the structure and function of the United Nations and other international organizations in order to promote, interrelatedly, the principles of equity and reciprocal interests in international affairs. Only in such ways as these, Ramírez concludes, will the new world order be premised on a just international economic system.

Two

Costa Rica in the 1980s:
A Balance of Social Development
José Luis Vega Carballo

INTRODUCTION

This chapter has two main objectives. First, to assess the socioeconomic evolution of Costa Rica during the past decade so as to better understand its role in Central American economic development. Second, to provide an answer in response to the question of why and how this small republic has survived its most severe economic depression of this century. Costa Rica has preserved its liberal-democratic institutions and its traditional social peace, in spite of stagnation in its economic sectors. This stagnation did not result in popular protest and violent insurgency, which many had predicted would be so strong that it would destroy the stability of the regime. As early as 1983, there was a sense that the political agreements and alliances that led to a thirty year period of social peace in the country could be jeopardized by the conflicts that would arise due to deteriorating economic conditions.

Other authors (such as Booth [1984] and Diamond et al. [1989], chapter 9) also argued that social conflicts, including class conflict, would probably intensify over this period. Generally, they predicted that internal political instability might eventually lead to a multiplication of the pressures resulting from socioeconomic deterioration and cause a corresponding increment in tension-tolerance levels within the democratic system. Some even believed that this would provoke social protest against the elites, using the regime's own participatory and pluralistic structure. This phenomenon, paradoxically, could move against the debilitated and shaken democratic institutions, destroying extant tension management mechanisms, such as the satisfaction of basic necessities and opportunities for "personal self-realization." (Nelson, 1989).

However, it is appropriate now, with the advantage of hindsight on the passing of a decade of abrupt internal and international changes to try to explain in the broadest terms the notable and, for many, the inexplicable continuity of Costa Rican democracy. A series of factors or conditions are operating historically, which have intertwined structural, normative, or ideological roots. One could attribute scientific properties, such as causality or responsibility, to the means by which the local elites planned to invalidate the expected "catastrophe" of an inexorable sociopolitical radicalization and polarization. This supports the prevailing thesis about apolitical convulsions and inevitable precipitations of Costa Rica in the midst of the Central American chaos.

On the other hand, it is important to clarify how conditions at the international level favored the leading sectors of this small nation. These sectors were now not only able to steer in a relatively stable manner in an atmosphere of regional revolts and undeniable dangers of destabilization, but also advantageously use it to maneuver their government to the head of a distinguished, regional pro-peace effort that has produced, and continues to produce, positive results (Rodríguez, 1989). According to Reuben (1989), those in government circles have, thus, been able to move, with a high level of security and prestige, towards the application of the "Programs of Structural Adjustment," which now have captured so much public attention. Thus, the evolution of exterior politics during the 1980s was firmly tied to the Central American regional crisis, and, in that regard, must be judged as a coherent exterior projection of the global or strategic interests of the dominant power bloc (Vega Carballo, 1987).

In this chapter, certain historical processes whose development is already known will not be touched on, since they have been the subject of abundant descriptions and critical judgment in widely dispersed, high-caliber works (Rovira, 1987; Edelman and Kenen, 1989). Neither will this chapter be overly ambitious, by rigorously pursuing the data and details of the socioeconomic situation previous to the crisis, since that has been done in other works (Vega Carballo, 1986, 1990a). Although watered-down descriptions or anecdotes will be avoided when possible, it will be indispensable at times to make parsimonious use of narrative and historic chronologies for analytical purposes, or to benefit the reader unfamiliar with the case.

The author will also attempt to draw some conclusions that will shed light on the Costa Rican case, which has been the subject of only a few comparative political and sociological studies (with the exception of Peeler [1985] who contrasts it with Columbia and Venezuela). This may be because Costa Rica may have been (or still is) considered insignificant, possibly because of its physical size. In this chapter, the author hopes to demonstrate the importance of studying the Costa Rican case to researchers and politicians who are affected by the politics of stabilization or by transitions to democracy.

THE REGIONAL AND CONTINENTAL GEOPOLITICAL CONTEXT: QUESTIONS AND DANGERS

In 1979, with the heightening of political and military instability in the Central American region, caused by the fall of the Somoza dynasty and the ascent of the Sandinistas in Nicaragua, many analysts (including Vega Carballo, 1983) asked questions about the future of Costa Rica. The first question was as follows: Will the "Switzerland of Central America" be able to survive in the midst of such convulsion? More precisely, will its hundreds of democratic institutions survive the onslaughts of diverse "communicant vessels" or "collapses of domain" caused by the unleashing of new, or intensification of old, domestic wars in almost all neighboring countries? The upheavals in civil society were unlike other historic circumstances in the Central American states because of the involvement of third actors and the great powers. Perhaps these events would not annul Costa Rica's traditional autonomy, which originated decades ago. Its democracy had been cultivated with great pains by liberal and social democratic elites as a symbol of a nationalist orientation of the highest order. In this respect Costa Rica was little understood.

Because of the acute internationalization that accompanied the conflagration of Costa Rica's neighbors, a parallel anxiety arose concerning the successive and powerful foreign interventions that were undertaken in the region by the two greatest world powers during the time known as the "Reagan Era." There existed a dangerous level of confrontation, which heated up the Cold War excessively and could have eliminated the peace and tranquillity to which the Costa Ricans were so accustomed. Destabilizing waves occurred under the general framework of a "war of low intensity," the novel military strategy that was tested in a post- Vietnam type of "tropical laboratory" (Vergara et al., 1987). Others argued that it was illogical to hope that these destabilizing waves would not produce a great upheaval, but instead a series of prolonged small-scale clashes, which would still leave the country in a state of "Lebanonization." This would irrevocably impact Costa Rican factional strife, which proliferated in many places beyond the porous frontiers of what a North American author qualified as our fragile "mini city-state" (Ebel, 1972).

These and similar questions were raised during the Reagan Era and were surrounded by great fears. Geopolitical tension could be noted at both regional and world levels. What is certain is that the dangerous coincidence of intermixing external and internal turbulences was creating an unprecedented crisis that brought international attention because of its strategic and military implications. As Booth (1984) and Reding (1986) recognized, there was also a preoccupation for Costa Rica's historical survival as a peaceful constitutional democracy; pluralistic, participatory and dangerously located in an explosive zone in the continent. How was it possible to survive and continue advancing at the same time?

Before entering into a full response to the questions posed, it is equally fitting to investigate, by way of a brief parenthesis, why the state was not defeated and irreparable polarizations and fissures in Costa Rican civil society did not occur, as had occurred in the past with at least two of the oldest and most admired liberal Latin American democracies, similar in many respects to that of Costa Rica. The question was worrisome, principally because those countries had been, or continued to be, immersed in the continental or Latin American crisis that ran through a period of instability, which many in the Economic Commission for Latin America have called "the lost decade."

This period refers principally to the Chilean and Uruguayan democracies (cases well analyzed from the contemporary perspective by Diamond et. al., 1989), which were victims of the contradictions inherent in post-war development and a wave of terrible bureaucratic-authoritarian repression in the southern cone. These regimes were created as much to combat the real or supposed onslaughts of the "evil empire" that neither the Pentagon nor the North Atlantic Treaty Organization (NATO) could contain, as to combat the existent or foreseeable wave of pressures from below that would hamper the continuation of rapid economic growth, confirming Olsen's (1963) hypothesis. Such turbulence could foster the arrival of the "highest stage" of developmentalism or South American populism, according to various well-known authors (O'Donnell, 1973, 1978; Collier, 1979; and especially, O'Donnell et al. 1986).

At this juncture, a tense opening was formed between social demands and the real possibility of response by the United States. The ruling regimes felt so beset that the actors that backed "law and order" ended up with hardhanded responses in order to break the vestiges of whatever centrist equilibrium was left. This was a well-known strategy in the Chilean case (Valenzuela (1978). Sights were set at implanting true would-be fascist Gulags or "National Security States" governed by authentic systems of terror, as set forth by Walter (1969) and which have been applied to Central America in some of the writings by Torres-Rivas (1980), and by Corradi (1985) in reference to the southern cone.

It is not that a "party" or fringe interest group of this type would not have looked to rise to power in San José. Nor would such a group have abandoned a drive for true "psychological warfare" and "militarization without militarism," with the support of paramilitary groups and a vocal coalition of business-sector plotters (Vargas Cullell, 1987; Hopfensperger, 1986), or even a coup d'etat—we know that there was almost a coup d'etat against President Monge in 1984 (Gutiérrez and Vargas Cullell, 1986; Sobrado et al., 1988). Many such initiatives failed because they were not sufficiently backed by political parties and the most influential civil actors, who were committed to sustain a coalition of democratic forces. What those who promoted the doctrine of "limited" national security for Costa Rica (in other words, "protected democracy" and even "restricted" democracy if tensions became acute) lacked in their repertoire was a decisive instrument that could be used to defend the weak democratic state in the face of the subversive forces and doctrines that surrounded it, an instrument that the counterinsurgent actors could count on to carry out the execution of the repressive-neoliberal experiment in the southern cone: the military.[1]

If it had not been for the constitutional abolition of the armed forces and their anti-democratic and destabilizing potential (effected by José Figueres when he was chief of the founding junta of the Second Republic in 1948, maintained only with difficulty), in the mid 1980s, when they found themselves at a conspirative apogee and enormously fearful, the ultraconservatives, or "pro-coup" sectors, would likely have tried to strike the mortal or preventive blow of "dictatorship" or "*dictablanda*"—as O'Donnell et al. (1986) call it—to the Costa Rican democracy. Had this occurred, at best Costa Ricans would than have been subjected to a "programmed resurrection," following one of the many schemes of transition in vogue throughout the continent.

Additionally, despite contrasts between Costa Rica and other Central and Latin American countries, it would be imprudent to neglect examining the Costa Rican case through the extra-continental mirror of the 1980s. Cultural and structural parallels stand out within the framework of the regional security crisis; and, despite their geographic distance, other apparently fragile Western democracies, having been victims of inherent difficulties, were reflecting on Costa Rica.

Authors such as Huntington (1966) have examined the crucial factors that lead to "non-governability" of similar contemporary democratic regimes. A North American political scientist has pessimistically asserted that the collapse of the Central American region's "state minisocieties" was due to the contradictions of a "post-agricultural era," which could not withstand the transition to sustained industrialization with stable and participatory regimes (Ebel, 1982). Other theories in vogue during the 1960s and 1970s in the wide body of literature about state breakdowns or collapses (Linz and Stepan, 1979) included options for recomposition or transition. They became the subject of much discussion in later years as well (O'Donnell et al., 1986). The alternatives which Central America has witnessed under controll "from the top down," (i.e., by the military and the diverse groups that make up the "despotic coalition" (Baloyra, 1982)) include what Torres-Rivas (1988) has called the paradoxical "authoritarian transitions to democracy" and other democracies, which despite any illusions, continue to be precarious or weak. As Huntington, who opened the debate on democratic stability a couple of decades ago, put it, "the most important lesson to be derived from the history of democratization is that the difficult part is not ending the nondemocratic regime, but to develop stable democratic institutions" (Huntington, 1988).

One must not lose sight of the lack of confidence in the survival of Latin American democracies that prevails in the left flank of the dependency theorists. As Diamond, Linz, and Lipset (1989) have noted in the preface to a recent work, most of the dependency school continues to insist on the Marxist assumption that the political systems and the other components of the superstructures of "bourgeoisie democracies" were illusional constructs or mere epi-phenomena—that exclusion and political repression and diverse forms of authoritarianism were the inevitable result (although undesirable) of the policies of defense and aggression, which the dominant classes practiced against the people and the new reformist or revolutionary social movements that emerged throughout the continent. Intermediately developed peripheral countries, such as Costa Rica, were put in the same disadvantageous position in the international division of labor as the other countries, and subject to the same wearing-down processes and subsequent fall to authoritarianism or fascism.

In order to avoid that ill-fated route, it is clear that these countries should opt for the "difficult transition to socialism." As previously noted, this perspective has been modified in its initial mix of skepticism and radicalism in the face of pseudo-bourgeoisie democracies and other mixed forms. Its supporters have now become more accepting of the outcome of some of the transitions that have occurred in and outside of Latin America. This has highlighted the existence of a "sane revisionism" (which had been preceded from afar by perestroika) in the heart of the left, which Ellner (1989) has noted in a recent review. However, in the early 1980s, when this change in position had just started to occur, the dependency school still had a distressing vision of the possibilities for the survival of the few liberal democracies, or those trying in vain to resuscitate democracy. A similar environment has emerged in recent years (Menjívar et al., 1986; Torres-Rivas, 1987).

In the case of Costa Rica and the other Central American countries, Kirkpatrick (1979) departed from these assumed Huntingonian radicals in an aggressively savage stance against the disarmed government of Costa

Rica. She insolently attacked the Monge administration (1982-86) as weak and irresponsible for its refusal to convert itself into a "garrison state" or at least a "police state." The central strategic idea was the defense of the state in unison with the Reagan establishment, entrenched at the time in the government of the United States—a spineless national democracy would form part of the North American backyard fence which, similar to other Reaganist strategies, would fence in the region and draw the line on communism. To this end, Costa Rica would protect the interests of the United States as if they were its own, keeping in mind that, among other things, it was located almost at the locks of the Panama Canal and had a common frontier with Daniel Ortega's Nicaraguan commanders. In other words, in the Reaganist vision this was nothing less than a frontier with Fidel Castro and the Managua-Havana-Moscow axis.

In the final account, and in spite of these and other right-wing Republican attacks and threats that went even further than the theoretical plan both inside and outside of Costa Rica (Blachman et al., 1986), anticipated ungovernability and a defenseless military did not undermine the bases of the democratic system. Local progressive elites were not intimidated either, and rejected many external pressures, whether open or covert, from the White House, the Pentagon, the Central Intelligence Agency (CIA) and the southern command. Various international assistance organizations also apparently took on a similar function in backing counterinsurgency, low intensity warfare, and the fight against the "Vietnam Syndrome" (Vergara et al., 1987).

Consequently, it is important to examine the Costa Rican resistance and its relative success more fully. This can be done from today's perspective, since Costa Rica has to a great extent been able to jump the hurdles of the 1980s, and has moved toward a distinct stage in the readjustment process. The internal and external dimensions of this stage are being debated intensely (Reuben, 1988; Rodríquez et al., 1989) because of the negative social costs. In this stage of readjustment Costa Rica obviously faces new challenges, new international circumstances, and a new context of regional reintegration (including the U.S. initiative for the formation of a huge free market encompassing all of North America). Thus, in the years ahead, Costa Rica faces enormous obstacles to ending the recession that continues to disturb its small and fragile productive apparatus.

THREATS FROM WITHIN: LIMITS TO GROWTH

Curiously, at the beginning of the past decade, most of the Costa Rican leadership straightforwardly asserted that it had successfully cultivated the country's relative isolation within the region. It believed that it had established a solid barrier protecting both national sovereignty and liberal democracy. It also believed that it had achieved this through redistributive measures and social reform. Such measures had been in effect since the 1940s and had withstood the short civil war of 1948, and were later expanded and implemented by the victorious socialist democrats to consolidate the political system over which they have presided for about three generations (Vega, 1982).

However, it should be mentioned that at the beginning of the 1980s this strategic distancing was totally, or in great part, overwhelmed. At present it is seriously threatened. This has permitted some political and business circles to rethink, in more pessimistic terms, the possibilities for salvation by way of isolation.

Recent tendencies in the productive framework of civil society and in the Costa Rican state have brought the strategy of stable democratic domination (which the leading sectors have employed since the nineteenth century) into question. These tendencies have also made the redistributive or socialist policies, which have been previously described elsewhere (Vega Carballo, 1986; Guendel and Rivera, 1987; Sojo, 1990) and traditionally prescribed by socialist democrats of the Partido de Liberación Nacional (PLN), especially difficult to administer. Accumulated tensions did not arise exclusively from the disorder of the 1980s, even though some were associated with structural transformation and resistance to change throughout the region. This argument has also been made by some economists (CEPAL, 1979; Edelman and Kenen, 1983; and especially Ulate and Rodríguez, 1983).

It must be recognized thoroughly that some of these tensions have existed since 1963. At that time, under strong opposition by the most conservative business groups, the national economy was inserted into the Central American Common Market (CACM) in order to end the region's traditional separatism. This measure caused a swift increase in the number of exchanges among CACM countries and promoted import substitution industrialization which, in less than a decade, increased the participation of industrial goods in the gross domestic product (GDP) from 12% to about 20%. This firmly established the modernizing process in Central American societies and economies, and, as will be examined later, also modified their socio-occupational and class structure. Of more immediate interest is that Costa Rica could no longer affirm that, whether politically or economically, it was at the margin of regional integration. In fact, the opposite was true.

In 1969, when El Salvador and Honduras fought the so-called "Soccer War," it became even clearer that almost a decade of commercial exchange and widening industrial markets had increased regional integration. It was also obvious that market interdependence could drive other cyclical factors and states of disequilibrium, all or most of which could undermine the stability so desired by the diverse modernizing elites of Costa Rica, who conducted peaceful power disputes amidst local turmoil.

The decision to integrate can also be viewed in light of the state industrial development model, which by the end of the 1970s manifested signs of exhaustion. These signs of exhaustion included tendencies to reduce investment; decrease interregional commercial expansion; and increases in deficits in current accounts despite strong tendencies to concentrate and marginalize growth (Rivera et al., 1986; Ulate and Rodríguez, 1983). The state industrial model also depended in good measure on a continuing increase in the size of the regional market, which needed further support through changes in regional demography and the implementation of agrarian reform or land redistribution in the other Central American countries. Also necessary was concurrent softening or restriction of many groups in society, especially the military-oligarchic and anti-reform elites' grasp on the model, which Baloyra has classified as reactionary despotism (based on Giner's conceptualization [Baloyra, ch. 5, 1982]). Others have termed them simple military dictators or counterinsurgents dressed in democrat's clothes. Many normally optimistic theoreticians were thereby put on the defensive about the question of regional development and integration. Existing forms were inadequate to create coalitions, realign forces in the power blocs, or to make the transformations necessary to promote and deepen industrialization and democratization, which they had hoped would trickle down from capitalist modernization. Unfortunately, the truth was that the "mini city-states" of the region, whether jointly or separately, were not able to revamp what Ebel would call the "post-agricultural" state. Given the various types of insurgents who were pressuring the state (Ebel, 1982), an economic and sociopolitical collapse was foreseeable.

Additionally, it is evident that the economic expansion was similar in style to that of the 1950s and 1960s, during which time import substitution industrialization and the growth of the benefactor state under the Costa Rican socialist democrats also occurred. Import substitution industrialization was later attacked for its various failings. In the first place, as will be shown, it could not rid itself of the ups and downs of the traditional agro-export cycle, nor of the massive importation of primary materials, technologies, patents, and so forth. This generated disequilibrium in the terms of exchange, the balance of payments, and foreign currency funds in a manner very similar to what had happened at the end of the fifties and the beginning of the sixties in Uruguay. As has been made clear by various studies (Vega Carballo, 1986; Fallas, 1982), a series of severe bottlenecks or disalignments occurred, which were not

easily overcome. Costa Rican agricultural and industrial sectors highlighted the dangerously high degree of vulnerability to exterior events to
which the local economic model was subject. Enormous fiscal outflows
occurred, in addition to poor monetary equilibrium and terms of trade. The
rest of the economies of the isthmus experienced similar problems, where
the central elements of the old structures collapsed on top of those that had
exhausted the accumulative process, namely, the diversification of the
productive structure—the boom in traditional exports; the growing exportation of industrial goods within the Common Market; and the stability of
the foreign currency exchange through inflationary rates. This has been
well examined by Bulmer-Thomas (1987, 1988) in his two most recent and
exhaustive studies.

Such "external dependency" is a cause of backwardness and
disequilibrium, according to a classic study by Torres-Rivas (Torres-
Rivas, 1989). This theory can be illustrated by examining the unfortunate
economic impact of the increase in petroleum prices between 1973 and
1975 and 1978 and 1981. Moreover, it was exacerbated by a no less
traumatic increase in external debt. In the case of Costa Rica, external
indebtedness rose to about $4.1 million over a short period of time,
causing an economy-wide collapse. There were only superficial differences in how this impacted other countries throughout the region. Certainly, serious repercussions were felt in Costa Rica. (Williams, 1986;
Rivera et al., 1986; Perez Brignolli, 1985).

THE GREAT CRISIS HITS: THE SITUATION DURING THE "LOST DECADE"

At the beginning of the 1980s, all of the indicators of a poorly
functioning economy were evident as the economy suffered severe rever-
sals. For example, Costa Rican per capita gross domestic product (GDP)
fell by 2% from 1979 to 1980, by 4.1% from 1980 to 1981, and by 11.5%
from 1981 to 1982. Internal demand also fell by 26% and gross capital
formation decreased by 46%. Whereas in 1977, 39,700 new jobs had been
created, only 3,900 were created in 1981. Open unemployment increased
from 5.9% in 1980 to 9.4% in 1982. Between 1979 and 1982, average real
salaries fell 40%, total production fell by 6%, and per capita production
decreased by 16%. This was happening in the midst of an unprecedented
inflation, which fluctuated between 80% and 100% (García-Huidrobo,
1989). Such was Costa Rica's abrupt and tragic entrance to the 1980s—the
economy deteriorated to such an extent that the economic indicators were
more similar to those of the 1970s than the 1980s (Hugo Céspedes et al.,
1984; Fallas, 1982). According to a 1983 report by the Interamerican

Development Bank (IDB), the steepest decline for all the Central American countries occurred between 1978 and 1983.

If a sensitive indicator such as Costa Rica's average per capita consumption is examined, a decline of 5.6% in 1978 to -15.3% in 1983 is observed. This stands out in comparison to the economic stagnation that affected Nicaragua and El Salvador, which showed declines of -9.8% and -10.6% for 1883, respectively (IDB, Economic Report, 1983). On top of all this, according to a recent retrospective study (Lizano et al., BCCR, 1989), external debt shot up dramatically during that period. Costa Rica's external public debt rose in current dollars from $551.2 million between 1970 and 1979 to $3,536,600 between 1983 and 1988, while payments as a percent of exports rose from 28.2% to 43.6% of GDP. Only debt repayment, which went from 24.1% to 88.6% of GDP during the same time period, moved in a positive direction.

This was not the only alarming occurrence. Just as worrisome was the impact of the debt crisis on power relations and the social structure of society (among others, Seligson and Muller, 1987). Social structure, and especially socio-occupational stratification, is, as Parkin (1978, p. 25) asserts, "the main support of class hierarchy." Social stratification had been showing signs of regression and stagnation for some time, according to measures of growth in social inequality based on occupational and salary structure. This was no secret both within and outside of Costa Rica (Baldares, 1985; Rourk, 1979; Herrick and Hudson, 1981). Since the mid-1970s, some economists warned of increasing imbalances in the social structure, and they continued to sound the alarm throughout the 1980s.

A number of new studies on the Costa Rican economy have revealed a growing concentration of wealth, widening inequality, and increasing indebtedness—all indicators of the growing level of poverty under which large sectors of the population currently live (Céspedes and Jiménez Acuña, 1988; Sauma and Trejos, 1990). These and several other inquiries commissioned by the Friedrich Ebert Foundation all verified a number of disquieting social trends during the 1980s. For example, it was shown that between 1977 and 1983, 20% of the wealthiest families increased their share of national income from 47% to 48.5%, largely at the expense of middle income families. The gap increases when considering differences between rural and urban areas, which is one illustration of the degree to which the income of the wealthiest sectors of the population increased at a time of stagnation and economic crisis. The growing income inequality increased the prospects of further social tensions, which did occur at the beginning of the decade, but diminished later on.

Other indicators, including those from official but previously unexamined sources, illustrate precisely the extent of economic depression to which reference has been made.[2] Some key indicators, such as the average nominal salary and the monthly consumer price index, point to a distressing picture as Table 2.1 shows.[3] In 1977 a nominal salary could acquire 77.7% of the consumer price index, but by 1982 this fell to 53.2 %, and only by 1990 did this figure return to levels comparable to the 1970s. This tendency is equally observable in other indexes as well. Open unemployment jumped from 5.92% in 1980 to 9.37% by 1982, and then declined to 5.46% by 1988. The underemployment rate, which largely reflects changes in the composition of the informal labor market, went from 26.38% in 1980 to 47.65% in 1982, and then declined considerably to 21.44% by 1988. There was additional evidence of severe housing shortages and declining rates of scholastic participation throughout the 1980s, according to the Ministry of Planning (MIDEPLAN, 1990).

Poverty and indigence also increased dramatically during the initial years of the 1980s. The household surveys of the Dirección General de Estadística y Censos (DGEC) indicated (using methodology of the Economic Commission on Latin America [ECLA]) that the percent of indigent families increased dramatically, from 17.7% in 1980 to 36.8% in 1982, but decreased to 14.9% by 1988. A similar pattern was evident for the percent of families who could not afford to satisfy their basic needs. This figure went from more than 27.2% of the population to some 47.4%, only to decrease later to 24.5%. Although this statistic followed an oscillating pattern, the absolute number continued to increase during the 1980s.

It is interesting to note how the Interamerican Development Bank (IDB) analyzed the above situation, since its methodology is somewhat different from ECLA's. It found a similar tendency percentage-wise, locating the percent of Costa Rican families under the "limit of well-being" within the following ranges: 41.7%, 70.7%, and 45.6%. But, whereas the proportion of poor in rural areas stood at 74% of all families in 1977, it decreased during the worst years of Costa Rica's depression, falling to 60% in 1983. The ratio subsequently rose to a high of 75% by 1986, a trend which runs counter to that witnessed in the urban zones, possibly because of seasonal and cyclical factors and institutional wage policies.

Another important source, the Institute of Economic Research at the University of Costa Rica, follows ECLA methods in its own research on poverty and income distribution (Sauma and Trejos, 1990). It recently announced that in 1977 poor families comprised 17.5% of the population, by 1983 that ratio had risen to 30.5%, but by 1986 had descended to 17.0%. As in other reports, significant differences were evident between urban and rural zones, with less concentration of average income in rural areas—this despite the fact that incomes in rural areas were less than 43% of those in urban areas. This data, besides confirming an interesting

Table 2.1
Consumer Price Index and Nominal Average Salary for Costa Rica
(June, 1976-1990)

Years	(1) Consumer Price Index	(2) Nominal Average Wages	(3) Ratio (2)/(1)	(4) Gap [(1)-(2)]/(1)
1976	2456.2	1472.1	59.9	40.1
1977	2573.0	1714.3	66.7	33.4
1978	2716.9	1964.7	72.3	27.7
1979	2936.1	2281.3	77.7	22.3
1980	3487.0	2579.4	74.0	26.0
1981	4551.5	3182.4	69.9	30.1
1982	8671.8	4612.8	53.2	46.8
1983	12310.7	7238.5	58.8	41.2
1984	13390.0	8637.3	64.5	35.5
1985	15373.2	10610.6	69.0	31.0
1986	17162.9	12966.6	75.6	24.4
1987	20181.4	14607.1	72.4	27.6
1988	24174.0	17213.2	71.2	28.8
1989	28270.3	21518.4	76.1	23.9
1990	33371.9	25356.1	76.0	24.0

Sources: Dirección General de Estadística y Censos (DGEC) and Caja
Costarricense del Seguro Social (CCSS).

pattern of decline and general improvement in the economic situation
during the 1980s, also suggest that it is unlikely that the general prosperity
of the 1970s will resume any time soon. The findings also show that
although urban/rural differences diminished during 1982-83, they later
recurred.

In summary, even though many Costa Rican authorities continue to
assert that the country is an example of recuperation or adjustment with
a "human face," they assert this from an overly optimistic or triumphant,
if not distorted, stance. Severe problems of internal inequality persist. For
example, it has recently been necessary to increase the per capita income

of indigent families by almost 100% and the incomes of those who cannot satisfy basic needs by 25%, in order to extract them from the depths of economic despair. However, of most interest at present is the question of why these economic dislocations, accompanied by persistent deterioration in the indicators of social well-being, did not provoke the sociopolitical convulsions so common in the region. These conditions certainly could have destabilized the political-institutional regime, its legitimate values, and all of the hierarchical structure of class domination.

STRUCTURAL RESISTANCE AND RESILIENCE: THE INVARIANT SAVIORS

Table 2.2 provides a profile of the socio-occupational structure of the employed and unemployed Costa Rican population between 1980 and 1989. It is clear that the composition of the socio-occupational structure of the economically active population between 1980 and 1989 grew in the middle and upper strata of secondary and tertiary occupations, with emphasis on management occupations, independent professionals, and especially self-employed workers, whose numbers doubled in the period immediately after the 1982 depression. There was a tendency for the proportion of dependent professionals to remain constant, the majority of which were probably tied to the public bureaucratic sector. Generally, one can perceive that the middle and upper strata increased from a quarter to a third of the population at the end of the last decade.

Meanwhile, among the lowest strata of the occupational profile there is a marked tendency toward the opposite—a proportional reduction of this sector with the exception of unpaid family labor, which proliferated in the informal and artisan markets, which grew during the worst years of the crisis. For example, in secondary occupations, the proportion of self-employed during the 1980s grew from 5.0% to 7.1% from 1980 to 1989. This did not occur among salaried workers, principally those in industrial occupations, whose relative share of the employed and out of work population declined from 22.5% to 21.3% in this period. This occurred despite the fact that industry suffered highly from contraction in both internal and external demand (especially that of the Central American Common Market). It is possible to conclude that at the beginning of the period participation by the lowest occupational strata increased in the low productivity tertiary sector, which peaked in 1982 at 17.1% and subsequently fell to 13.2% in 1989.

If we consider all Costa Rican families from 1977 to 1986, these socio-occupational changes were not sufficiently significant to alter the degree of inequality, as the Gini coefficient remained relatively constant

Table 2.2
Socio-Occupational Structure of the Employed and Unemployed Costa Rican Population (1980-1989)

Occupational Strata	1980	1982	1985	1987	1988	1989
Total Employed and Unemployed	760,058	822,542	875,930	965,948	995,698	1,018,07
I. High and Medium Strata (% of total)	31.4	27.6	31.1	32	33.7	33.6
I.1 Secondary and Tertiary	30.1	26.3	30.3	30.9	31.9	32.2
a. Owners, industry, commerce, and services	3.1	2.7	2.1	2.7	2.9	2.5
b. Managers, industry, commerce, and services	2	2.1	2.4	2.5	2.4	2.4
c. Self-employed Professionals	0.2	0.3	0.5	0.8	0.3	0.9
d. Dependent Professionals	8.1	7	8.8	7.7	8.4	8.5
e. Self-employed in commerce	3.5	2.1	2.7	4.5	4.5	4.3
f. Employees, Salespersons, Clerical Workers	13.3	12.1	13.9	12.8	13.1	13.1
I.2 Primary Occupations	1.3	1.3	0.8	1.1	1.8	1.4
II. Lower Strata (% of total)	68.4	71.9	68.4	67.2	65.4	65.4
II.1 Secondary Occupations	27.5	26.8	26.4	27.4	26.7	28.4
a. Salaried Workers	22.5	20.5	19.9	21.2	20.4	21.3
b. Self-employed and Unpaid Family Workers	5	6.3	6.5	6.2	6.4	7.1
II.2 Tertiary Occupations	14.9	17.1	15.5	13.7	13.5	13.2
a. Salaried Workers	13.1	14.8	13.7	12.8	12.6	12.1
b. Self-employed and Unpaid Family Workers	1.8	2.3	1.7	0.9	0.9	1.1
II.3 Primary Occupations	26	28.1	26.6	26	25.2	23.8
a. Salaried Workers	17.4	19.6	17.2	14.4	14.8	13.3
b. Self-employed and Unpaid Family Workers	8.7	8.4	9.4	11.6	10.4	10

Notes: Based on the methodology of Filgueira and Geneletti, "Estratificación y movilidad ocupacional en América Latina," *Cuadernos de la CEPAL*, No. 39, Santiago de Chile, 1981. After 1987 the methodology of the household survey was modified.

Source: Household Survey of Employment and Unemployment, Dirección General de Estadística y Censos (DGEC).

at 0.42. Data from 1977 show that the richest 20% of families had claims on 47% of average monthly income. This figure rose to 48.5% in 1983 and to 48.6% in 1986. The bottom 20% increased its share of income from 14.9% to 15.7% by 1983, dropping to 14.9 by 1986. The data do not indicate a catastrophic regressive trend. However, there were differences between urban and rural populations, and the wealthy increased their share of total income to a larger degree than the poor in some of those years. Also, during the years of economic decline, both the poorest and the wealthiest sectors increased their share of wealth at the expense of the middle income sectors, without provoking a dramatic decline in the share of income going to the rural sector. Moreover, the rural sector was able to mitigate the effects of the economic decline that followed the 1982 shock—their average income grew by 38.4% from 1983 to 1986, a higher rate than the 30.9% found in urban areas. One explanation for this tendency is that, as has been traditionally the case in Costa Rican history, small and medium agro-business played a stabilizing role in the face of economic decline. In the long term this stabilizing role counterbalances cyclical increases in urban-rural tensions, thus alleviating a persistent problem that has bred violence and insurgency in many Latin American countries such as El Salvador and Peru.

A similar phenomenon in the evolution of the middle-high occupational sectors was observed in research undertaken by the Programa Regional del Empleo para America Latina y el Caribe and the International Labor Organization (Garcia Huidrobo et al., 1990). It was found that wage policies following the 1982 decline were geared to increasing average wages in the private sector, which rose 49.3% between 1982 and 1986. However, since this sector contains about 80% of wage-earning workers, and since public sector wages increased only 25.8%, the wage structure was made worse at the high and middle levels of the occupational scale through the end of the decade. As expected, this wage policy lowered the income and the standards of living of the professional or techno-bureaucratic occupations, which endured wage cuts of 15% to 20%. These events led to promotion of the theory of "discriminating wage recovery," in which the purchasing power of the lowest sectors was increased, leaving them in a situation similar to that of the late 1970s. Simultaneously, those enjoying much higher incomes saw increases, but at much lower rates, because of differences in geography and social strata.

The data indicate that long-term structural factors involving wages and occupations were used by Costa Rica as a form of resistance to the crisis and the changes brought about by disruptive internal and external factors. In sum, the relative continuity and rigidity of the social system ensured long-term social stability. This was especially true for class and occupational structures, social mobility and income distribution, and in mitigating urban-rural differences. The framework offered opportunities for social mobility among different groups and elites, which compensated for the economic hardship suffered by the entire population at the hands of structural adjustment, which many studies predicted would result in social instability.

POLITICAL AND IDEOLOGICAL CENTRISM: THE OTHER BALANCING FACTOR

Despite what has been asserted here, collective behavior observed during the crisis cannot be explained only through economic and structural analyses. There are many balancing factors at the political, electoral, and social levels that must necessarily be taken into account. These factors not only brought stability by sustaining institutional balance and a consensus favorable to regional pacification, but they also supported the status quo. The elites and other groups unfavorable to democracy found it difficult to take advantage of a politicized and institutionalized military. Most leaders were not inclined to break off dialogue and pushed quickly and efficiently for the creation of a two-party system.

A two-party system tends to weaken conflicting electoral and ideological platforms, while it personalizes political battles and condemns labor and community disputes as destabilizing forces at times of economic crisis. Furthermore, when foreign policy problems became more complicated, this inter-elite game contributed to the weakening of subversive internal forces, creating cohesion as a widely accepted goal and thus opening the door to the acceptance of more severe economic measures. All social classes were asked to make sacrifices. This illustrates the important role that political leaders can play at times of crisis or cleavage.

After analyzing public opinion surveys, Seligson and Muller (1987) concluded that from 1978 to 1983 most of the population supported the political system as the best possible, though most criticized the group in power. This, Seligson and Muller argue, was due to the cumulative effect that the elites' defense of democratic and legalistic traditions has had on the cultural and ideological beliefs of Costa Ricans. Seligson and Muller also argue that the level of support for the political system was very high, regardless of the economic measures taken. Support among those who had the highest opinion of the system fell from 79.7% in 1978 to 70.2% in 1983. For those who supported the system the least, discontent rose only slightly, from 2.3% to 3.7% during the same period. Once the government launched socioeconomic compensation programs in 1983, popular support rose considerably at all levels.

The four-year term promotes patience in the electorate, which then exercises the "punitive vote" to punish failed or damaging policies, thus placing the blame on the politicians and not on the system. Multi- or two-party pluralism, together with the highly legitimized cycle of electoral politics (which stimulates high levels of electoral participation) directly maintains the legitimacy of the system during times of crisis, as concep-tualized by Max Weber. High levels of legitimacy prevent the system from diverting from normative and constitutional channels. This phenomenon was also observed by Booth (1984, 1989) and confirmed by Seligson and Gómez (1989).

Moreover, once economic crises and foreign threats dissipated, especially after the end of the Nicaraguan conflict, the leaders of the political parties introduced state reforms that allowed for a large-scale overhaul of the productive sector. Supposedly, the ultimate goal was to liberalize or to give new energies to a dormant civil society by eliminating a suffocating bureaucracy through cuts in social spending and in the personnel of state agencies and state owned companies. These reforms left the economy in the hands of foreign and domestic markets. The purpose was to eliminate distortions, promote exports, and lower or freeze real average wages. The reform of the productive system was supported by the International Monetary Fund (IMF), the World Bank, and the United States Agency for International Development (USAID). It is similar to the strategy currently followed by many countries, including former socialist countries.

What was noteworthy about the process was that it was undertaken at an accelerated pace, without paying the "social debt" generated by such reforms (García-Huidrobo, PREAL-OIT, 1989), and without experienc-ing the emergence of the repressive type of apparatus common in the southern cone and in other Central American countries. This occurred because the reforms were made by elites who enjoyed the support of a center-oriented electorate, whose composition and dynamics are striking to observers.

The origin of the competitive-pluralist party system in Costa Rica can be traced to 1889, when an opposition party first came into power. The evolution of political parties and inclusive policies in Costa Rica (remem-ber, exclusion, and not inclusion, has been the norm elsewhere in Central America) occurred in two major phases. There were also two phases in the efforts of the local elites to build and expand, through aggregation and absorption of factions, a political center, which became the locus around which public and private policies revolved in Costa Rica. The first of these phases extended from 1889 to the short civil war of 1948. The war removed the liberal elite from its hegemonic position, from which it had been obstructing social-Christian and social democratic reforms initiated dur-ing the 1940s and accelerated by the *Junta Fundadora* of the Second

Republic under the leadership of José Figueres. The political realignment that took place during this phase was made possible by the active participation of the urban middle classes, which had been preparing for its incorporation for decades. The reforms revived public education, stressing democratic values and the need to defend civil liberties. The strengthening of the center-periphery axis led to an opening of the political process, which became still more evident in 1951 when the PLN was founded. The PLN became the nucleus of a highly participatory system, with a dominant party and statist-modernizing policies, which deepened and stabilized liberal democracy in Costa Rica (Vega Carballo, 1982, 1987).

During the postwar years, a high level of state intervention supported the extended political participation of civil society. State intervention geared the integration of the petit bourgeoisie and the popular classes toward stable center-periphery exchanges. The petit bourgeoisie and the popular sectors had backed the reforms of the 1940s and the inter-elite agreements of 1948-49 which allowed for the approval of a new constitution and the removal from power of the old coffee oligarchy founded during the First Republic. The reforms did not eliminate the elite, nor did they suppress its economic power, but instead opened the door to forces loyal to liberal-democratic ideals that had supported social-Christian and social-democratic reforms. (Ameringer, 1982.)

In this manner, social peripheries gathered around stimuli from the state and the dominant political party. They were incorporated and absorbed, some say asphyxiated, by a huge protective bureaucracy, which was mainly concerned with the redistribution of wealth toward the less favored classes. Redistributive practices were aided by an economic surplus generated by the sustained growth of the agro-industrial economy, which contributed 6% of the average annual growth from 1950 until the 1982 crisis. Social movements, such as trade unions and professional associations, could make demands in an atmosphere of civil liberty which, albeit limited, had no precedent in Costa Rica. In exchange, these organizations had to support and participate in a dense net of clientelistic interests. Often, base organizations were created directly from "above" by the higher spheres of the paternalistic bureaucracy. The bureaucracy could, from its high position, exercise still another function: granting favors, licenses, finances, and privileges to the private sector. It had controlled the banking system since 1948, as well as both legislative chambers, even when the dominant party lost elections, and thus controlled the budgetary process (Rovira, 1990).

At the same time, the ruling sector successfully promoted its own ideology, which supported civil and human rights, the rule of law, social mobility and equal opportunity, medium and small business, and especially the extension of formal political participation amidst a general consensus and social peace. The First Republic's old conservative motto of "order and progress" was thereby respected, but the ideological mix and the platform of newly dominant groups was incorporated into it. The regime carefully implemented state-led socioeconomic development policies, which met the demands of the middle sectors and the emerging industries. As Gaetano Mosca would have put it, it was a skillfully knit, splendid political formula, in agreement with the times when Keynesian policies still dominated, and when the American New Deal and its successors—John F. Kennedy's Alliance for Progress and Lyndon B. Johnson's Great Society—still had considerable influence.

The PLN therefore controlled the electoral and political processes from above through the bureaucracy and from below through the masses. It was able to create a small empire whose objective was the promotion of state-led development policies while incorporating civil society and the ideological superstructures in a democratic manner. This was in sharp contrast with several failed reform movements that had proliferated in Central America during the 1945-52 period. (Torres-Rivas, 1987). These failed movements eventually led to repression and to the violent exclusion of the middle and popular classes from the political-electoral process and from involvement in the functioning and organization of the state. Elsewhere in the Central American isthmus, the rule was cyclic and worsening crises of participation and departicipation, which have been analyzed elsewhere (Vega Carballo, 1983).

From 1982 to 1983, the leftist coalition *Pueblo Unido* lost much of the strength it had enjoyed during the previous decade. This was due to the division of the Communist party and the collapse of the union movement. The center-right movement, however, gained coherence as the Social Christian Unity Party (*Partido Unidad Social Cristiana*), which was created through an agreement backed by the PLN in order to consolidate the two-party system and allow them to share the benefits of controlling the state. From another perspective, this agreement could be seen as an effort to counterbalance the centrifugal tensions of center-periphery relations by adding stability to the system. This was initiated precisely at the time when the economic crisis was at its worst, and when the external threat was most alarming to the people in power. The relationship between these circumstances and the defensive unification of the different group has been described previously (Vega Carballo, 1987). The "centrist" agreement can be explained not only as the defense of a democratic regime under threat, but also as a foreign policy tool toward a Central America immersed in the Esquipulas agreement. The purpose, therefore, would be twofold: to defend democracy and to address a key issue of national security.

PUBLIC POLICIES AND FOREIGN AID

The policies of public spending changed at the same time that the pacts creating the new two-party system were adopted. Under the old system such policies were promoted through pressure from organizations linked to international banking. Additionally, the extent of the foreign debt (close to $4.5 billion) played a crucial role. The change in direction, however, did not bring to an end the social programs—in contrast to what is happening now, when the less tense atmosphere allows for a climate in which new reforms and new models of development are being proposed for the 1990s. With emergency programs, such as Social Compensation under the Monge administration, and Social Housing under the Arias administration, the government avoided leaving the most impoverished and severely affected sectors of society without protection. (García-Huidobro, 1990).

For military and geopolitical reasons, the United States and other Western capitalist countries increased foreign aid to Costa Rica, considered a "bastion of democracy" to be protected at all costs. The total amount of foreign aid to Costa Rican public coffers grew from $312 million in 1981, to a maximum of $404 million in 1983, followed by a slight descent later on. Victor Hugo Céspedes (1985, p. 124) has estimated that the total amount of foreign aid delivered to Costa Rica from 1981 to 1984 was $3 billion. Funding from the U.S. government alone jumped from $14 million in 1980 to $157 million in 1983. The figure was still above $120 million in 1986 (Rovira, 1987, p. 71; Fagen, 1988, p. 151). This indicates the importance of foreign aid in allowing the Costa Rican government to keep the programs that preserved minimum standards of living for the popular classes at a time of deep economic crisis. So-called "social expenses," which constituted 23.3% of the gross national product (GNP) in 1980, only decreased to 15.8% in 1983, recovering after 1987 to almost 20%. Per capita expenditures went from 728.2 constant *colones* in 1966 to 495.9 *colones* in 1983 and close to 550 *colones* toward the end of the decade, despite the severe financial recession triggered by foreign debt negotiations and the adoption of new development models.

As Guendell and Rivero (1987) argue, this strategy was built following the framework of the agreements with the IMF, the World Bank, and the USAID. Many of the demands made by these organisms had to be implemented. What makes the Costa Rican case unique, Guendell and Rivero argue, is that the demands of the popular sectors were also incorporated, as the social policies clearly indicate (see Guendell and Rivero, in Rojas et al, 1989, p. 115). There were, nevertheless, some negative effects. For one, research has indicated that services have deteriorated substantially. The state has maintained its role as institutional mediator in social conflicts in a more limited, although perhaps, more effective way. It has achieved this by embracing the neoliberal strategies that advocate limiting assistance to only 20% of families, thus covering only the very poor and excluding the middle class, and even the bureaucracy. This is also an attack on the clientelistic practices and the patronage of the political parties.

Surprisingly, the system of political parties and electoral dynamics followed opposite paths instead of splintering and polarizing with the crisis. The public sector, in the mean time, attempted to avoid catastrophe by maintaining emergency programs and basic social services targeted to the middle and popular classes, which constituted the base of the clientelism net. The most surprising result of this process was civil society's rejection of the "incorporation" scheme as a model of political development and the substitution of a "deincorporation" model. This so-called "neoliberalization" of state-society links turned, by the mid-1980s, into a counterattack from the private business sector with clear anti-development and anti-state components. Backed by multiple international organisms still intoxicated by Reaganomics, this process continues unobstructed today.

The two-party system counterbalances the impoverishing economic policies followed since 1982, which have decimated much of the periphery. A series of private corporative agencies with easy access to the mass media has provided backing for these policies. They have dismantled all forms of opposition and have fueled an atmosphere of resignation, as well as of mere survival at the individual, family, small business, and informal levels. Under increasingly more difficult conditions, privileged groups, especially in the urban sector, are adopting survival strategies that range from participation in fundamentalist religious groups, in competition with the state's official Catholic church, or participation in magical and esoteric sects, to diet variations and restrictions. In suburban and rural areas, some families have entered a survival home economy. Time spent on recreation, hobbies, or the arts has decreased. Larger numbers of family members have entered the labor market, especially the informal sector. Small craft shops, family shops, street vending and door to door vending have also flourished. Armed gangs trying out new forms of organized crime have appeared. All these changes have contributed to a de facto depoliticization of civil society, rooted on a different view of the state, which is now necessary, since its capabilities of redistributing goods and services vanished.

This "informalization" of the economy has been a response to generalized adverse physical, emotional, and social conditions. However, it has also been the result of the changing role of the state and of its weakening societal links. This point deserves more attention from researchers, who, up to now, have focused their attention on labor and economic aspects. Complete parallel systems have appeared as the functioning of the crippled state has deteriorated. These parallel systems, whether they are considered legal or illegal, are usually tolerated or even encouraged, even by agents of change connected to the patronage net working with the bureaucracy and the bi-party system. This generates new and endemic forms of corruption. It has also contributed to the failure of all serious attempts to mobilize and radicalize the population undertaken by a labor movement anchored to obsolete vertical models of mobilization (Vega Carballo, 1990).

It is possible that these changes in state-society links have had little or no impact on the formal and widespread aspects of the democratic, pluralist, and highly participatory political system of Costa Rica. They have also not modified the highly conformist roots of the system. The efforts made to obtain large amounts of foreign aid have helped ease budgetary and current account deficits and other economic problems of basic social programs. Stabilization and internal contention efforts were launched, sometimes even in contradiction of the suggestions of the more radical negotiators of neoliberal policies. Foreign policy maintained a high degree of stability as the fight for a negotiated solution to the Central American crisis, and for a halt to the influx of refugees from Nicaragua and El Salvador continued to be main goals. The policies of the PLN administrations (Monge, 1982 and Arias, 1986-90) were continued, albeit with some changes made by the PSUC (Calderón, 1990-94), which enjoys the invaluable support of the strengthened political center.

CONCLUSIONS

By now it has become clear that only a political structure with wide, highly institutionalized and legitimate power can serve as the framework for the alignment of heterogeneous forces. The simplistic and catastrophistic theories of those who predicted that the Costa Rican democratic regime would collapse in the short term have thus been disproved. Nonetheless, a weaker political structure would have to face the same alignments, which combat the standard political party system, that plague other nations of the Central American isthmus.

However, none of the threats of insurgence, or of authoritarianism in dealing with insurgence, has materialized so far in Costa Rica. If the combination of psycho-cultural and structural factors explained earlier in the chapter does not change, it is unlikely that Costa Rica will follow the political path of many of its neighbors. Likewise, if the current PSUC administration of President Calderón is careful not to destroy (with the help of the ''Chicago Boys'') the buffers so carefully built in Costa Rica against the impoverishment and radicalization of the worker-peasant sectors, the present political structure should remain unchanged. Currently, the movements on the right, whether traditional or neoliberal in origin, cannot reach out for a professionalized and politicized army to assist them in the ideological prosecution and police repression that would be necessary to eliminate Costa Rica's social achievements. This is also a significant difference between Costa Rica and its neighboring nations.

The abolishment of the armed forces and the resistance of the political leaders to centralize police forces or to transfer funds from social programs to military expending will still play an essential role in protecting the democratic regime. At the same time, disarmament in the neighboring countries of Panama and Nicaragua will provide a more positive environment. Finally, it is encouraging that international organizations such as the World Bank are beginning to recognize that the demilitarized Costa Rican model should be implemented in other nations and should receive more international support (Associated Press cable which appeared in *La República*, July 8, 1991).

The survival of the democratic regime in Costa Rica is not a mere product of historical or sociological good luck. What are the possible causes of its survival? The Costa Rican case indicates that democracy is not a mere stage of development, as suggested by a North American empiricist school of thought (Neubauer, 1967; Smith, Jr., 1969). This school attempts to explain the origin and predict the viability and collapse of democracy through the analysis of interconnected economic variables. Most of the variables usually associated with economic success and modernization collapsed in Costa Rica after 1982, and have still not fully recovered. They deteriorated to the point of not meeting the ideal requirements to sustain the so called ''democratic regime.'' Therefore, the thesis that democracy is a stage of development is wrong. Furthermore, democracy is not a final product. Democracy is not an object or a fixed system, but rather a series of fluid processes, which paradoxically do not appear to have any linear correlation with any preconceived socioeconomic system. If there were a correlation it would not make sense to talk about democratization of closed, authoritarian, or military economic or political systems - in the east, south, north or west.

Democracies are something much closer to what we have in Costa Rica: the expression of real and practical historical efforts, procedures, and specially flexible strategies so that the political leaders develop through trial and error, in a slow process, ways to adjust and readjust. In the case of Costa Rica such strategies were based in interrelated premises, such as (1) the attempt to balance economic growth with distributive fairness and with widespread and pluralist political participation—all within a unitary model in which none of the elements becomes dominant at the expense of the others; (2) the need for political leaders to make conscious efforts to promote mutual trust of the political actors, stimulate a cultural compromise, and provide channels for negotiation and permanent dialogue. In other words, the creation of a consensual political culture; and (3) the need to sustain a highly legitimized political "center" with strong incentives to achieve lasting inter-elite political formulas, in Gaetano Mosca's words, or agreements. This center should be subjected periodically to the vote of the masses of the cities or the countryside. Although these formulas are far from perfect, they offer high levels of usefulness and security.

There is another aspect of the Costa Rican case worth emphasizing because of its theoretical and practical implications. It involves the capacity of a relatively homogeneous society to change its model of production and accumulation without fractures or social upheaval. Costa Rica does not have the ethno-cultural, linguistic, and other cleavages that have marked other Central American nations, particularly El Salvador or Guatemala. It also has not received the destabilizing waves of immigrants that South American nations, Argentina in particular, have had to confront. It can also be demonstrated that economic changes do not necessarily produce symmetrical changes in society. Furthermore, changes resulting from an economic crisis may take a direction opposite of the one that might be expected.

To the surprise of those who sustain mechanistic or linear paradigms, the Costa Rican case is evidence that a political-institutional superstructure, with its correlative value, opinion, and belief systems, can outlast or even be reinforced by economic crises and changes in external factors. It also shows how it can survive the process of modernization through the support of the dominant value system by the dominated classes and its real or apparent pluralism, or through apathy, alienation, or resignation to the lack of options. It could also be argued that it is normal to go through periods of crisis and structural change, since they are inevitable; or that these swings are technical in nature, and not sociopolitical, thus requiring impersonal, aseptic, and politically neutral treatment. This invalidates many deterministic and fatalist predictions regarding relations in social systems. Since the events of the 1980s, these theories are now obsolete, although they played an important role in the eighteenth and nineteenth centuries.

Finally, it is necessary to focus attention on another point brought up in this chapter: How is it possible that a concatenation of postmodern circumstances, which appear to be external to a society protective of its legal and geographic borders is actually not well predicted by some theories, for example, the once-famous dependency theory? This refers to what was once called the internationalization of the Central American crisis. What escaped the attention of many observers is that this time the situation was quite different from the situation in previous conflicts, such as the war between El Salvador and Honduras in 1969, or the less far-reaching conflicts which arose from the Cold War. It is hoped that this dimension will emerge under new light from the shadows of empiricist research and theory. This would help explain how small countries, particularly those located in areas with high strategic value, such as Israel and Costa Rica (Avinera, 1987), can provide substantial flexibility for change, and why other much larger and more powerful countries, such as the former Union of Soviet Socialist Republics, are unable to do so.

The connection between these successful strategies and transnational interdependence helps to invalidate many restrictive hypotheses based only on the internal dynamics of the nations-states. Physical, legal, and economic borders are being dismantled, overwhelmed by the processes of transnational integration-disintegration found in the New World order that was described earlier. Whether the new order will tend toward democracy or authoritarianism, toward economies that repress or encourage egalitarian economic development, will depend on the evolution of the mechanisms of international cooperation, which had tremendous importance in the case of Costa Rica. This is not a theoretical problem, but a practical one, directly linked to the policies of industrialized nations, especially in levels of protectionism and the way in which the foreign debt problem is addressed. In Lipset's (1989) words, "In the possible and necessary New World Order the wealthy and advanced democracies cannot impose their vision of the world to the developing world. They can, nevertheless, create an international political and economic climate which strengthens the position of democratic leaders and organizations in the Third World. This would increase the chance of success of democracy in those Third World countries."

The near future will tell us if we are right on this, and whether we can advance to new areas of research and thought. In political science we must not only seek relevance, but also a commitment with practical applications, in handling the issues of political development and social welfare. After all, we may one day realize that the primary goal of political science is the same as the best goals of humanism and healthy socialism, which have only one purpose: to send the human mind in search of universal formulas of coexistence that will allow maximum levels of well-being in all levels of social and human existence.

NOTES

1. It is now known that the armed forces of many of the major South American states employing the repressive model willingly offered to cooperate with their counterparts in the isthmus. Thus, their designs for total ideological war would resonate on a continental scale. This was the motive for their pushing for acceptance of their offer of continuity in the military-oligarchic dictatorships of Costa Rica's neighbors (remember the "travels" of the military "advisors" of the Chilean and Argentine armed forces to various sensitive areas in Central America). It has been well documented that they, along with the United States, contributed to military activities in Honduras and Costa Rica (Flynn, 1985; Edelman and Kenen, 1989, especially pages 269-78; Reding, 1986). Moreover, this contributed to the national insurgency of the bloc of *criollo* power, or at least to factions of it. Vargas Cullell rightfully classifies these factions as "coup-favoring," traditionally conservative, liberal equilibrium, nationalizing reformists (1987, pp. 134-38). They refused to continue on the anti-democratic path in spite of the great surrounding pressures that fanned the winds of war and obstructed peace processes and regional demilitarization.

2. Other useful information comes from the Costa Rican Social Security Register (CRSS, Planillas Nacionales) and the General Director of Statistics and Census (DGEC), whose statistics on Price Index, Basic and Nonbasic Consumer Basket, and especially the annual data bases of "Household Surveys of Multiple Items" I have recombined and recalculated for the entire decade of the 1980s.

3. The CPI for Costa Rica measures the current cost of 158 goods and basic services for a typical family of five.

II

Themes in the Restructuring of the Political Economy

Three

External Debt, Structural Adjustment, and the Labor Market

Carlos E. Santiago

The 1980s is seen as another lost decade for Latin American and Caribbean economic development. The dramatic fall in international private lending to the region after 1981, and the subsequent reliance on conditional lending from multilateral public institutions such as the International Monetary Fund and the World Bank, has resulted in alternative approaches to economic revitalization and growth. The ability of the state to pursue countercyclical economic policies and expand its influence over economic matters has been substantially curtailed by external lending conditions and by domestic constraints that arise as a consequence of long-term budgetary deficits. As a result, economic liberalization policies of the 1980s pursued, among other things, privatization of government assets, deregulation of commercial activity, promotion of non-traditional exports, wage repression, and long-term balance of payments equilibrium.

The objective of this chapter is to discuss the general state of liberalization and structural adjustment in Latin America and the Caribbean, its links to the labor market, and the potential limits to the current export promotion development strategy. These limits are partially attributed to inconsistencies between the pursuit of macroeconomic policies and microeconomic behavior. The cases of Jamaica, the Dominican Republic, Costa Rica, and Puerto Rico are discussed. Although there are considerable structural differences between these countries, there are also similarities in the scope of liberalization policies that were enacted during the 1980s.

The chapter is divided into four sections. The first section surveys the recent experience of Latin America and the Caribbean with respect to external debt and economic performance. In addition, the labor market effects of liberalization policies in Jamaica, the Dominican Republic,

Costa Rica, and Puerto Rico during the 1980s are examined. Similarities
and contrasts among the four are highlighted. The second sections
reviews existing approaches to the study of liberalization and labor market
adjustment and presents a useful, descriptive framework for identifying
target groups most affected by these policies. The third section discusses
the use of a modified household production approach to the study of labor
market phenomena. The model presented is applicable to household non-
farm small-scale producers, such as those found in the urban informal
sector. Finally, section four provides concluding comments and direc-
tions for further research.

EXTERNAL DEBT AND STRUCTURAL ADJUSTMENT—
HOW FAR HAVE WE COME?

In some respects, the crisis of external debt in Latin America and
the Caribbean, which reached its depth in 1982, has abated. Indicators of
external trade and indebtedness certainly show improvement for the
region. Yet there is considerable doubt that these gains have translated
into broad-based and consistent increases in standards of living. The
principal issue is whether efforts to expand foreign trade and reduce
international indebtedness via structural adjustment, ten years hence,
have been worth the increased inequality and relative and absolute poverty
that have accompanied them. These policies can be justified only if one
can argue that, in the medium term, standards of living will rise.
Table 3.1 shows some principal economic indicators for Latin
America and the Caribbean between 1980 and 1990. From 1983 to 1990,
exports and imports of goods and services from the region increased at
relatively similar rates—approximately 4.3% annually. The growth of
foreign trade has certainly surpassed the growth of the gross domestic
product (GDP) for the region. The balance on current account has also
improved as the gap between exports and imports of goods and services has
narrowed and net receipts of transfer payments have increased. In
addition, indicators of the impact of foreign debt servicing, such as the
ratio of interest and amortization to total exports or the ratio of interest
payments to exports, have declined. The former from 37% to 27% between
1980 and 1989 and the latter from 20% to 14% over that same time period.
It is also true that the implementation of structural adjustment
programs in the region is not uniform. Mexico, Chile, and Bolivia have
embraced more radical efforts at overhauling their domestic economies
while Peru, Haiti, and the Dominican Republic have come rather late to
the process. The disparity of efforts at structural adjustment is also
reflected in the disparity of outcomes. Certainly, some countries have

Table 3.1
Principal Economic Indicators for Latin America and the Caribbean, 1980-1990

	1980	1983	1984	1985	1986	1987	1988	1989	1990
I. Growth Rate of GDP (%)	5.8	-2.3	3.2	2.8	3.8	3.0	0.8	1.1	-0.7
II. Balance of Payments (billions of U.S. $)									
Exports of Goods and Services	123.1	116.8	129.4	123.6	107.8	120.6	135.4	148.5	164.2
Imports of Goods and Services	154.2	126.3	131.8	128.3	126.5	132.8	147.7	158.3	177.7
Current Account Balance	-30.5	-8.4	-0.7	-2.0	-16.6	-9.4	-8.3	-5.8	-6.8
III. Total External Debt (billions of U.S. $)	242.5	361.0	377.5	390.0	409.7	445.1	427.6	422.2	428.6
Long-term Public and Publicly Guaranteed Debt	129.7	221.8	249.8	275.4	309.6	341.5	332.5	324.6	317.6
Long-term Private Non-guaranteed Debt	43.1	69.0	65.7	55.5	49.8	43.2	30.6	23.5	21.5
Short-term Debt	68.3	61.3	50.4	44.5	33.9	42.2	48.1	58.4	68.8
IV. Foreign Debt Servicing									
Interest and Amortization (billions of $)	46.0	50.2	51.6	47.7	47.5	45.9	54.6	45.3	44.4
Interest and Amortization (% of Exports)	37.4	43.0	39.9	38.6	44.1	38.1	40.3	30.5	27.0
Interest (% of Exports)	19.7	29.8	27.2	28.1	27.7	23.4	24.6	17.4	14.2
V. Gross Domestic Investment (% of GDP)	24.3	---	16.7	17.7	17.7	20.4	20.9	19.5	---
VI. Total External Financing (billions of U.S. $)	29.3	20.3	17.0	12.9	9.6	12.6	13.4	8.9	---
Net External Credit (excl. IMF)	22.9	16.0	12.7	7.4	4.8	5.4	3.8	0.6	10.3
Direct Foreign Investment	6.1	3.5	3.2	4.3	3.5	5.6	8.0	6.6	---
Grants (excl. technical assistance)	0.3	0.8	1.0	1.2	1.3	1.5	1.6	1.7	---

Source: World Bank, *World Development Report 1992* (Johns Hopkins University Press, Baltimore, 1992).

showed more improvement than others. We need to begin documenting those instances where specific interventions of structural adjustment have resulted in particular consequences. The link between macroeconomic policy and economic effect is not always clear, and the claims that structural adjustment policies have resulted in specific outcomes must be examined carefully. One could certainly argue that economic recuperation and recovery might simply represent improvements in the international arena which have only limited ties to a particular economic restructuring package. On the other hand, we must also highlight those circumstances where economic inefficiencies have been surmounted and market opportunities augmented by structural adjustment policies.

One of the objectives of structural adjustment is to "rationalize" the domestic economy and promote exports of non-traditional goods and services. This involves providing a stimulus to the export sector and eliminating exchange rate and tariff biases that might inhibit development of these activities. Presumably, foreign direct investment would provide the needed capital and technology to compete in the international arena. A question that has not been raised is whether there are limits to export promotion of non-traditional goods and services—much like the limits to import substituting industrialization that emerged in the 1970s and that preceded the debt crisis.

A major difficulty in continuing a policy of export promotion of non-traditional goods and services is that (1) debt servicing remains high in the region, (2) the public resources necessary to support subsidies to the export sector are scarce, and (3) the availability of external financing to import capital goods to maintain the export initiative is unpredictable. Much of the success of an export promotion strategy is the ability to expand into new markets without the hindrance of tariff barriers or other forms of protection. Sluggishness in the industrial economies or increased protectionism will reduce the prospects for export promotion of non-traditional exports from Latin America.

The inability to continuously finance imports, in the face of an already compressed import bundle made up largely of hard to import substitute capital goods (so needed to sustain economic growth), led to economic collapse during the early 1980s. Thus, the limits of an inward-looking, import-substituting industrialization development strategy lie in the difficulty in acquiring technology and training a skilled labor force to produce those more difficult to substitute capital goods. This same phenomenon may lead to the demise of the outward-looking export promotion strategy currently popular in the region. Fiscal discipline and austerity have led to declining expenditures on education and infrastructure, endangering prospects for the development of human capital. How long can these countries afford to subsidize exports and foreign direct investment, at the expense of other societal needs?

Structural Adjustment in Jamaica, the Dominican Republic, Costa Rica, and Puerto Rico

The economic stagnation that befell Latin America and the Caribbean during the 1980s was acutely felt in the Dominican Republic and Jamaica. In 1988, per capita gross national product (GNP, in current dollars) in the Dominican Republic was less than two-thirds of its 1980 level. Jamaica did show some recuperation during the late 1980s, but nominal per capita GNP was still 93% of 1980 levels and 85% of 1975 levels in 1988. Both Costa Rica and Puerto Rico showed a greater capacity for recuperation from the 1979 recession. Still, per capita GNP in Costa Rica in 1988 was 87% of 1980 levels. The Costa Rican labor market demonstrated a greater capacity for recovery than did other countries. Puerto Rico was not adversely affected by falling primary product prices (it gained from lower oil prices) and benefited from improved economic conditions in the United States. Nonetheless, the 1970s showed that Puerto Rican economic growth was unsteady and that economic downturns in the United States resulted in longer periods of stagnation on the island.

Jamaica, the Dominican Republic, Costa Rica, and Puerto Rico all invoked liberalization measures during the 1980s, although some with greater commitment than others. In the case of Jamaica, the Dominican Republic, and Costa Rica, liberalization was prompted by international public institutions before additional lending would take place. In the case of Puerto Rico, liberalization was spurred by conservative administrations in the United States. For Puerto Rico this generally meant tax reform, revisions to the Internal Revenue Code that regulates U.S. subsidiaries on the island, reform of the banking sector, and increased privatization of public assets.

Jamaica, the Dominican Republic, and Costa Rica undertook policies more directly associated with conditional structural adjustment lending (Worrell, 1990). The Jamaican dollar was devaluated periodically after the Seaga government was elected in 1980. In liberalizing the tightly controlled Jamaican economy the island was able to reschedule earlier debt and receive considerable loans and Special Drawing Rights from the International Monetary Fund and the World Bank. Some external financing went to promote non-traditional manufacturing and agricultural exports. In 1984, the Jamaican dollar was allowed to float daily against the U.S. dollar. That same year, the government imposed surcharges on banks and trust companies, increased taxes on tourism, travel, and cigarettes to cut its deficit by $44 million. An agreement was reached with the IMF in 1987 to provide loans to aid the country during the restructuring process. Rather than continuing the devaluation of the Jamaican dollar, the government offered subsidies to exporters, wage increases were limited to 10%, existing price controls were maintained, import duties and corporate tax rates were cut, and major banks were denationalized. Exports remained sluggish, and additional lending from public international institutions was required. The government embarked on an ambitious program of capital spending in 1987 and combined it with continued divestment of state-owned enterprises. By 1987 recuperation had begun as gross domestic product increased 4%—its highest level in four years. The devastation caused by Hurricane Gilbert in 1988 proved a real setback to economic expansion, but considerable international aid and insurance payments enabled the economy to recover more rapidly than expected. Debt was rescheduled with the Paris Club in 1990, allowing Jamaica a five-year grace period on existing debt, with ten years to repay.

The Dominican Republic also underwent an orthodox liberalization program during the 1980s. Its economic crisis was precipitated in the early 1980s by falling sugar prices (its main export) and a lack of diversification of its export sector. The shortage of foreign exchange became acute as external debt servicing payments rose dramatically, import substitutes were overemphasized (many were foreign exchange dependent) and capital flight grew. Some efforts were made to reduce fiscal deficits, but the results were disappointing. Likewise, exchange rate policies failed to reverse a situation of continued depreciation and domestic inflation. The IMF increased its lending in 1983 on conditional terms, and previous debt was rescheduled. Public opposition to rising food and gasoline prices following continued devaluation grew violent. The recovery proved extremely slow as sugar prices lagged and U.S. sugar import quotas were reduced. The little recovery that was noted by 1985 was attributed to the growth of the tourist sector and investment in free trade zones. Cheap labor costs and low rental fees for plant and office space were major inducements to foreign investors to expand or initiate operations in the Dominican Republic. By 1988 the government requested a refinancing of its more than $4 billion foreign debt.

The government of Costa Rica acted quickly to address the worsening economic crisis of 1980-82. A set of policy initiatives was adopted in 1982, and standby agreements were signed with the International Monetary Fund with the purpose of implementing stabilization programs. Structural adjustment loans were obtained from the World Bank in 1985 and again in 1988 to further the process of economic reorientation. Costa Rica agreed to join the General Agreement on Tariffs and Trade (GATT) in 1989. The result of these efforts has been to reduce the scope of public sector intervention and stimulate the growth of non-traditional exports.

The Puerto Rican economy was certainly not invulnerable to adverse economic conditions during the 1980s, and there were parallels with changes occurring in the labor markets of both the Dominican Republic and Jamaica. One common feature of all these economies is the pattern of demographic change observed during the 1980s. In effect, changes in the rate of natural increase in the population were far greater than the rate of population growth. The equalizer was obviously a net out-migration of labor during the decade of the 1980s.

The economic downturn experienced by these countries did not appreciably affect the natural increase in the population, as mortality rates reached a low-level plateau and birth rates continued a steady decline that preceded the 1980s. In 1988, the natural increase in the Dominican population was 24 per thousand, while Costa Rica had a 23 per thousand rate, Jamaica a 20 per thousand rate, and Puerto Rico a 12 per thousand rate. These differences reflect, more than anything else, disparate standards of living in the four countries.

Over the period of stagnation and uneven growth of the 1980s, a growing divergence was observed between the rate of population growth and the natural rate of increase, particularly for the three Caribbean economies. In effect, the population growth rate remained "artificially" low as net emigration began to dominate population growth dynamics. This phenomenon was quite apparent in Puerto Rico during the years of mass emigration of the 1950s. That emigration resurged on the island during the 1980s is symptomatic of present economic difficulties. However, to equate the emigration of the 1950s with that of the 1980s is incorrect, inasmuch as the nature of circular migration has changed. One proposition, not fully elaborated upon in this chapter, is that Puerto Rican migration has become more cyclically sensitive compared to the 1950s.

Documentation on Dominican and Jamaican migration during the 1980s is poor, and research in this area is scanty. However, the 1990 U.S. Census will probably bear out that a critical mass of Dominicans and Jamaicans has taken up residence in the United States, opening the way for continued migration from the Caribbean. As individuals from these countries move to the United States, their families and relatives are increasingly likely to join them abroad. Likewise, information is easily processed and transmitted by return migrants.

The case of Dominican migration to the United States during the 1980s is a particularly interesting phenomenon inasmuch as Puerto Rico often plays the role of way station between the Dominican Republic and the United States. Duany (1990) provides an insightful study on Dominican workers in the Puerto Rican labor market. Estimates of Dominican migration, both to Puerto Rico and the United States, indicate that the 1980s represents a period of substantial net emigration compared to earlier decades. Moreover, Duany argues that the nature of Dominican migration to the United States is fundamentally different from that to Puerto Rico. Dominican workers disproportionately enter low-wage tertiary sector activities in Puerto Rico, while those that gravitate to the United States exhibit higher educational attainment and skill levels more suitable for manufacturing and public sector employment. These differences have important implications for understanding labor market dynamics in Puerto Rico and the United States.

A related phenomenon is the simultaneous decline of real wages, particularly in informal sector activities, and the increase in labor underutilization as a result of economic stagnation. This seemingly contradictory result highlights the segmented nature of labor markets in all four countries. During the 1980s, real wages declined precipitously in the Dominican Republic and Jamaica, and to a lesser extent in Puerto Rico. Although wage data are notoriously poor, there seems little to contradict the notion that wage levels were eroded by inflation (often resulting from repeated devaluations) and a lack of government support (induced by conditional lending practices) for increasing nominal minimum wage levels. By 1988 the average hourly wage rate in the Dominican Republic was 62% of the Jamaican wage rate and 13% of the Puerto Rican wage rate (Cearra-Hatton, 1989). During the worst years of the economic crisis in Costa Rica, real wages declined while labor underutilization increased. But this pattern was short-lived, as recovery took place and inflation ebbed. This was due to the particular dynamic of inflation, indexation, and minimum wage change that is institutionally ingrained in the Costa Rican society.

Although Puerto Rico and Costa Rica fared better than Jamaica and the Dominican Republic during the 1980s, there is some evidence (Santiago and Thorbecke, 1988; Santiago, 1989) that earnings in the urban informal sector in Puerto Rico declined to low levels—partial proof of the expansion of labor supply to this sector. Gindling (1991) and Gindling and Berry (1991) also show that considerable segmentation exists between formal and informal sectors in San José, Costa Rica. Labor costs in Jamaica and the Dominican Republic were extremely competitive compared to those in Puerto Rico, and some formal sector employment did occur in response to the establishment of free trade zones, but it would be naive to assume that the informal sectors did not expand in these countries as well. The economic stagnation was simply too prolonged, and governments had virtually no resources for a sustained program of countercyclical employment generation. That informal sector activities grew in spite of substantial emigration and declining wages in the formal sector is further evidence of the economic stagnation that affected Jamaica and the Dominican Republic.

A FRAMEWORK FOR THE STUDY OF AGGREGATE LABOR MARKET ADJUSTMENTS

Resistance to the implementation of structural adjustment policies on the part of Latin American and Caribbean governments is generally linked to the view that the labor market will bear the brunt of adverse effects of liberalization. This will be reflected in falling real wages, slow employment growth, and more frequent and longer spells of unemployment. In Williamson (1990), Patricio Meller highlights the importance of analyzing the potential effects of structural adjustment policies on the market for labor: "All too often it is the labor market that serves as the residual through which almost all the *structural* (author's insert) adjustment is achieved. It would be good to see inclusion of these issues in the next formulation of the Washington policy consensus," (p. 35).

It is ironic that this important conclusion comes after a decade of falling incomes and declining standards of living for considerable sectors of the population in Latin America and the Caribbean. On a more positive note, while most recent research focuses on domestic and external macroeconomic adjustment and equilibrium, there is a growing body of literature concerned with the effects of structural adjustment on the labor market. It is especially crucial that this emphasis continue if we are to address the difficulties of moving to a development path with "equitable growth" (Ranis, 1987).

Perhaps the most explicit consideration of the effects of economic liberalization on labor markets is found in Edwards and Van Wijnbergen (1988) and Edwards and Edwards (1990). Using a trade theoretic model based on three principal sectors (importables, exportables, and non-tradables) and two factors of production (labor and capital), they show that import tariff reductions can result in non-trivial unemployment. This partly justifies the general reluctance of many Latin Americans to embrace structural adjustment policies. Moreover, it highlights the precarious position of newly emerging democratic regimes, given scenarios of medium- to long-term economic hardship.

What makes the trade-theoretic approach of considerable relevance to understanding labor market adjustment to economic liberalization is the introduction of practical assumptions, such as the existence of (1) a fixed minimum wage in the importables and non-tradables sector; (2) an uncovered (free or informal) non-tradables sector; (3) Harris-Todaro-type quasi-voluntary and queuing unemployment for non-tradable and importable covered-sector employment; (4) a labor-intensive exports sector; and (5) non-perfectly inelastic labor supply. These characteristics of labor markets in less-developed countries (LDCs) have found support in the theoretical and empirical literature.

Trade liberalization is initially reflected in a decline in the price of importables in response to a reduction in tariffs (the terms of trade effect). Labor gravitates away from the importables sector and toward the exportables and non-tradable goods sectors.[1] This increases the waiting time for relatively ''high wage'' employment in the covered non-tradables and importables goods sector. Simultaneously, the outward shift of the labor supply function in the uncovered non-tradable goods sector will depress wages while total employment in the non-tradables sector expands.[2]

In the long run, the fixed minimum wage cannot be sustained because political pressure works against the protected (covered) sectors.[3] The initial effect is to reduce labor force participation for agents whose wage falls below their reservation wage. In addition, the probability of obtaining covered-sector employment increases as the gains from involuntary queuing unemployment falls. The longer the period of adjustment, the greater the fall in involuntary unemployment as the free and protected sector wages converge.

This conceptualization of labor market dynamics is consistent with traditional views of the mechanisms of labor mobility and market-clearing adjustments. The few empirical/policy-oriented studies (Mann and Sánchez, 1984, 1985; Riveros and Sánchez, 1990) on this subject support the theoretical postulates. Many of these studies focus on the experience of southern cone countries, particularly Argentina, Chile, and Uruguay; and the findings are consistent throughout. The dichotomies that are highlighted include differences between (1) tradables and non-tradables sectors, (2) urban and rural areas, (3) skilled and unskilled labor, and (4) formal and informal sectors.

Some of the more interesting findings are that the wage gap between formal and informal sectors has increased, that wages are generally rigid in the formal sector, and that the degree of labor mobility between the two is limited. Moreover, the manner in which liberalization policies were implemented exacerbated the urban-bias that characterized earlier periods. In most cases, open unemployment did not become a serious problem until the early 1980s when the non-tradables sector expanded relative to the tradables sector. It is also noteworthy that the movement of labor market aggregates suggested an ''added-worker'' phenomenon in which women were entering the labor market in increasing numbers while the participation of men declined, often because of early retirement from formal sector occupations. Increases in female labor force participation were evident during the 1980s. These findings lend support to elements of the basic theoretical structure discussed above.

Revisiting the 'Dual-Dual' Framework

A useful approach to better illustrate the sectoral impact of liberalization policies is to employ a multisectoral framework such as that often found as a component of a modified Social Accounting Matrix (SAM) model.[4] To be relevant, the framework must assist in the identification of "stylized facts" as guides to help understand labor market phenomenon. Important dimensions of the framework include the location of economic activity and the nature and technological sophistication of that activity. A related consideration is the amount of human capital endowed in the labor required to carry out various activities. Such a schematic framework appears as Figure 3.1.

In these multisectoral models, sector differentiation is often associated with dualistic development. The general notion of dualism highlights the interdependency between modern (formal) industry and traditional (informal) agriculture as expressed in surplus labor models. In contrast, a "dual-dual" framework extends the standard model by incorporating regional dimensions.[5] The distribution of modern sector activities between urban and rural areas is often not stressed enough. The role of traditional non-farm activities in rural areas is also often underestimated. The latter is often viewed simply as a repository of non-migrating agricultural labor during the off-season. However, research (Anderson and Leiserson, 1980) suggests that this sector is not only large, but also important in sustaining rural incomes.

The urban informal sector is recognized as critically important in any discussion of labor markets in Latin America. This recognition exists even though there is considerable disagreement concerning the characteristics, role, and functions of the urban informal sector. Moreover, there is little interest in incorporating informal sector activities into standard national income accounting frameworks or much of a consensus on the most appropriate way to accomplish this. This has led to snapshots of the urban informal sector in particular metropolitan areas with considerably less information available on longer-term trends in the growth of these activities. An important notion regarding urban informal sector activities, which will be discussed in greater detail later in this chapter, is that informal sector activities often encompass the production of goods and services for both the market and the household, often with the use of family and wage labor.[6]

A major paradox in the study of the labor market experience of Latin American and Caribbean countries over the past decade is the coexistence of declining real wages in both formal and informal sectors, with continued sluggish growth of formal sector employment. A contributing factor is the growth of labor supply—impulsed as it is by the demographic

Figure 3.1
A Multisectoral Framework for the Analysis of Labor Market Change

Location	Type of Activity		
	Formal		Informal
Urban	Skilled	Unskilled	3
	1	2	
Rural Non-Farm	4		5
Rural Farm	6		7
External	Skilled	Unskilled	10
	8	9	

transition. It also reflects a process of rapid urbanization owing to massive rural-urban migration that is fueled largely by difficulties in maintaining living standards in rural areas. These supply-side factors often over-shadow any substantive gains in the growth of formal sector employment.

The inability of the formal sector to promote employment to keep pace with labor supply is related to the structure of the wage cum skill locus. The likelihood of obtaining formal sector employment and the prospects for moving between formal and informal sector occupations are tied to the variety of skills and attributes that the worker brings to the job. Surely, workers with more skills have better opportunities for obtaining formal sector employment. But they may also be the most likely to experience open spells of unemployment because (1) they would generally have more resources to "afford" longer spells of unemployment and (2) their reservation wages are higher, leading them to resist acceptance of lower-paying informal sector jobs.

One factor that has complicated formal sector labor absorption over the past decade has been the combination of general economic stagnation with the inability of the state to promote employment at past rates. Countercyclical spending on the part of government is limited by budget deficits and enforced by conditional lending policies of international public institutions. Certainly, part of the justification of past public sector employment growth was to forestall social unrest and political upheaval. But, given the limited options available to many countries, the declining role of the state in these activities may be viewed as a necessary price to pay for stabilization and long-term growth. It is also conceivable that a political consensus has been reached wherein the pendulum of a political-economic trade-off has swung in the direction of democratic reform and reduced state intervention.

Another crucial component of the multisectoral framework of Figure 3.1, especially for Caribbean societies and Central American societies, is the existence of a migratory outlet. Communities of Caribbean-born residents have long resided in the northeast United States, serving as hosts for new immigrants. Central American immigrants to the United States have quickly carved out communities. Information about employment earning and income-generating opportunities travels quickly to the region, and family networks foment a support system for the new immigrants. Governments often promote, both implicitly and explicitly, emigration of their labor force because it reduces pressures on local labor markets and provides needed remittances to help sustain incomes of the non-migrant population. A feature of Caribbean and Central American migration that deserves further exploration and research is the potential for continuous and circular migration, principally between the islands of the Caribbean and the United States. This back-and-forth migration is fundamentally different from the place-to-place migration that is characteristic of rural-urban migration. The circular nature of Caribbean migration manifests itself both in continuous moves of different people and multiple moves of the same individuals. This phenomenon has important implications for labor markets in regions of origin and destination.

A MICROECONOMIC APPROACH TO THE STUDY OF LABOR
MARKET ADJUSTMENT

The preceding analysis focused on aggregate or sectoral labor markets, with little concern for the microeconomic behavior that underlies the macroeconomic phenomena. To understand the full ramifications of structural adjustment it is necessary to examine the household and individual responses to policies that impact labor markets. What is sought is a consistent microeconomic link to the macroeconomic patterns that emerge. A potentially useful direction is to use the household production model, which is commonly applied to agricultural activities, to examine non-agricultural household activities similar to those that occur in predominantly urban informal settings. Melmed-Sanjak and Santiago (1990) have developed this application.

The household production model poses a problem in which household utility is maximized subject to a full-income budget constraint. This constraint differs from the conventional budget constraint by the incorporation of household profits from the family enterprise and of exogenous income. Thus, the key is that consumption and production decisions are made interdependently. One consequence of the assumptions concerning the imperfect substitutability of family labor in the home enterprise in both consumption and production is that the wage rate for home labor activities, w_1, is determined endogenously.[7] Considering the comparative statics of family labor, (L_1), and of hired labor demand in the home enterprise, (L_3), Melmed-Sanjak and Santiago (1990) demonstrate that both are functionally related to the parameters of both the profit function and the utility function. Another implication is that L_3 varies with w_2, family labor's alternative employment opportunity cost. It also proves interesting to consider simultaneously changes in w_3, the wage rate for hired labor employed in the home enterprise, and w_2, the wage rate that family labor receives in non-home enterprise employment.[8] Because family labor and wage labor are imperfect substitutes in production, changes in the market wage will impact the mix of unpaid family workers and wage labor within the household enterprise. This, in turn, affects the ability of the informal sector to play a role as employer of last resort.

The following four propositions, derived in Melmed-Sanjak and Santiago (1990), highlight the usefulness of applying the household production framework.

Proposition 1: *Family labor supply will vary positively with the price of hired labor.*

Proposition 2: *The response of hired labor demand to changes in the wage rate is not unambiguously negative.*

This result of the application of the household production model to non-farm activities is contrary to standard results from the theory of the firm.[9] Interestingly, empirical estimates of the elasticity of demand for labor in farm enterprises are quite small compared to values estimated using conventional models. In the context of the household production model, hired labor demand may be predictably inelastic if substitution possibilities are limited by the quasi-fixed character of family labor supply.

Proposition 3: *The demand for hired labor will vary positively with the market wage rate for family members in outside employment.*[10]

Proposition 4: *The supply of family labor to the home enterprise is expected to vary inversely with changes in its market earnings opportunities.*

The four propositions can be summarized in terms of the following expressions: dL_3/dw_3 is indeterminate; $dL_3/dw_2 > 0$; $dL_1/dw_3 > 0$; and $dL_1/dw_2 < 0$. These results illustrate the potential usefulness of moving to a framework of analysis that differs from conventional models, and provides insight into the behavior of small-scale non-farm household units such as those found in the informal sector in Latin America and the Caribbean. In particular, they admit the possibility that using traditional employment models to evaluate hired labor demand may result in "perverse" or biased results if agents actually make decisions in a household framework. Moreover, they can help explain contradictory results that arise out of macroeconomic policies formulated in the guise of structural adjustment reforms.

One example of the contradiction between macroeconomic structural adjustment policies and microeconomic behavior is the continued unemployment and persistent immiserization of informal sectors in the face of considerable wage repression. If we assume that the economy is closed, such that migration is prohibited, w_2 and w_3 will be influenced by similar forces and they will move in a parallel fashion. Further assume that wage repression results in a downward trend of w_2 and w_1. Family labor supply to the home enterprise will fall (rise) if the decline in the opportunity cost of outside employment for family members w_2 has a greater (smaller) impact on family labor supply than does the decline in the wage rate for hired labor w_3. In addition, it is conceivable that the effect of a decline in w_2 on hired labor demand will reinforce or overcome the effect of a decline in w_3 on hired labor demand, resulting in no improvement in informal sector employment opportunities in response to wage repression.

On the other hand, if we now examine the situation of an open economy with external migration, and further assume that wage repression results in a fall in w_3 but not w_2, the results suggest the following:[11] (1) family labor supply to the home enterprise will unequivocally decline in the face of opposite movements of w_2 and w_3, and (2) hired labor demand will be more elastic in the open economy compared to the closed economy. The case of the open economy, which is more characteristic of Jamaica, the Dominican Republic, Costa Rica, and Puerto Rico, provides a rationale why, in the household enterprise, family members are often "exported" and furnish remittances to the household while the household hires non-family wage labor. The extent to which this phenomenon is actually occurring will have to be left to empirical analysis.

The consistency between structural adjustment policies and labor supply/demand decisions in the context of the household production model needs to be reconciled. If the informal sector is as large as most studies suggest, then to invoke structural adjustment without accounting for the role of the informal sector as employer may lead to unexpected consequences. One runs the risk of further marginalizing large sectors of the labor force if structural adjustment does not lead to growth with equity.

CONCLUSIONS

This chapter serves to point out the need to focus on three different areas for understanding the dynamics of Latin American and Caribbean labor markets over the past decade. The first is the comparative evaluation of labor market phenomena across different Latin American and Caribbean economies. There are few studies of this sort, but it is important to reconcile theoretical propositions with empirical evidence. The second involves analytical work that combines trade and labor theoretic approaches. The existing literature is scanty, but has proved quite useful. In particular, the sectoral differentiation and the assumptions regarding the coexistence of market clearing processes and queues are noteworthy. The third is the need to study the microeconomic underpinnings of observed macroeconomic phenomena. Again, very little has been done in this area, particularly with regard to labor markets in Latin America and the Caribbean. The household production model does provide a useful framework for integrating small-scale production activities with the broader labor markets in which they operate and offers some interesting hypotheses for empirical evaluation.

NOTES

An earlier version of this chapter was presented at the XVI International Congress of the Latin American Studies Association held in Washington, D.C., April 1991. The comments of R. Albert Berry, Tim Gindling, Katherine Terrell, and, especially, Jolyne Melmed-Sanjak are greatly appreciated.

1. The relative price of non-tradables will be affected to the extent that non-tradables can be substituted in consumption with importables and exportables.

2. The uncovered non-tradables goods sector is akin to the informal or free market sector often discussed in the development literature. It should also be pointed out that workers may opt for labor force withdrawal in the event that informal sector wages fall below reservation levels.

3. The fixed wage can be due to explicit government legislation or might simply reflect union negotiated wage floors.

4. A recent example of the use of a SAM model to assess the impact of recent agricultural development policies in Mexico is found in Adelman and Taylor (1990). One particular aspect of the empirical exercise is to assess the alternative impacts of unimodal and bimodal agricultural development strategies.

5. The term ''dual-dual'' was first coined by Erik Thorbecke (1965). Subsequent elaborations within a development planning framework are discussed in Graham Pyatt and Erik Thorbecke (1976) and Erik Thorbecke (1980).

6. In this regard, Bhagwati (1982) argues that the urban informal sector constitutes the ''urban counterpart of the traditional sector in the rural areas.''

7. w_1 is the return to labor that equates the household's (*cum producer*) demand for family labor derived by profit maximization with the household's (*cum consumer*) supply of family labor derived by utility maximization. It is referred to as ''the virtual wage'' in the literature on agricultural household behavior (Singh, Squire, and Strauss, 1986).

8. The assumption is maintained that family labor is an imperfect substitute in production of the goods marketed by the family business and that, when entering the labor force, family labor seeks employment in a different labor market. Hence, two wage rates are specified. However, it is not unrealistic to presume that factors which affect the wage rate in one non-farm occupation may also influence the wage rate in alternative non-farm activities (especially when one recalls that these activities, while different, are substitutes in the utility function).

9. The response of hired labor demand to a change in the market wage rate will be unambiguously negative only if the ''substitution'' effect on the virtual wage is smaller than the ''income'' effect on the virtual wage. Otherwise, the elasticity of hired labor demand may be dampened.

10. Intuitively, as w_2 increases, the demand for leisure and outside work increases, implying that the family labor supply to the home enterprise decreases,

inducing an increase in the virtual wage. Because L_1 and L_3 are substitutes in production, the increased price of L_1 will imply an increased demand for L_3.

11. Assume that w_2 is the wage the migrant receives in the place of destination.

Four

The Dynamics of Agrarian Policy in United States History: Implications for Contemporary Central America

Jolyne Melmed-Sanjak

INTRODUCTION

The agrarian structure of a nation influences the participation of the agrarian population in the political economy and agrarian policy is determined by the forces of political economy. The character of this circular influence has important ramifications for economic development. Therefore, in the contemporary Central American context of stabilization and structural adjustment policy (SA), it is useful to look (again) at land policy, with an eye toward its implications for economic growth. Noe Pino (1981) notes that from the point of view of the defenders of SA, the answer to the question of how SA will resolve problems of land tenure [and associated agricultural development problems], income distribution, and un- and underemployment is that market forces will reassign resources in such a manner that economic growth will produce spillover effects which will benefit all of the population (i.e., trickle down). This is at best a tenuous conclusion, as the contemporary worsening of the distribution of income in the United States illustrates. In the context of Latin America, Berry (1991) shows the short-run distributional consequences of SA. Carter and Mesbah suggest a permanence to these tendencies in their recent work on land markets and agrarian structure in Chile (Carter and Mesbah, 1992).

Without contesting the merit in policies of market liberalization and export promotion, one can observe that the espoused vision of market salvation is supported based on a naive or incomplete view of the model behind the miracle growth experiences in East Asia. There is an unfortunate tendency to forget the historical context in which liberal market policies were adopted in East Asia (see Lin, 1988). Of particular relevance is the fact that in the 1950s both Taiwan and South Korea witnessed extensive redistribution of land through agrarian reform programs oriented toward ownership in family-sized units. In Taiwan, the agrarian reform was followed by policies of support to the agricultural sector (e.g., infrastructural investment, fertilizer subsidy, and modernization programs), which implied substantial increases in productivity and incomes. In contrast, the Korean government did not invest so much in agriculture, depending more on external funds to finance its industrialization. Could this difference have contributed to greater macroeconomic and distributional problems for South Korea? It is also worth noting that, historically, the East Asian governments have also put much emphasis in human resource development, that is, education.

Interestingly, a review of U.S. history leads to the inference that the economic success of our country similarly has roots in a set of family farm-oriented land policies and in continuous policies of education, agricultural research, and agricultural sector subsidization. Together, the forces behind and the development of the profound policy initiatives adopted in the United States in the late nineteenth century can be viewed as analogous to an agrarian reform. Our "agrarian reform" received its greatest impulse in the Homestead Act and in the Morrill Act, both enacted in 1862. These acts recognized the political commitment of a family farm-oriented agrarian structure and set the stage for the development, dissemination, and adoption of modern agricultural practices.

Through an investigation of the dynamics of agricultural policy and economic progress in the history of the United States, this chapter will draw conclusions regarding the contemporary problem of economic development and its relation to agrarian policy in Central America. The chapter proceeds as follows. A conceptual discussion of the implications of land distribution policy and agrarian structure in the process of economic development is provided in section two. In section three, a review is presented of the history of U.S. agrarian policy through the early twentieth century. This review is used to analyze the role of particular agrarian policy choices in the process of growth and development of the United States. In section four, support is given to Owen's (1966) argument that the operation of the Mill-Marshallian model of agricultural development fueled the growth process in the United States in a very successful way.[1] Furthermore, the implications of the legacy of Jeffersonian agrarianism for political power and institutional development were a critical factor in shaping the successful transformation of the United States to an industrialized nation. An initial broad distribution of land across the population was necessary for the transformation of the economy to proceed and for growth to be inclusionary.

In section five, these arguments are extended to the contemporary

Central American context. Recently, political and academic thinking about agrarian policy has been colored by the notion that land reform in Latin America is dead; however, this chapter argues that SA has created a niche for reevaluation of land policy. Historically, egalitarian or redistributive agrarian policies have not occurred without a matching of popular agitation and political openings, for example, as in both East Asian and U.S. history. The contention here is that land reform (albeit of a different nature than in the past) can be consistent with the goals of SA. Moreover, the extent to which land access is made a priority will critically influence the degree of success attained in the long run with the regime of policies imposed as SA. The dynamics of SA should, in this light, release the political deadlock on land policy in Latin America that de Janvry and Sadoulet (1989) have recently characterized as entrenched; i.e., programs of SA should incorporate reform and extension of the previous agrarian reform programs in Central America. The chapter concludes with a discussion of whether and to what extent efforts to address problems of land distribution will be pursued within the new policy environment.

LAND DISTRIBUTION AND EMPOWERMENT EXTERNALITIES

The extensive literature on land distribution focuses on the debate about the equity and productivity implications of particular distributional and tenurial patterns in the process of growth (Koo, 1982; Putterman, 1983; de Janvry and Sadoulet, 1983; Carter, 1984). The productive impacts of reforms that favor more broad-based ownership of land espouse the incentive-theoretic benefits on resource use and allocation.[2] It is also generally accepted that the payoff from any land policy is limited in the absence of comprehensive policy actions including (in addition to land redistribution) credit programs, technical assistance, and education. Speaking in regard to agrarian reform in Asia, Ladejinsky (1966) demonstrates the success of comprehensive agrarian reform. He asserts that in Taiwan agrarian reform meant the following: sharp increases in security of tenure, investment in land improvement, improved agricultural technology, expansion of productivity, and increased standard of living in rural areas.

In the past, based on equity and productivity considerations, economists have said that reform must be made without paying particular attention to the dynamics which drive the necessary institutional change. In their recent epitaph for Latin American land reform, de Janvry and Sadoulet recognized the dynamic problem of implementing agrarian reform: " . . . the episode of Latin American land reforms which failed to achieve the promised net social gains by asset redistribution because they were rendered economically unfeasible by the shifting political power induced by the very land reform institutions'' (de Janvry and Sadoulet, 1989, p. 1398). Thus, they assert, in Latin America, the dynamics of political economy put the brakes on the process of structural change in agriculture.

Drazen and Eckstein (1989), albeit from a very different standpoint, also critically comment on the long-run dynamic of redistributive, ownership-oriented land reform. Their main point is that, in fact, such reform may not be welfare improving because of the ''crowding-out'' effects of land accumulation on physical capital accumulation. While their theory seems correct, it ignores the possibility of land distribution without large land debt burdens accruing to individuals. The historical precedent of subsidizing or eliminating private payment for land distribution programs would reduce or eliminate the crowding out effect. Moreover, the case of Taiwan demonstrates the possibility of making the transfer of land a stimulus to the industrial sector by paying the land debt through the granting of industrial bonds.

Finally, extending the logic of de Janvry and Sadoulet to the United States and Taiwanese experiences, one observes that the very process of land distribution empowered the rural populous. Ladejinsky (1966) notes the reshuffling of local political power that followed as a consequence of agrarian reform in Taiwan. Hayami and Ruttan (1986) recount a similar story of political power shift following tenurial reform in a Philippine village. Through this empowerment, the institutional change necessary to ensure modernization and accumulation of productive capital in agriculture was set in force. In Latin America, in contrast, agrarian reform policies, as implemented, yielded greater empowerment to the larger-scale, commercial farm enterprises. Therefore, institutional development and the extension of modernization have been concentrated and relatively limited.

Speaking of Latin America, de Janvry and Sadoulet classify the results of empowerment via property ownership as institutional rent-seeking: ''It takes the form of tax advantages, the location of public works projects, the nature and availability of technical progress, selective price support programs, access to subsidized credit, all of which are allocated by the forces of political economy'' (de Janvry and Sadoulet, 1989, p. 1406). A similar statement could be made in reference to the evolution of U.S. agricultural policy and institutions. However, because of the difference in the distribution of empowerment, the behavior of farmers is more appropriately labeled ''profit-seeking.'' (Nabli and Nugent [1989] refer to the distinction between rent-seeking and profit-seeking. Rent-seeking is viewed as a socially wasteful means to individual gain.) In other words, during the period of active land settlement policy, the "rents" favored the family farm sector, which constituted the mass of the rural population (even though our current regime of agricultural policy may favor the large farm sector and corporate interests). The difference in the institutional paths of the United States and Latin America reflects the importance of coincidence, in time, of economic and political logic. In the United States, the geopolitics of settling the new nation created an opening favorable to popular agrarian politics. Whereas, in Latin America, the influence of rent-seeking behaviors on institutional development changed the cost-benefit calculus of land reform policy so as to prevent its comprehensive implementation.

In the literature, the effect of competitive profit-seeking behavior in agricultural development is known as the agricultural treadmill. Owen notes the importance of institutional development in the functioning of this treadmill:

The speed of this 'agricultural treadmill,' which a family farming system inherits along with market opportunity, quite obviously tends mainly to be conditioned by the degree to which knowledge and access to new methods and techniques are generally available to farmers. Thus, the Mill-Marshallian model provides a framework within which increased agricultural production, on a cumulative basis, can be rendered essentially automatic and almost a direct function of public investment in agricultural research and rural education and of the adequacy of complementary rural financial institutions and farmer's financial reserves. (Owen, 1966, p. 53)

What is missing from his discussion is the question of under what circumstances a government will make these necessary investments. One might infer the existence of an omnipotent government that would extend the institutional support necessary to the functioning of the treadmill in foresight of social gains. However, in the Latin American context, such investments are notoriously lacking.

Hayami and Ruttan (1986) assert that greater understanding of the process of modernization is gained by viewing changes in institutions, as well as technology, as endogenous to the economic system. They assert that the demand for institutional change is responsive to changes in factor supply and demand. The example is given of farmers pressuring public researchers to develop appropriate technologies in response to market conditions. However, the question of what leads to the existence and maintenance of a public research system still remains to be addressed. In general, say Hayami and Ruttan, "the sources of supply of institutional innovation are less well understood" (Hayami and Ruttan, 1986, p. 107). The argument can be made that the family farm-based agrarian structure,

itself, yields the   political climate in which appropriate institutional
development will be supplied (of course, demand-side incentives, as
explained via the treadmill effect, will also exist). This argument makes
explicit the circular dynamic between distribution and modernization.[3]

In the context of agrarian policy, the existence of such institutional
rents or profits can be considered as empowerment externalities. The term
"externality," while used loosely here, captures both the source of the
evolution of early U.S. agricultural institutions and their crucial role in
our enjoyment of a modern economy. It is appropriate in the sense that the
investment cost of making land productive (and, prior to the Homestead
Act, paying a purchase price) gave the family-farm sector significant
propertied interest which secured its political stature. Thus, while the
broad distribution in land ownership stemmed from the geopolitical
position of rural people vis-à-vis the newly forming democratic government, once established it carved a particular political niche for the farm
population in national policy (which was, as it happened, in line with
Jeffersonian ideals[4]). As a group, then, family farmers had a common
interest in promoting legislation that would increase their individual
profit. The payoff, therefore, for investing in land was greater than its
immediate agricultural yield. Thus, using the label of empowerment
externalities appropriately emphasizes land distribution as a force behind
the supply of institutional and technological development.

In sum, more equity in resource distribution, in addition to its direct
merit and impact on production, has indirect implications for the dynamics of growth. The profit motive in a competitive economy will induce
those empowered by ownership to demand institutional support for their
enterprise. More important, the location and distribution of the supply of
public institutions will be qualitatively different under different distribu-
tions of property. This difference is implicitly recognized in the observation that a highly decentralized system of agricultural research centers
yields greater response to the farmer's demands (Hayami and Ruttan,
1986). Unlike the case of Latin America, the productive benefits of
induced technological and institutional change can widely characterize
the agricultural sector.[5]

AGRARIAN STRUCTURE AND INSTITUTIONAL DEVELOPMENT IN THE UNITED STATES: AN HISTORICAL SYNOPSIS

In this section, a brief synopsis is presented of U.S. agricultural
history, with an emphasis on agrarian structure and institutional evolution. The discussion demonstrates how, historically, these two facets of
agrarian economy were interlinked. It also notes the role of education in

the process of empowerment. It is important to recognize education as a productive asset whose distribution is, as is that of land, a relevant issue that tends to be determined within the realm of political economy.

Albrecht and Murdock (1990) provide a useful schematic presentation of U.S. agricultural policy history: (1) the period from 1776 to 1862, characterized by infrastructural development (i.e., canals, railroads, surveying and titling); (2) the period from 1862 to 1933, characterized by agricultural development fostered by research and education; (3) the period from 1933 to 1965, characterized by commodity program development; and (4) the current period, characterized by concern for consumer issues. The discussion in this section will subdivide history in a similar fashion, although the latter two periods will be reviewed together and only in a cursory manner.

Prior to the revolution of independence in the United States, the rural-land tenure system had feudal characteristics (Cochrane, 1979)[6] and much land lay idle. With independence, feudal land holdings became state land holdings and the question of an appropriate tenure system to govern these lands was a major policy concern. Thus, the earliest land policies of the United States evolved from the debate about control of state lands in the east. Cochrane identifies a purpose in the ensuing policies of erasing the essentials of feudalism and stimulating a small farm-oriented, private ownership rural economy[7]. Once the westward expansion began and the states turned over much of their landholding to the federal government, the issue of appropriate land tenure was the focus of debate in the process of disposal of the national public domain. The policy pattern established in the East was not automatically accepted as the basis for land distribution in the frontier regions. In fact, the political mood favored a more conservative large farm-based distribution policy.

The process of liberalization of land policies is earmarked by the passage of the land ordinance of 1785, which was mainly supported by western politicians. This ordinance set in motion the process of surveying the domain and marking 640-acre sections for public disposal by auction. Interestingly, the 1785 ordinance required that one section be retained for the purpose of education in each township. This reflected the prevailing Puritan philosophy of the Northeast, which saw education as a keeper of religion.[8] Agitation to further liberalize the land settlement policies and make lands available to families with little resources continued as the initial tendency for lands to be bought by wealthy speculators clashed with the tendency of squatters claiming lands.

National interest in attracting immigrants and increasing urban tensions eventually swayed the political arena in favor of the squatter, and the United States witnessed a series of land ordinances and acts that progressively made land available in smaller parcels at more accessible prices (Bertrand and Corty, 1962). The Distribution-Preemption Act of 1841, which endorsed the claims of settlement by squatters before actual purchase, was a noteworthy part of these legislative initiatives. This act also allocated more public lands for the support of public schools.

This turbulent epoch in agrarian history culminated[9] in the Homestead Act of 1862, with its provision for free disposal of the public domain in 160-acre lots to those who could settle and make productive a parcel of land. The political forces behind the passage of this act represent an interesting set of alliances. The Homestead Act was mainly supported by easterners concerned with the poor condition of life for the urban working class and by squatters on the frontier. It was opposed by eastern industrialists who viewed it as opening the doors for labor migration and by western farmers who viewed it as driving down land values.

In summary, the pre-revolutionary period of U.S. history was essentially feudal in ownership structure with the majority of the population living by subsistence farming (Albrecht and Murdock, 1990). (In fact, despite the fact that agricultural modernization and commercialization had begun, Kirkendall [1987] suggests that ours was basically a peasant society until the Civil War era.) By the Civil War, the debates and struggle over land policy were resolved in favor of a family farm-oriented agrarian structure.

A POLITICAL ECONOMY INTERPRETATION OF AGRARIAN CHANGE IN UNITED STATES HISTORY

From the perspective of the arguments made earlier in the chapter, one can say that a relatively broad distribution of empowerment had been achieved by the late 1800s in the United States. That is, because of the historically unique broad distribution of land ownership, the family farmer was a force forming a political constituency. The landed masses also had access to public grammar school education, and some pursued secondary education. It can be argued that farm ownership generates the income base to allow effective demand for education. Koo argues this way in the context of East Asian development: "But one must not overlook what land reform has done in raising the income of the farmers, which, in turn, places education within reach" (Koo, 1968, p. 43). Yet it should be noted that the farm families in the United States did not wholeheartedly endorse the educational agenda being promoted during the era of school reform in the 1800s, as witnessed in their reluctance to sufficiently tax themselves to pay for more than minimal school operation (Binder, 1974). In fact, however, its existence meant a rural constituency that was both political and literate. As Cochrane states, education made it possible for a rural person "to become an informed citizen acting in his own best interests" (Cochrane, 1979, p. 311).

The force of this empowerment is evident in the legislative record during the late nineteenth century when economic pressure[10] led farmers to organize and push forward significant and innovative institutional developments. The Granger movement, as well as other farmer organizations, grew in membership and was influential in the ensuing changes in the social, educational, and economic conditions of the farmers (Albrecht and Murdock, 1990). Increasing agricultural productivity and "priming the pump of industrialization" were, at the same time, a national concern (Bonano, 1990). The particularly significant developments in this era were the regulation of interstate rail commerce, the institution of a land grant system for agricultural education and research (each state was to create an agricultural college that would provide an education more catered to the needs of rural people as opposed to the education offered by the private higher education institutions), the creation of the United States Department of Agriculture and its extension service (the land grant college system was oriented toward research with the creation, in each state, of an agricultural experiment station, with research results disseminated to the public via extension agents), and farm credit institutions. Thus, the institutions necessary for the functioning of the Mill-Marshallian model were created, and the technological change that drives the agricultural treadmill was rendered feasible because of the public sponsorship of research and dissemination. According to the literature on technology adoption, the existence of secure tenure and of credit institutions also played a key role in the process of agricultural modernization.[11]

By the early twentieth century, the process of modernization of agriculture had succeeded. Market-oriented surplus production was characteristic, and only 25% of the total U.S. population was engaged in agricultural production. United States agriculture entered a new epoch of agrarian policy oriented toward control of oversupply and the social ramifications of low product prices, which were exaggerated by the national economic conditions in the era of the great depression. More currently, the 1980s brought a debate about market-oriented policy and export enhancement efforts. As indicated in the introduction, contemporary questions regarding government intervention in the agricultural sector are not of particular interest for the theme of this chapter. However, the evolution of the land tenure system during the current century is relevant in explaining the movement of farm policy away from the interests of the small family unit and toward the interests of the larger commercial farm sector (Bonano, 1990).

The broadening effects of land settlement and the subsequent reconcentration of farms are evident in the historical comparison of the number and the average size of farms presented by Bonano (1990). He tells us that in 1850, there were 1.5 million farms averaging 203 acres in size; in 1930, there were 6.5 million farms averaging 151 acres in size; and by 1987, there were only 2.1 million farms averaging 462 acres in size.[12] Bonano argues that "U.S. agriculture is steadily moving toward a dual-structure" (Bonano, 1990, p. 18), with, in 1983, the largest 4.5% of farms generating 49.3% of the value of production and "rural residence" farms (50% of all farms were so categorized) producing only 3% of sales. The picture is even clearer in the data provided by Albrecht and Murdock (1990) who tell us that in 1982, 1.2% of farms had sales greater than $500,000, and that their sales represented 33% of total farm sales; 13.5% of farms had sales greater than $100,000, and their sales represented 75% of total sales; and nearly 50% of farms had sales less than $10,000, and their sales represented 3% of total sales. In fact, for the last group, farm-derived income constitutes less than half of the typical family's total earnings; part-time farming is a characteristic of the U.S. agrarian structure. Finally, in line with the arguments of de Janvry and Sadoulet (1989) regarding Latin America, institutional rent-seeking by the large farm sector seems evident in the distribution of the U.S. farm subsidies (Kahn, 1989).

While these figures are striking, the dualism is fundamentally different from the dual structure of agriculture in Latin America, where the large farm sector does not produce a correspondingly high percentage of agricultural value (Thiesenhusen and Melmed-Sanjak, 1990). Also, there are crucial differences in the size of small farms and the quality of life of the "land-poor" in the United States. While the smallest 50% of U.S. farms rely on off-farm employment for roughly half of their income as do the sub-family farm units prevalent in Latin America, the necessity of such work is less tied to basic subsistence in most of the United States (i.e., without denying the shameful existence of extreme poverty in the Appalachian and Ozark regions, the average quality of rural life is better in the United States than in most less-developed countries [LDCs]).

AGRARIAN POLICY IN CONTEMPORARY CENTRAL AMERICA: IMPLICATIONS OF STRUCTURAL ADJUSTMENT

In this section, the discussion focuses on the context of agrarian problems in contemporary Central America. The context for discussing land policy and growth is the macroeconomic environment of stabilization and structural adjustment. First, attention is given to the impact of land policy reform for the process of SA. The chapter focuses exclusively on the privatization component of SA, as it is directly related to the question of the linkage between land policy and economic growth. (Noe Pino [1991] provides a comprehensive discussion of the impact of SA on the agricultural sector.)

It cannot be said that SA is completely bad or completely good for the agricultural sector. Rather, experience is suggesting that some segments of the farm economy are gaining while others are losing, thus worsening the already skewed distribution of income. In this environment of deteriorating social well-being for the rural poor, the demand for access to secure land holdings and to agricultural services is growing. Can we say what the ramifications of more active and progressive or liberal land policies might be for the process of structural adjustment?

One can, without much imagination, observe the limited nature of SA which excludes such fundamental restructuring as that implied by agrarian reform. Lele (1990) rather forcefully suggests this in her empirical analysis of the impact of SA in Malawi's agricultural sector.[13] Furthermore, Adelman and Taylor (1990), using simulation analysis, demonstrate that SA accompanied by agrarian reform would have increased the benefits of macroeconomic restructuring in Mexico. Specifically, they demonstrate that while SA policies which failed to restructure agrarian policies were successful in relieving some of the macroeconomic concerns (by 1986, Mexico had a trade surplus, GDP had increased 2.4% from 1980, and the government was able to service its debt), the socioeconomic costs of SA were also apparent (by 1986, poverty had reached 51% of the population). They then show that SA accompanied by investment in small farm-sector development would yield significantly more improvement in macroeconomic variables without the associated deterioration in living standards. More important, they observe that the required government spending to fund rural development more than paid for itself by increased government receipts yielding a 6.4% bigger deficit reduction than SA without such investment.

Thus, cost-benefit calculation should support the goals of agrarian reform. Perhaps more importantly, the relationship between the goals of agrarian reform and the goals of SA can be characterized as symbiotic. That is, in addition to the just-mentioned benefits that an agrarian reform could contribute to the success of SA, the process of land reform in Latin American countries needs restructuring and, as will be explained in the following paragraphs, the SA initiatives toward privatization can be viewed as healthy for the success of agrarian reform.

As mentioned earlier in this chapter, the take-off stage of economic development in the United States and in the East Asian high growth countries was preceded by small farm, ownership-oriented agrarian policy. In contrast, in Latin America the orientation of reform attempts has been in favor of collective farming. This orientation carried an ideological face

that was often maintained rigidly in the reform legislation and/or administration. It now carries a popular face of failure. It makes one wonder
whether the specific form of agrarian reform determines whether or not
such reform will yield a positive contribution to the growth process. More
specifically, a relevant question is whether cooperative organization can
play a role in an agrarian reform that is both viable and consistent with the
overall objectives of SA.

In the case of Honduras, for example, the popular notions of cooperative failure exaggerate the problems of the reform sector (Melmed-
Sanjak, 1991). Instead, notwithstanding some problems, the reform
sector has shown an ability to adapt its institutional structure to the
economic reality in which it operates and, on average, is competitive with
the productivity of non-reform sector farms. Furthermore, the cooperatives play a key role in creating access to both social and productive
services.

The promotion of privatization as part of the programs of SA could
be extended to modifying reform laws in such a way that makes legal a
variety of uses of group organization, ranging from complete cooperation
in ownership and production to parcelized tenure with cooperation only in
services, as does the new agrarian legislation just passed in Honduras. We
cannot forget the importance of various forms of producer cooperation in
both the United States and Taiwan, nor can we overlook the ineffective-
ness of non-voluntary cooperation in a market economy. Interestingly, the
parcelization of cooperatives formed under prior agrarian reforms could
create a nascent capitalized family farm sector (see discussion of
parcelization in Peru in Melmed-Sanjak and Carter, 1991). Thusly
restructured, agrarian reform could bring about a broad distribution of
empowerment. However, it seems that this possibility rapidly evaporates
with land reconcentration (e.g., the Chilean experience). A functioning
system of service cooperatives and rural credit access could help prevent
this.

Simultaneously, agrarian reform is being reoriented toward policies
of land market stimulation and subsidization rather than relying on
expropriation as a means of land redistribution. In today's political
climate, this could make land access feasible for the many who were
excluded from prior land reforms. Surveying and titling of land holdings
is another action that would fall under the rubric of privatization and is
something that agricultural economists have argued would enhance productivity and promote modernization. Titling would also make land
holdings more useful as collateral. As mentioned earlier in this chapter
the first land ordinances in the United States provided for surveying, thus
setting the stage for a relatively expedient titling process. In fact, it was
precisely land market development and control that were the object of the

most "transitional period" of agrarian policy in the United States.

Finally, privatization of certain institutions is argued to be efficiency enhancing, assuming inefficiency arises from bureaucratic and, sometimes, corrupt management. Such inefficiency is particularly characteristic of some of the agencies that were created in efforts at agrarian reform, agencies which are known for poor management of funds, for not providing adequate incentive for repayment of debts, and for not extending services such as technical assistance. Making the agencies that are responsible for credit and other agricultural services more accountable would make them more effective. Complete privatization, however, may not be appropriate given that the private sector traditionally has not wanted to bear the risk associated with many agricultural operations. In the Central America context, the problem for private banks is worsened by the lack of secure title, which limits the use of land as a collateral base for loans. As mentioned, however, land titling is also a form of privatization.

CONCLUSIONS

The introduction of this chapter suggested that the early set of United States agricultural policy initiatives could be viewed as being analogous to an agrarian reform. "Agrarian reform" was viewed as a critical determinant of the path of economic development that the United States followed. Reiterating, the basic argument is as follows: The resolution of the debates over how to settle the state and national public domains favored the creation of relatively small, family-operated farms. At the same time, the leading political philosophy ensured that the settlement incorporated the development of an accessible system of public education. This meant the existence of a propertied mass of literate farmers who had a voice in national politics. Driven by competition and profit-seeking, they pushed forward innovative institutional change. The institutions that evolved made possible rapid and widespread modernization of agricultural technique. Of particular uniqueness is the socio-geographic pattern of location of and access to higher education, research, and public services. (In contrast, urban bias in institutional development is more pronounced in Latin American countries [see Schultz, 1968]). Agricultural development in the United States was, in fact, over successful—since the 1930s our agrarian problems have been largely related to overproduction and overinvestment. This pattern of agricultural development meant that the agrarian question was resolved relatively painlessly, that is, cheap food was abundant, the pace of migration to urban areas was more in sync with the pace of industrialization, and the gap between rural and urban development was not as exaggerated as in other parts of the world.

Remember, however, this happy process was not automatic, but rather the result of the dynamics of both the popular struggles and the political economy that characterized the newly independent country. Although Albrecht and Murdock note that the "privilege to own land became enshrined in the Declaration of Independence and the Bill of Rights, and has been historically the basis of American Farm Policy" (Albrecht and Murdock, 1990, p. 53), it was a struggle to create the uniquely egalitarian system characteristic of that time. There was much controversy, in fact, about the nature of agrarian policy.

Some particularly important qualifications and peculiarities of the United States example remain to be discussed. First, one must recognize that the agrarian history of the U.S. South differs significantly from what has been described herein as our national history. In fact, its characteristic was a bimodal structure of commercial crop-oriented plantations, which relied on slavery and indentured servants for labor, coexisting with very small farms. After the Civil War, there was an increase in tenant-farming arrangements. The history of the Suoth more closely parallels the export-oriented bimodal structures of Latin America. Perhaps it is not surprising that the incidence of poverty is relatively high in the South (Schiller, 1989, tells us that less than one-third of the U.S. population resides in the South, yet forty percent of the poor live there).

Second, one has to acknowledge that the U.S. land policy occurred in a context of relative abundance. Thus, the issue of the scale of production units that is prevalent in the debates about a unimodal, private ownership agrarian structure did not arise. The Homestead act gave land in 160-acre lots, an amount that is likely beyond the imagination of most individual *campesinos*. Moreover, Cochrane (1979) points to the importance of abundant land resources in providing a tax base from which to fund education, infrastructure, war and so forth. In his view, in fact, abundant land "drove the entire process of agricultural development in the US in the 19th century" (Cochrane, 1979, p. 311). The case of Brazil, however, tempers this conclusion. It demonstrates that abundant land is not sufficient for agricultural development to happen as it did in the United States.

Finally, the transfer of land from a landed elite, an important issue in the implementation of agrarian reform plans that was raised by de Janvry and Sadoulet (1989), was also a non-issue in the history of the United States. Our "expropriation" was of native American land. There was a general unity across white political interests concerning this issue, and the native Americans had no political clout nor comparable military strength.

Thus, an examination of the agrarian policy history of the United States illustrates clearly the dynamic interaction between the forces of politics and economics. Land policies were both determined by and influential in the political economy of our nation during its pre-modern era. This circular dynamic is a good example of Hayami and Ruttan's (1986) notion of the process of induced technical and institutional innovation. Moreover, explicit attention to the question of land distribution contributes to understanding the supply-side of the process of innovation in institutions.[14]

In a recent essay on institutions and economic growth, North notes that "the contrasting histories of North and South America are perhaps the best comparative case that we have of the consequences of divergent institutional paths for political and economic performance" (North, 1989). In that essay, North also questions what determines the path of institutional development. De Janvry and Sadoulet (1989) characterize the path-dependent development of institutions in Latin American agrarian policy and this chapter presents a similar discussion with respect to U.S. agrarian history.

The path-dependent nature of the process of development combined with irreproducible historical circumstances implies that the U.S. model, with its more favorable performance record, cannot (perhaps, should not) be directly transferred to Latin American policy. Nevertheless, it is clear that some model of "agrarian reform" must happen in the development of the region's nations. The advent of SA seems to provide an historical juncture[15] in which appropriate change could be implemented. With regard to contemporary Central America, in particular, there is a compatibility between two apparent strangers—structural adjustment and agrarian reform. SA needs agrarian reform, and the remnants of past attempts at agrarian reform need to be structurally adjusted.

Thus, in response to the conclusion that land reform in Latin America is dead, it was suggested in this chapter that SA brings the political opening for its rebirth, albeit in the guise of "market mechanisms." Whether and to what extent this opening will be realized, however, is a serious challenge to any optimism that this analysis may have stimulated. On the one hand, in reference to the economic unfeasibility of agrarian reform generated by the historical path of agricultural development in Latin America, the implications of SA can be read as swaying the cost-benefit calculus in favor of progressive rural development. In other words, the myopic policy horizon that "rationally" promotes large farm- biased agricultural development ignores the long-run consequences of this choice on fundamental factors, such as the composition of farm output and the accumulation of human capital, and, hence, for the macroeconomic growth process. The debt-crisis was, to some extent, a manifestation of this myopia. The Mexican case is illustrative, as shown by Adelman and Taylor (1990); the macroeconomic benefits of small farm-oriented agrarian policy would outweigh the costs. Additionally, Santiago (1991) indicates that there is now some evidence that the expansion based on "myopic" structural reform is now reaching its limits. Mexico, for example, is not completely free of its macroeconomic problems. The limits of an agricultural export-promotion-led growth strategy are likely to be even more limited in Central America given the nature of demand for non-traditional tropical produce.   More important, if the crisis of short-run decline in living standards and income distribution escalates social tension (e.g., Venezuela, Costa Rica, Honduras), self-interested politicians can no longer afford to be myopic. However, on the other hand, the changed global political economy may mean that such social tensions can be even more easily ignored or repressed than in the past.

In conclusion, issues relating to land distribution, or more broadly, agrarian structure, are being brought back to the policy arena in the wake of structural adjustment. And the contemporary mood of liberal economics is consistent with more extensive and enduring agricultural development than that which transpired in the past two decades of largely semantic attempts at agrarian reform. Might Central American nations witness the historically necessary match of popular struggle and political interest and act upon promoting inclusionary rural growth, or will we witness the solidification of the division between the haves and the have-nots? Might the increased social and economic tensions spawned by the debt crisis and SA break the institutional monopoly of large-scale agricultural interests (as in the 1960s the power of the landed oligarchy was challenged and land reforms enacted), or do the macroeconomic changes of SA only fortify these interests? Might the largesse of the agrarian bureaucracy be stirred such that broadly distributed rural progress can occur, or will "band-aid" social welfare programs appease growing tensions? The importance of such questions is epitomized in the debate surrounding the passage of the Agricultural Modernization Law in Honduras in 1992. This law restructures agrarian policy in a manner which proposes to make the Mill-Marshallian model accessible and viable. However, upon closer view, the law appears to be a double-edged sword that could just as easily fall on the side of redistribution in favor of the bimodal, export-dominated agricultural development path.

Can we be optimistic about the removal of long-run, long-standing structural impediments to the process of growth and development in Central America as a consequence of structural adjustment and stabilization? Not while ideological baggage haunts the intonation of agrarian reform (and the implementation of the neoliberal model of growth); and not while the contemporary competition for a share in the globalization of capital and technology overshadows and distorts cost-benefit calculus.

Rather, the trend may be toward macroeconomic progress that is exclusionary and of limited duration.

NOTES

1. The Mill-Marshallian model is one in which land is relatively equally distributed among farmers and, therefore, the farm sector is characterized by competition. The drive for profits leads a technological treadmill with decreasing average costs of production. Thus, cheap food is abundantly available during the process of industrialization. Bertrand and Corty (1962) similarly argue that the family farm system served as a stimulant to capital formation and moderization in agriculture.

2. There is also debate in the literature about the form of redistribution. Arguments are made in favor of production and/or service cooperatives based on imperfections in access to credit, insurance, and other productive inputs as well as advantages to scale in marketing. Arguments are made against cooperative institutions based on the potential disincentives for labor effort and long-run investment.

3. Hayami and Ruttan (1986) recognize that the distribution of economic and political power may bias the direction of institutional change. Yet, they do not connect this observation to their conclusion that growth in agricultural productivity is necessary for resolving problems of income level and distribution.

4. Owen (1966) diminishes the importance that Jeffersonian philosophy had in defining agrarian structure in the United States. He argues that geography and demographics played a larger role.

5. It cannot be said that broad access to research and technical assistance will assure the widespread benefits of modernization. Review of the impact of the Green Revolution in India indicates that available technologies may not be adopted under the constraints of subsistence. (Hayami and Ruttan, 1986, offer a succinct review of the critiques of the Green Revolution.) The effects of land distribution on the development of other agricultural institutions (e.g., for credit and infrastructure) may be equally important.

6. The material in the following paragraphs is primarily a summary of the historical accounts provided by Cochrane (1979).

7. The mechanisms for creating such a system included allowing individuals with limited capital to purchase small parcels of land and granting land as an inducement for military service.

8. This was in contrast with the view of the southern elite who agrued that popular education would create a political threat. In practice, the latter view seems correct; popular education is a keystone in the process of democracy. Basic education of the population, in this sense, is a critical piece in the argument about the development of institutions that favor the functioning of the Mill-Marshallian

model.

9. The term "culminated" refers strictly to the particular epoch of agrarian history already discussed. Land settlement policies continued to evolve and the Homestead Act was modified repeatedly, perhaps reducing its effectiveness in creating a unimodal agrarian structure.

10. The Civil War caused a labor shortage which helped induce mechanization even at the cost of high debt (Bonano, 1990). The resulting increased productivity meant low product prices. The rail monopoly added to the economic stress of the farmer by imposing high tariff rates.

11. Kirkendall (1987) argues that this technological bias in the land grant system meant that, eventually, it has failed to serve the interest of promoting rural welfare. This is not inconsistent with the argument made herein in which these institutions are seen as having developed in response to the profit motivation of the family farm sector and by the national need to promote agricultural modernization. As Schultz (Schultz, 1968, p. 160) states in reference to the system of land grant institutions ". . . . is not efficient in promoting the welfare of rural people, it promotes agriculture."

12. Furthermore, the United State, despite its Jeffersonian ideals, experienced a period in which tenant farms were prevalent. In the 1930s, 42% of all farms were tenant operated. However, after 1939, tenancy diminished in importance as new institutions such as co-ownership partnerships and cooperatives evolved. (Albrecht and Murdock, 1990).

13. Castel (1991), in his discussion of Latin America's debt crisis, makes a convincing argument in support of this assertion.

14. History also tells us that the position of a nation *vis à vis* the global market and global politics has important influence on the supply of institutions. Comparison of the development of East Asia and Latin America might be used to examine the importance of global factors.

15. Hayami and Ruttan (1986) give numerous other examples in which changes in economic realities (e.g., the opening of Thailand's economy to international trade) induced changes in property rights structures.

Five

Structural Adjustment and Honduran Agriculture: Some Considerations

Hugo Noé Pino

INTRODUCTION

Changes in commercial trends at the world level, the rise of external debt, and the formation of economic blocs are some of the external factors that have conditioned the behavior of the economies of underdeveloped countries during the past decade. Those changes translated into a loss of dynamism in traditional exports at a time when debt repayments were pressing. These changes produced serious disequilibria in the balance of payments for many countries that, in turn, created economic crises, which lead to, among other things, stagnation, inflation, and unemployment. Unlike in the past, these disequilibria did not constitute temporary changes in economic and financial trends among nations, but reflected new facets in the world economy. One of the most significant aspects was the substantial increase in the technological gap between developed and underdeveloped countries. This was manifested in advances in biotechnology, electronics, cybernetics, and other fields of applied science.

Even though the diagnoses regarding the economic crises in underdeveloped countries took into account the new world context, much emphasis was placed on the assertion that the crisis was also a product of distortion-producing state interventions in the economy. These diagnoses were put forth principally by international financial organizations (IFOs) that recommended a reinsertion in the world economy based on economic liberalization processes. Consequently, the structural adjustment programs (SAPs), well known and debated in the Latin American context, were designed and promoted. They included both traditional policies of stabilization as well as adjustment policies that sought to increase the efficiency of the economy based on economic liberalization (e.g., commercial, financial, exchange, and pricing). It is in this context that Honduras and other Central American countries began at the end of the last decade and the beginning of the present to apply such programs.

One important component of the SAPs is sectoral-level adjustment for the agricultural, energy, financial, and social sectors. The objective of this chapter is to analyze and discuss the program of structural adjustment in the Honduran agricultural sector. The first section will present a brief history of agriculture in the post-war period, with the goal of understanding the modifications introduced by the agricultural structural adjustment program. The second section discusses some general considerations about the structural adjustment program in Honduras, detailing the principal methods adopted up to the present. This permits a better understanding of the links between macroeconomic and sectoral policies. The third section analyzes structural adjustment policies that specifically affect the agricultural sector. New policies are described, along with the processes by which they were created. This is important because it clearly demonstrates the influence of IFOs in the determination of the national political economy, while, at the same time, highlighting technical and political weaknesses in the government sector. Finally, some preliminary comments are made about the effects that such programs could have on the Honduran agricultural sector. Concern about the effects on clearly heterogeneous commercial agents is emphasized, calling attention to the political and social effects of the implementation of the proposals.

A BRIEF HISTORY OF AGRARIAN POLICY IN HONDURAS

Since the 1950s, Honduras has experienced an important economic expansion, stimulated by international demand and reinforced by the political economy of the state. The agricultural sector, which during the 1950s had contributed about 50% of the gross domestic product (GDP), had reduced its participation to some 30% by the first half of the 1980s. Simultaneously, the agricultural sector's great dependence on the production and exportation of bananas underwent change. Banana exports, which between 1925 and 1952 represented 80% of total exports, fell to 31% of exports between 1980 and 1984 (Noé Pino, 1988). This behavior can be explained by the breakthrough of new agricultural exports, such as coffee, cotton, refrigerated meat, wood, and others. An increase in industrial production, reinforced by the Central American Common Market, created a similar effect.

The process of economic diversification was backed by a series of societal and state-level institutional reforms, which substantively differed from the first half of the century. In the 1950s, the state created the Central

Bank of Honduras, the National Bank of Public Works, the National Economic Council, and other governmental agencies, in anticipation of a more active state role in economic activity and, therefore, in the agricultural sector. In this regard, Posas states, "The State promotes the creation of general conditions for capitalist production and reproduction, not only through the construction of vital public infrastructure which makes possible, even though only partially, the integration of a secularly divided internal market, but that also provides easy financing for the development of agriculturally productive activities" (Posas, 1979).

It should be pointed out that during that decade the National Bank of Public Works (BANAFOM)[1] offered credit assistance, and the Ministry of Natural Resources offered technical assistance, principally under the headings of exportation and national agro-industrial consumption. Examining the increase in loans authorized gives an idea of the importance of this financing. In 1950, the National Bank of Public Works (BANAFOM) authorized a total of 397,325 lempiras in loans. By 1960, this had increased to 7 million lempiras, and to 39 million lempiras by 1970. The products that derived the most benefit were cotton, coffee, tobacco, rice, sugar cane, and to a lesser extent, rice and beans (Posas, 1979, p. 46).

Another important aspect of state agricultural policies was the creation of the National Agrarian Institute in 1961, and the first Agrarian Reform Law of 1962. The principal objectives of the law were to transform gradually the traditional landowners tied to the non-productive *latifundio* into modern capitalist agricultural enterprises, and to create a stratum of small landowners in agricultural colonization projects. These changes were promoted by the state, which preferred to use national lands and induce the interregional migration of landless peasants (Posas, 1979, p. 58) rather than expropriate private lands.

As a consequence of the reformist government of López Arrellano (1972-75), the institutional framework for land reform was considerably strengthened during the 1970s. During this period, not only was the new Agrarian Reform Law (Legal Decree 170) promoted, but state intervention related to agricultural and forest activities was expanded. For example, the Honduran Institute of Agricultural Marketing was created with the objectives of regulating the commercialization of basic grains in the country, using price guarantees as its instruments; creating and controlling silos; and monopolizing the external commercialization of basic grains. During the same period, the Honduran Forest Development Corporation (COHDEFOR) was founded. Its goal was to control and preserve national forests, as well as to monopolize the commercialization of wood. At the same time, provisions stores for basic consumer goods (BANASUPROs) were created with the objective of eliminating speculation on the part of merchants. To the same end, various businesses were financed by the Honduran Corporation of Investments (CONADI), some of which were directly related to the agricultural sector.

During this period, agrarian reform was strongly pushed, as can be seen by the large number of land adjudications that occurred. This process, however, had begun to diminish by the end of the 1970s.[2] Highlights of the period include the process of agricultural colonization, utilizing national lands in the Aguan Valley zone; the promotion of the assignment of lands on the basis of collective forms of peasant organization, such as cooperatives and associated enterprises; and the heightened development and negotiating capacity of the peasant organizations.

In practice, since the end of the 1970s, interest in agrarian reform as a widespread process has diminished given changes in the character of government and of legal institutions. At this point, effort was oriented toward the consolidation rather than an extension of agrarian reform, that is priority was given to extant groups and not to new adjudications. In practice, this meant that most of the agricultural support policies were steered toward groups dedicated to production for export or to agro-industrial consumption.

In sum, then, during the past four decades, state agricultural policy has been characterized by the promotion of capitalist agricultural development, which has motivated the transformation of landholdings into agricultural enterprises, and created a differentiated peasant sector. The necessary support for this transformation has been provided, while the rest of the rural population has been marginalized as *minifundia* or remains landless.[3] In the 1980s, the loss of enthusiasm for the agrarian reform process was heightened by the acute economic crisis that Honduras experienced beginning in 1982, and which continued throughout the decade.[4]

THE GENERAL FRAMEWORK OF STRUCTURAL ADJUSTMENT

Beginning in 1992, Honduras experienced a deepening of the program of structural adjustment. Its implementation was brought on by the acute economic crisis that the country had been experiencing since 1982. For example, the gross national product (GNP), which at the end of the 1970s had been growing at an average annual rate of 8.8%, grew less than 1% during the first five years of the 1980s. In per capita terms, this signified a fall of 2.4%. The abrupt fall in production was strongly influenced by the fall in exports and investment levels. In effect, exports of goods and services that were growing 9.8% at the end of the 1970s, fell to -0.7% in the first half of the 1980s. Additionally, gross domestic capital formation grew by 10% and 2.3%, in the 1970s and 1980s, respectively.

Although there was a recovery in economic activity during the period of 1986 to 1988 as a result of better international coffee prices, by the end of the last decade there was a renewed deterioration in key macroeconomic indicators. For 1989, the fiscal deficit grew to about 13% of GNP, inflation grew by 9.8%, and the balance of payments deficit worsened, manifesting itself in a foreign exchange shortage. Faced with this situation, the new government of Rafael Leonardo Callejas expanded the structural adjustment program initiated by the previous governments.

Analysis of Honduras' structural adjustment program requires that a distinction be made between short-term stabilization policies and economic reactivation policies, the effects of which must be evaluated in the medium and long term.[5] Short-term stabilization policies principally seek to diminish such macroeconomic disequilibria as inflation, the federal deficit, and balance of payments deficits. Economic reactivation policies seek to increase the efficiency of the economy and its reinsertion into the world market. Currently, economic reactivation policies are also termed structural adjustment policies because they do not imply a reactivation under the same conditions as they did in the past, but presuppose a substantial modification of the manner in which the economy operates. This implies a reduction in state intervention because of its supposed distorting effects on economic activity, as well as a redefinition of which productive sectors must lead the economic reactivation.

In the case of small economies, such as the Honduran one, structural adjustment emphasizes economic liberalization processes and an increase in outward orientation. These two fundamental aspects are based on the diagnosis that the current crisis is the product of strong distortions in economic activity introduced by state intervention and of changes occurring in the international environment. The first factor requires the liberalization of markets, while the second requires a growth strategy based on export agriculture, given Honduras' greater comparative advantage in this area. Basically, then, commercial, financial, price, and exchange rate liberalization are the central elements of the new strategy. Additionally, the promotion of traditional and non-traditional exports and the privatization of state enterprises complements the reactivation phase. In Honduras, two principal phases of adjustment can be distinguished. The first involves those economic stabilization attempts shaped for the most part by the Law of Structural Regulation of the Economy, approved in March of 1990, and the sectoral adjustment programs, some of which are just beginning to be implemented, such as those pertaining to agriculture and energy. The second phase involves other sectors, such as the financial and social sectors.[6]

The Law of Structural Regulation of 1990 contains principally short-term measures; in other words, it leans toward economic stabilization.

The majority of these measures are of a fiscal nature and have as their objective the reduction of the fiscal deficit and the generation of enough resources to comply with the requirements of Honduras' external debt. Even though there is a general belief that structural adjustment in Honduras began with the approval of this law, the truth is that some important measures were taken during previous administrations. Decree 18-90 does not, therefore, constitute the beginning or the end of the structural adjustment program. Yet the importance of this legal framework should not be downplayed, since it accelerates and expands the range of short-term neoliberal policies, which have had detrimental effects on the living conditions of the population.

More specifically, the principal measures of Decree 18-90 include (1) modifications in exonerations and exemptions; (2) elimination of surcharges on tariffs; (3) modifications in the calculation of profit taxes; (4) an increase in the sales tax from 5% to 7% for the majority of goods and to 10% for alcoholic beverages; (5) increases in taxes on the production and consumption of petroleum derivatives; and (6) a temporary tax (to be eliminated at the end of 1991) of 12% on extraordinary profits from traditional exports and 7% for non-traditional exports.

The law further asserts that, of the additional state revenues derived through tax reform, 98 million lempiras will be dedicated to social expenses, such as subsidies for urban transport, an allotment for families with school age children, subsidies for the consumption of foodstuffs, an allotment to the land bank for housing, and a transfer to the Honduran Fund for Social Investment (FHIS).

The law also includes an accelerated process of tariff reduction that would reduce import taxes until they reach a floor of 5% and a ceiling of 20% for 1992. However, the most important measure, owing to its aftereffects, was the devaluation of the lempira. The nominal exchange rate of two lempiras for one dollar was changed in March of 1990 to four lempiras for one dollar, which was increased to 5.50 to one at the end of November of that year.

Another important element of restructuring was the modification of the price structure for petroleum derivatives, causing a price increase of about 150% by October of 1990, which essentially meant an increase in taxes on the production and consumption of these products. Likewise, there was a change in the taxes on public services, such as water, telephone, and electricity, which were increased considerably. The objective of all these measures was the elimination of what public officials have called "false prices," or, in other words, prices under conditions of disequilibrium.

Finally, at the same time that stabilization measures were undertaken, they were accompanied by adjustment policies, including, among others, the privatization of public enterprises; the formation of a legal framework to modernize public administration; price liberalization; structural adjustment in the agricultural sector; the intensification of export promotion; and financial liberalization. Together, they formed a new framework for economic activity, whose effects were not only limited to the short term, but were also not easily reversible. Furthermore, as a response to the negative social consequences of structural adjustment, programs of social compensation were enacted. The Honduran Fund of Social Investment (FHIS) and the Family Allotment Program (PRAF) are the heart of social compensation policy in Honduras.[7]

STRUCTURAL ADJUSTMENT IN THE HONDURAN AGRICULTURAL SECTOR

Some Theoretical Considerations

Even though many of the macroeconomic policies contained in the Law of Structural Regulation of the Economy indirectly affect the agricultural sector, the process of structural adjustment explicitly includes particular sectoral cum structural adjustment plans. IFOs require the creation of sectoral programs before they approve external financing for certain sectors. These include the agricultural, industrial, energy, financial, and social sectors. But, without doubt, the priority from the point of view of the Honduran government has been the agricultural sector.

Even though the basic elements of the structural adjustment program have been strongly influenced by the IFOs, especially the U.S. Agency for International Development (USAID), its theoretical foundations have been developed by the group of countries that continue on a path of post-war policies of import substitution.[8]

A point of departure is that the growth of the agricultural sector has been found to be strongly determined by the development of other sectors of the economy, particularly through macroeconomic policies. In this manner, changes in the protection of industries, public spending, external financial flows, salary levels, and nominal exchange rates can reinforce or neutralize agricultural support policies.

The best way to study how macroeconomic policy decisions affect the agricultural sector is through evaluation of the impact of such policies on the real exchange rate, since it has such a profound effect on foreign trade. The real exchange rate is defined as the relation between the price of tradable goods and non-tradable goods. The price of tradable goods is determined by international prices, nominal exchange rates and commercial policies, while non-tradable goods (those only for domestic consumption) are determined by domestic changes in supply and demand (Valdés, 1986, p. 162).

The following general premises result from this analysis: (1) industrial protection helps industry at the expense of agriculture; (2) deficit spending increases the relative price of non-tradable goods, consequently affecting the real exchange rate and profitability of tradable goods; and (3) movements of financial capital substantially affect the real exchange rate. In summary, the price of tradable agricultural products, so important in stimulating their production, is determined fundamentally by the real exchange rate and by macroeconomic policies.[9]

All of the analyses that support structural adjustment describe how state intervention, a product of the import substitution model, has produced distortions in the allocation of resources with an anti-export/anti-agriculture bias. Therefore, in order to avoid crises that are characterized by balance of payments disequilibria, it is necessary to apply economic liberalization measures. The structural adjustment program (SAP) for the Honduran agricultural sector reflects these considerations.

History of the Modernization Law and the Development of Agriculture

The nature and content of SAP for the agricultural sector was shaped by what initially was called the Law for the Reactivation and Development of the Agricultural Sector, which was originally to be sent to the Congress of the Republic in July of 1991 for approval. However, strong opposition to the plan forced the government to initiate dialogues with peasant groups, the National Federation of Honduran Cattlemen (FENAGH), and with representatives of large estate owners and ranchers. In this manner, an agreement on the content of the law was eventually reached.[10] Negotiations took nearly six months and resulted in the following: (1) a new name for the law (the Law for the Modernization and Development of the Agricultural Sector), (2) a profoundly divided peasant movement, and (3) an alliance between government and cattle ranchers to openly support the new law. The law was approved and promulgated during the first third of 1992.

The process undertaken in order to reach a consensus on the agrarian policies of the new government took a route similar to the design of the macroeconomic policies referred to previously. The drafting of documents, and the creation of seminars, conferences and other types of activities served as the framework in which public functionaries, producers, politicians, and other interested groups influenced the law.

USAID has been one of the most influential agencies in determining the country's agricultural policy, as it was in the designing the macroeconomic restructuring program. The agency's document titled "A Strategy for the Agricultural Sector in Honduras" (USAID Honduras, 1990) became the general framework for the creation of Honduras' agricultural sector policies.

The document had many major revisions—one in April of 1989, and another in October of that year. It is important to note that the first draft, in referring to the obstacles to agricultural development, mentions that "the quantity of cultivable land is the principal factor limiting the growth of the sector [and thus] greater attention is given to mechanisms different from agrarian reform for increasing the efficiency of land use." In the second draft, this had been changed to "other mechanisms *instead of* agrarian reform"—the final report completely eliminates any reference to agrarian reform.[11]

The document asserts that, in its implementation phase, USAID should use the proposed program as well as instruments of assistance in the promotion of its projects, which "implies a high degree of emphasis on policy reforms with the backing of programs [e.g., ESF and PL-480] tied to policies of conditionality." [12] In other words, the structural adjustment program was based on proposals created with the solid support of negotiated settlements.

The report also includes the following: a global vision of Honduran agriculture; the sector's objectives and restrictions; an agricultural development strategy for Honduras; the sector's institutional framework; behavioral goals; economic policy recommendations; and assistance plans. In this strategy, restrictions on agricultural growth are divided into three principal categories: (1) agricultural price structures; (2) the resource base; and (3) access to markets and technology. In each case, the emphasis is on the need for reforms in pricing policies (including macroeconomic policies) and in land tenure. The report also mentions that all of the policies affecting the agricultural sector had been intensively debated by the new government and representatives of the private sector.

With regard to the structure of prices, the report details two aspects—intersectoral prices and intrasectoral prices. The first entails a decrease in real agricultural prices, and the second conforms to inefficiencies within the agricultural sector's pricing structure. It is proposed that macroeconomic policy changes will be necessary to solve the first problem, while sectoral policies will be necessary to solve the second.[13] At the intersectoral level, an overvalued exchange rate and industrial protection are two elements that must be modified in order to eliminate the current anti-agricultural bias. With respect to the intrasectoral price structure, it is argued that all types of price controls on agricultural products must be eliminated.

The agricultural development strategy asserts that the expansion of the agricultural sector is constrained by the area of land under cultivation and its productivity. Improvements in agricultural productivity require intensification of land use, given limitation on arable land. Two ways in which to achieve better land use are to replace traditional export crops with non-traditional ones (since they have a higher value) and to intensify cattle ranching.[14] To intensify land use requires incentives such as lower taxes on land and guarantees of land tenure, without regard to the type of crop cultivated.[15] Additional constraints on agricultural productivity include costly access to local markets because of lack of transport and storage facilities, as well as inefficient and costly public services. The report also mentions inadequate credit for small producers, lack of access to affordable consumer goods, and deficient food assistance programs. In each case, the report presents both the political and economic effects and the potential impact of its recommendations to the government.

This is not the only document that USAID has written about the agricultural sector in Honduras. In February 1989, the international consulting division of the firm Chemonics, located in Washington D.C., published "The Agricultural Sector in Honduras: Diagnostic, Policies, and Recommendations" (Paz Cafferate et al., 1989). The report was written with the objective of determining those government policies that directly or indirectly affect the development of the agricultural sector in Honduras, of analyzing the relative development of the agricultural sector, and of generating recommendations for the future development of the sector. The report, in its analysis and conclusions, follows the same line of thinking as the USAID strategy just outlined.[16]

In April of that same year, the World Bank and USAID funded a seminar entitled "Economic Adjustment and Agricultural Policy." Attendees included analysts from the Central American Research Institute (IICA), public functionaries from other countries, and international consultants.[17] The seminar was aimed at intermediate-level functionaries from the principal public institutions connected with the agricultural sector, such as the National Agrarian Institute, BANADESA (National Bank for Development of the Agricultural Sector), and the Ministry of Natural Resources, among others. As a result of the seminar, an inter-institutional technical group on agricultural policy was created with the purpose of drafting a document on the reactivation of the agricultural sector in Honduras.

Roger Norton became the coordinator of the commission, though coordination of this group was nominally placed in the Planning Secretariat. The resulting report focused evenly between the structural factors and the political-economic factors that impede the development of the agricultural sector in Honduras. Among the structural factors they identified were the lack of secure land tenure; unresolved distributive questions; lack of efficient land use; lack of institutional coordination among public sector institutions in Honduras; lack of agricultural sector representation in macroeconomic policy-making institutions; excessive state intervention in product commercialization and agricultural consumption; intersectoral distortions in pricing policies disadvantageous to agriculture; lack of effective measures to conserve natural resources; and structural failures in agricultural banking institutions (Interinstitutional Technical Group, 1989). The recommendations were not unanimously supported, however, as different points of view were taken into account, including the views of various state agencies and interest groups.

The framework for agricultural policy under the new Callejas government was based on the commission's analysis. The IFOs were confident that the new government would promote a vision that would coincide with the agricultural strategy they advocated. As a last recourse, loans were to be available on conditional terms, which became necessary. What was necessary was the immediate implementation of macroeconomic policies, while avoiding a proliferation of different initiatives that would lead to political instability. This notwithstanding, the Law of Structural Ordering of the Economy, to which we have previously referred, together with other measures, satisfied the macroeconomic policy requirements for the structural adjustment program. For example, the devaluation of the lempira increased the competitiveness of exports, thereby stimulating the production of tradable goods. Additionally, tariff reductions improved the internal terms of trade for agriculture and eliminated the industrial sector bias that the tariffs had formerly produced. However, a comprehensive agricultural development plan was not yet complete, as it needed an appendage in the form of the previously referred to Reactivation of the Agricultural Sector bill, which was introduced in July 1991.

Changes in the Institutional Framework of the Honduran Agricultural Sector: The Approval of the New Law

The first draft of the Agricultural Reactivation Law, which articulated the macroeconomic aspects of the structural adjustment program for the agricultural sector and its component sectors, was to be approved by the legislature in July 1991, but it faced strong opposition. To enhance political support for the plan, the government initiated consultations with various peasant and producer organizations.[18] The consultations produced the support that the government sought; on December 16, 1991, the new agricultural policy was signed into law. It should be noted that landowners and cattle ranchers supported the law, while peasants were divided in their support for it.

There was also controversy among agricultural sector public officials regarding the new plan. Juan Ramón Martínez, director of INA (National Agrarian Institute) during the beginning of the Callejas administration, wrote:

It is necessary to affirm from the start that the Modernization Law is fundamentally "counter agrarian reform." It will result in limiting peasant access to land, which conforms to current practices in the country, and derail the peasant organizations, both economically and organizationally. It will put agrarian conflict management, currently in the hands of the government, into the hands of the private sector. Clearly, on the last point, the weakest will not have any alternative but to regroup at the level of agrarian confrontation, whose institutionalization is obvious to any observer, which will considerably increase and generate further unrest in the agricultural sector. (Martinez, 1990, p. 27)

In spite of these problems, the law was approved rapidly by the National Congress.[19] One could argue that, with a few exceptions, many deputies were unfamiliar with the contents of the law, as they were with the twenty laws, decrees, and regulations that the new law amended.

The new law has two well-defined general objectives: "to dynamize our agriculture in benefit to all of the nation; and to make sure that the fruits of development are shared as widely as possible among all families coexisting in the agricultural sector. These objectives will be met through a redefinition of the role of the State in agriculture. This new role will involve the establishment of a framework of favorable incentives for growth in production and employment, and the focusing of new governmental programs on the small producer."[20] Likewise, in order to establish a structure of incentives for the growth of production and employment, the law added the following: "make necessary reforms in the commercialization of agriculture; rescue the agricultural financial sector and restructure it on a viable base; convert agrarian reform enterprises, establishing secure land tenure while increasing access to land; decentralize research services and agricultural extension; redefine the role of the state in the forest sector; create a better atmosphere for improving coordination between agricultural policies and environmental protection; promote private initiative; and consolidate the institutional structure of the agriculture public sector."[21]

SOME COMMENTS ON STRUCTURAL ADJUSTMENT IN THE HONDURAN AGRICULTURAL SECTOR

The economic program of the current government can be evaluated at two distinct levels: one dealing with stabilization policies, the other dealing with changes in the structure of domestic production that tend to reinsert it in the global economy. The first type of policies are short term in nature—their evolution has been analyzed elsewhere (Noé Pino, 1991). The second type of policies are medium and long term; hence, an analysis of them would be premature at present.[22] Nonetheless, some evaluation is possible on their probable impact on the agricultural sector.

The New Law

As suggested earlier, the new law has two dimensions. The first dimension encourages agricultural production, in coordination with macroeconomic policies, and the second substantially modifies state participation in the agrarian sector. However, the law provides greater clarity and effectiveness in achieving the second than the first. In other words, the law is quite clear in its approach to eliminating state participation and regulation in various agricultural activities, but sufficiently vague in terms of what specific actions are necessary to encourage production, primarily in the peasant sector.

For example, in referring to peasant groups, the law prescribes a liberalization program for both agricultural enterprises and agro-industrial enterprises. Without specific programmatic definitions and without a time reference, the law proposes to consolidate enterprises within the cooperative movement. In the same manner, it does not establish specific mechanisms for allocating funds among various activities, such as the seed capital necessary for small farmers or guarantees that properties are properly titled (a lengthy process in itself). Thus, one could conclude that the process of deregulation is accelerating rapidly, while benefits, especially those related to the peasant sector, are left to traditional public-sector bureaucratic processes with their characteristic lack of financial support.

As has been suggested, the principal modifications to agricultural markets consist of liberalizing domestic and foreign trade, while decreasing state participation in stabilizing market and grain stocks. Although one must recognize the serious administrative deficiencies of the past (e.g., corruption), one must also realize that liberalization presents many problems in the agricultural sector. For example, there is little consideration of the role of intermediaries or "coyotes," who are often unnecessary but manage to lay claim on an important part of the final price of the product. In addition, one should realize that trade liberalization has benefited the import-sector economic agents to the detriment of domestic producers, as recent cases involving imports of rice and corn demonstrate.[23]

The new law also proposes the use of price bands to maintain stable food prices in the presence of substantial international price volatility. However, if adequate coordination of tariff policies is not achieved at the regional level, any advantages brought about by tariff reductions will be reduced or eliminated through intraregional commerce and different import taxes.

A few observations are in order with regard to the allocation of agricultural credit. First, the creation of a single credit institution for the agricultural sector avoids duplicity and poor coordination by the diverse public agencies involved in that sector. Second, the prohibition on interagency lending can be beneficial, given political pressures and the past history of disbursing grants improperly. Third, restructuring the National Agrarian Bank (BANADESA) will reduce its capacity to serve the agricultural sector. Its capital has already been reduced from 75 to 40 million lempiras and the bank's liquidity will no longer originate via new contributions, but rather through partial recuperation of the credit portfolio acquired by the government. Although there have been attempts to justify this reduction by asserting that the bank will benefit small and medium producers, the financial necessities of these producers suggest that the available amounts will be insufficient.

It is interesting to note that while the Minister of Natural Resources has stated that BANADESA's financial problems arise from the inability of small and medium producers to meet their obligations, the data demonstrate that it is the lack of repayment of the larger loans that has created financial difficulties for the bank. This indicates a substantial reduction in the state's provision of agricultural loans, with a concomitant desire for private banks to assume that function. Thus, although BANADESA will remain solvent, access to credit for small producers will become more difficult. The government's new prohibition on BANADESA's management of public trust funds, which served as its principal source of financing, lends further credence to this argument. Such action is telling, since the majority of the agrarian small-scale producers are not recipients of commercial bank or BANADESA (with its own funds) credit because they cannot meet basic guarantee conditions.[24]

The law also proposes the creation of rural credit houses, owned and managed by the peasant users of such institutions. Some 70% of the capital for such rural credit banks comes from the recovery of loans made from public funds held in trust. It is generally believed that this amount is not very significant compared to the financial needs of this sector. Additionally, given previous experience, there is real fear that political criteria will be used in administering these funds and that they will be mismanaged.

Changes have also been made to the Agrarian Reform Law—while not formally eliminating it, the changes substantially modify its intent. The new law eliminates the notion of the social function of land, which is an important basis for its taxation. Thus, this virtually guarantees that the land currently possessed by cattle ranchers, landowners, and peasants will not be expropriated.[25] Given the unequal distribution of land in Honduras, it is easy to see that the major beneficiaries of this measure will be large landholders. The logic behind such measures is that landowners and cattle ranchers do not invest in their property, not because they do not see it as a symbol of power and political control, but because the insecurity in land tenancy does not allow them to be agricultural capitalists. This logic is correct, but it does not fit reality. Moreover, it is expected that foreign investment will take advantage of land acquisition to a greater extent than domestic entrepreneurs.

The freezing of rural property and the legalization of the one-hectare *minifundia* also present many problems. First, it is foreseeable that the expansion of employment opportunities will be insufficient to reduce rural unemployment and underemployment, much less create enough jobs for the growing population. This is due to the nature of production of both traditional and non-traditional exports, which only slowly absorbs the surplus agricultural population. The alternative would be to accelerate agro-industrial development and/or absorb rural migrants through growth of urban industry. Nonetheless, neither of these approaches is the focus of structural adjustment programs. In addition, the legal definition of a *minifundia* of 1 hectare in size is controversial. While some have suggested that it is an adequate quantity of land to support a household, others argue that, given the limited fertility of Honduran soils, 7.2 hectares is a more appropriate size, taking into consideration the quality of the land (Thorpe, 1992, p. 17).

The law further suggests a rapid process of land titling. Expediting the land titling process has a two-fold objective—to strengthen tenure security for land and to guarantee access to agricultural credit. However, this, combined with the elimination of the rental prohibitions of the past, stimulates joint ventures between capitalists and landowners, and the assignment of land rights to individuals could lead to further concentration of land, be it through the credit system or by direct purchase. Moreover, attention should be called to land titling processes that require peasants to first group themselves under a legal form of incorporation (known as the *personeria juridica*), when it is well known that obtaining such status is bureaucratically difficult and subject to political favoritism. This, in turn, contradicts the Law's efforts to ease credit and seed capital funding for farmers.

Interestingly, on the surface the law considers women beneficiaries of agrarian reform, which would appear to be a positive development. However, the question arises as to how beneficial the new policies will be for women. Emelda Vallecillo, representative of the National Association of Women Peasants (ANAMUC) argues "that the Agricultural Modernization Law also affects women, since they are married to peasants who will be stripped of their land, or who will be deprived of the series of guarantees that they have acquired." [26] Additionally, the process of differentiating peasant women will be accentuated because it allows for the benefits of agrarian reform to be received by those who do not work the land, even if they reside in a rural area. This will contribute to the rise of different interest groups, which has already occurred in the agrarian sector.

A land bank and rental and coinvestment contracting are proposed as alternative mechanisms for access to land. These options need to be analyzed in more depth to determine their potential impact on the rural sector; however, some observations can be made if these options are viewed as a substitute for expropriation and land adjudication. First, a factor affecting the development of a land bank is, without doubt, the amount of financing it has available. Although the law provides funding for the bank from land sales, the amount has not yet been established. In reality, a land-bank program requires a great quantity of financial resources; which is evident, for example, in the case of Costa Rica, where there is a more equitable distribution of land than in Honduras. In Costa Rica, the Institute of Agrarian Development invested about $3 million in 1991, estimating that the total demand for parcels of land would absorb about $45 million, in addition to another $30 million necessary to guarantee the adequate exploitation of these parcels (Thorpe, 1992, p. 67). It is not known whether such a plan exists for Honduras, but it is likely that, under current budgetary restrictions, there are few possibilities for financing such an endeavor. Finally, a resurgence of external debt will leave the agrarian sector as vulnerable and subordinate as before.

One can deduce from the previous discussion that the law does not sufficiently address the problems affecting peasants, in contrast to the direct benefits it provides the export sector, landowners, and cattle ranchers. The same can be said for problems at the macroeconomic level. Moreover, the generation and transfer of technology are solely in the hands of the private sector, thus removing access for small producers to productivity-inducing services. In spite of what is considered the ability to subsidize the sale of such services through seed capital, there is no specific plan to determine the program's scope, or the source of its financing.

Similarly, commercial liberalization (the total exclusion of the state in the production and processing of wood) and the opening of the forestry sector to foreign capital conform to current adjustment programs. It is important to remember that the Forestry Development Corporation (CODEFOR) was created in response to overharvesting of the forests by private and, principally, foreign interests. This is contrary to the pressures by IFOs to promote the exploitation of our limited natural resource base. Even though civil society recently triumphed in impeding the ratification of the Stone Container agreement, new threats of exploitation of Honduran natural resources will arise again in the future.

One of the most interesting aspects of the process for approval of the modernization law was the distinct positions that various groups in the peasant movement took with respect to this law. The reasons for the various positions taken are beyond the scope of this chapter. However, some preliminary explanations can be given. For example, one of the results of the agrarian reform process was the economic and organizational consolidation of many groups linked to agricultural producers. The incentives for support of the modernization law was based on the privileges they received through land provisions, loans, and technical assistance, among other things.

In this manner, the problems currently facing peasant organizations have become diverse. One group, with sufficient land, is concerned with additional investment opportunities so that they may avoid violating the legal landholding limits. This group and those peasant enterprises with sufficient, but not excess land concentrate their attention on such things as credit and access to markets. They tend to forget the needs of other peasants and, in particular, end up adopting positions contrary to the interests of the land-poor and landless peasants. Furthering this division among the Honduran peasantry is the corruption/co-optation strategy subtly employed by the government to ensure the cooperation of the already privileged peasantry, thereby discrediting the continued calls for land invasions and adjudications.

For those who consider the legal framework a determinant of peaceful coexistence and collective interest, it is worthwhile to point out that, in spite of affirmations to the contrary, the new amendments to the agrarian reform law destroy its original intentions, substituting the market mechanism for them. In this respect, it would be more consistent to seek the abolition of the constitutional precepts that support the necessity of these processes, instead of insisting that the agrarian reform process is the goal being sought.

FINAL REFLECTIONS

A first observation is of a methodological nature and is derived from the analysis of the origins of the stagnation of Honduran agriculture in the 1980s. Proponents of structural adjustment in the agricultural sector confine their analyses to two elements: (1) the changes and vicissitudes of international trade, and (2) domestic economic policies. This analytical division is useful as long as a necessary synthesis is achieved, while permitting a global perspective. However, in practice, this analysis never goes beyond the superficial and ignores some important considerations.

For example, one concern is the nature of international trade. While a complete opening to external trade has been imposed upon Honduras, the developed countries have created new protectionist policies, detrimental to imports from the Third World. The recent decision by the European Economic Community to place barriers on the export of Latin American bananas, and the decision by the United States to impose import quotas and boycott agreements such as those involving coffee are evidence of this trend.

At the same time, worries arise about the promotion of non-traditional exports, whose principal destination is the United States. These concerns relate to price stability, market size, and competition with other countries that promote similar exports. With respect to this, Salvador Arias has noted:

The North American market for these products [non-traditional exports] is very small. Of the 28 products studied by the FHIA of Honduras, the only product with an important market, which is over 3,000 million dollars, is cacao, a product which is currently being replaced by another made from enzymes, thanks to the biotechnological revolution. The United States market for the other products is not more than 350 million dollars. Only five of these products can count on markets of over 100 million dollars. The market for flowers is 317 million dollars, that of cardamom 107 million dollars, and that of black pepper 200 million dollars. In sum, the potentials are not very big because many countries can produce these goods. (Arias, 1989, p. 135)

The concentration on non-traditional export production is another area of concern. For example, in Honduras, cultivated shrimp has become the third biggest export product, behind bananas and coffee. However, this production is highly concentrated in four or five businesses, with the strongest ones being tied to transnational corporations. Thus, the benefits of this growth will be concentrated in few hands, with limited effects on improving the distribution of income. There is little possibility of these crops being produced by small producers or peasants, given the amounts of capital, technology, market access, and other resources that make their production and sale profitable. These are the types of issues that must be considered when seeking a more equitable distribution of the benefits of growth.

In summary, we recognize that the small and open economies of Central America need to export. Traditional exports should be promoted as much as non-traditional ones. One should be cautious that these exports do not take on such importance that the economy loses its capacity for allocating resources, which later may be difficult to modify and thus cause serious bottlenecks in the external sector.

Additionally, support for exports must not be to the detriment of efficient import substitution and the development of the industrial sector. Development that harmonizes the two sectors would permit a better articulation of the productive sectors and a reduction in the negative effects produced by fluctuations in foreign trade. At the same time, and even though it seems contradictory, the promotion of exaggerated outward orientation weakens the production of basic grains, which is important for the nutritional security of the population. More precisely, in situations where resources are scarce, the promotion of exports can be at the expense of food production.

The significant reduction of state participation in the economy is another important element of discussion. No one can defend a corrupt and inefficient state, or deny its negative impact on the domestic economy, but it is a wide gulf between this situation and one where the state' role is marginalized. Such extreme positions have been taken that some of the positive aspects of state intervention, such as health services, education, and housing, have been largely ignored. These services can be provided only through income redistribution, which to now has been stymied.

The Honduran economy is characterized by a high degree of heterogeneity, which translates into a varied capacity for response to market forces. Therefore, it is necessary to establish selective policies which recognize these differences and allow for inefficient producers to improve. In other words, it is necessary to recognize that in Honduras an important part of rural agriculture is comprised of *minifundistas* (which will now increase in number) that possess poor quality lands and of landless peasants whose lot must be improved by an appropriate development strategy. In this sense, we share the Economic Commission for Latin America's (ECLA) conclusion:

To have markets set agricultural production prices would be the equivalent of forgetting the heterogeneity of the small producers and to eliminate peasants as producers. The fundamental problem with Latin American agriculture does not have anything to do with perfecting the functioning of the ex-ante markets, nor only with bettering the conditions of production in order to permit its agents to compete ex-post in the market. The elimination of the inefficient producers is a possibility when they are in the minority, but not when they constitute the most numerous groups in the population.[27]

   To summarize, structural adjustment in the Honduran agricultural sector seeks to resolve two fundamental problems: production incentives, and access to productive resources, which the new law defines widely as land, agricultural credit, technology, and channels of commercialization, among others. From the point of view of structural adjustment, the first problem arises from mistaken government policies on both the macroeconomic level (excessive industrial production) and the microeconomic level (control of agricultural prices). What this requires, therefore, is the elimination of market distortions. The price system is thereby converted into the optimal mechanism for resource allocation. On the other hand, problems of access are resolved through the same mechanism, the market. Consequently, the majority of productive state services must be privatized and restrictions placed on any efforts to provide access, as in, for example, agrarian reform.
   The policy prescription just described has two principal drawbacks. First, it ignores the lack of evolution of markets in countries such as Honduras. Second, it ignores the role of power relations in the flow of economic life. These two aspects are neglected, though necessary in any synthesis of the national economy, its participation in the international division of labor, and processes of globalization and recomposition of forces at the world politic level. The programs currently being promoted have the potential for renewing favorable conditions for the accumulation of capital in the short term, but do not guarantee their sustainability in the medium and long term, nor resolve traditional development problems. In other words, the participation of Central America in the new international context, on the basis of low wages and stabilization and adjustment policies, translates into a menu for misery, and not into sustainable economic growth whose benefits are shared by the majority of the population.

NOTES

   This chapter is based largely on ''Central American Campesinos in the Face of the Challenges of the 1990s,'' a monograph sponsored by POSCAE and OXFAM. I am grateful for the comments given by Andy Thorpe and Rigoberto Sandoval Corea.
   1. The National Bank of Public Works was created with the objective of

authorizing credit assistance in both agricultural and industrial activities. In 1980, it was turned into the National Bank for Agricultural Development (BANADESA) and is currently being restructured again, with its size and functions being greatly reduced.

2. "The assignments of lands during the agrarian reform period (1962-1986) involve a total area of 321,516 hectares, equivalent to 8.85% of total farm area. The major part of the adjudications happened between 1973 and 1976, during which more than 42% of the total lands were distributed." (Ruben, 1991, p. 32)

3. About the 1990s, Posas observes that "the demands of the majority of landless peasants, a group increasing due to the explosive growth of the population, fell into relative indifference of this nucleus of differentiated peasants, more interested in obtaining state credits and productively bettering its land 'acquisitions,' a view widely held by the former group." (Posas, 1979, p. 120)

4. A detailed account of the characteristics of the crisis and the political economy necessary for its resolution can be found in Noé Pino and Hernández (1991).

5. In some cases this distinction is difficult to make, for example, in the case of exchange rate policy. That is, devaluation produces changes in relative prices that should encourage exports and discourage imports; in other words, it is a short-term measure. On the other hand, an exchange policy tending to "manage" the real exchange rate stimulates export production over a long period than a short term.

6. The Law for Modernization and Agricultural Development, which contains the basic elements of adjustment, was finally approved in April of 1992.

7. For an evaluation of the results of the structural adjustment program in Honduras during the first two years of the Callejas administration, see Noé Pino (1992).

8. The arguments presented are based on an article by Valdés (1986).

9. For a detailed explanation of the effect of such policies on the agricultural sector see Norton (1988).

10. For an expanded account of the diverse social groups and their projects see Noé Pino and Posas (1991).

11. Op.cit. p. 2 The same page notes that agrarian reform has only marginally affected the distribution of land and that the agrarian reform cooperatives have not been very successful.

12. Op.cit. p. v. ESF funds refer to support for disequilibria in the balance of payments. PL-480 refers to funds provided as food aid.

13. USAID (1990, p. 8).

14. The document recognizes that great expanses of land are needed for extensive cattle ranching, but considers that its inefficient use is a product of agrarian reform, which needs modification.

15. The Agrarian Reform Law of 1975 declares lands in which the follow-

ing crops are cultivated as unaffected by the law: banana, plantain, sugar cane, african palm, coffee, pineapple, citrus, and tobacco.

16. The purpose of the report was to analyze the effects of economic policy on the agricultural sector, emphasizing its relationship to exchange rates, exterior commercial policies, agricultural pricing policies, sectoral credit policies, infrastructure and transportation policies, and land use and tenancy policies.

17. Among those consultants, the participation of Dr. Roger Norton, who had worked as a consultant for USAID/Honduras is significant. In the seminar, Dr. Norton presented the paper "Perspectives on Macroeconomic Policy and the Agricultural Sector," in which he summarized the principal aspects of structural adjustment. Some of the Honduran media have referred to the new Law of Modernization and Agricultural Development in Honduras as Norton's Law. Even though the promulgation of a law involves many complex economic and political factors, it is impossible to deny that Dr. Norton's influence has been extremely strong in the determination of Honduran agricultural policy.

18. Among the groups opposed to the bill were peasant organizations, urban workers' groups, and professional organizations.

19. The Liberal party, the principal opposition party, was unable to agree on a unified platform for discussion, precisely because many of its representatives represent the current hegemonic interests of Honduran agriculture.

20. These were words spoken by the Minister of Natural resources, Mario Nufeo Gamero, while disputing the agricultural law, which took place December 16, 1991, in the Presidential House. *Time,* January 6, 1992

21. Letter of the Minister of Natural Resources accompanying the delivery of the Law of Agricultural Modernization and Development to the National Congress, December 20, 1991.

22. It must also be taken into consideration that regulations for the implementation of the law are not completely drafted and approved. These regulations will more precisely set the conditions of agricultural sector activity.

23. "It is evident to the people that many government measures openly contradict the national interest. In this manner, it produces distortions in the market when it authorizes indiscriminate imports of rice, corn, wheat, or chicken in order to benefit the few at the expense of the many." Eduardo Facusse, President of the Chamber of Commerce and Industry of Tegucigalpa, *La Tribuna,* September 5, 1992.

24. Even though the land titling process hopes to resolve this problem it will not produce results in the short term.

25. This has also been reinforced by changes in the recuperation of national lands, in the expropriation of idle lands, and by the elimination of restrictions on indirect land exploitation.

26. "Association of Women Peasants Questions the Modernization Law" *El Heraldo,* September 5, 1992, p. 18.

27. CEPAL. "Methodological features of a strategy for food security." LC/ MEX/L. 48, May 1987.

Six

Industrial Democracy
and Reindustrialization:
Cross-Cultural Perspectives

Alvin Magid

The philosophical roots of industrial democracy can be traced to the Industrial Revolution. For some, the coming age aroused fears that the nation-state and the nascent factory system would succeed to the detriment of myriad smaller communities which had long been organized on ties of personal loyalty, on small trade, and on the routine of manual labor. The principle of industrial democracy was born partly of a notion that participatory democracy on a broad front must assert itself against the organizational power of the modern state and of industry and commerce (Rousseau, 1968, bk. 1, chs. 7 and 8; bk. 2, ch. 3; bk. 3, ch. 18; Mill, 1905, p. 114; Pateman, 1970, pp. 1-111; Lindblom, 1977, pp. 331-34).

In contemporary America, participatory democracy is fed by various elements of discontent. An important one concerns the growing dissatisfaction of industrial labor with how industrial workplaces are organized. For example, many workers greatly distrust the industrial organization philosophy known as Taylorism. Named for Frederick Winslow Taylor, a turn-of-the-century social theorist, Taylorism asserts that the job performance of industrial labor will be adequate where reasonable wages are paid as compensation for the numbing hierarchism of the factory, with its emphasis upon the scientific organization of work based on repetitive tasks and detailed instructions (Taylor, 1947, pp. 41-47). Wages and working conditions have since improved significantly, fueled mainly by the interaction of trade unions, management, and government. U.S. industries nevertheless continue to experience growing alienation of workers and decline of the work ethic; in many industries, absenteeism of workers is increasing and their productivity is falling.

Proponents of industrial democracy contend that traditional incentives, such as wages, fringe benefits, promotions, dismissals, and superiors' instructions, are not adequate. They have more confidence in worker participation in industrial decision making as a strategy for improving the quality of work life and stimulating worker decision makers to act more responsibly in the interest of greater productivity (Wootton, 1967, p. 106ff.; Blumberg, 1969, chs. 5 and 6). Some advocates of industrial democracy believe that labor will be more efficient in a participatory environment where resourcefulness and inventiveness are rewarded, not detailing the tasks performed by fellow workers. Labor productivity is expected to grow with the loosening of organizational fetters (Lindblom, 1977, p. 332). Even in management circles there is some qualified support for the notion of worker-participation-as-incentive (Roach, 1973, pp. 1-43).

FACTORS INFLUENCING INDUSTRIAL DEMOCRACY IN REINDUSTRIALIZATION

Dissatisfaction with the quality of work life is, by numerous accounts, endemic in American society (Ritzer, 1972, pp. 139-325; Terkel, 1974). Partly for that reason, and partly because many Americans feel themselves powerless to check the tedium at work, ideas for workplace reform advanced on behalf of any segment of the labor force are not likely to attract wide support. For example, the issue of dysfunction in the organization of the industrial workplace has yet to win over a large constituency to industrial democracy. The forces of bureaucratization, professionalization, specialization, and centralized control in U.S. industry are all geared to promote rationalization based on a particular model of efficient human behavior. They prevail over a countervailing derationalization whose stress is upon debureaucratization, deprofessionalization, and democratization (Ritzer, 1972, pp. 3-67).

But there is more reason to anticipate a growing interest in the United States in the principle of industrial democracy spurred by the play of economic forces at the local, regional, national, and international levels than by ennui in the workplace. Already those forces are seen to threaten an increasing number of American industrial workers as well as the survival of many communities tied to a traditional factory system economy.

Among the more significant economic forces that cast a long shadow over the landscape of American industry are the soaring deficits in international trade and the federal budget; high U.S. interest rates; American and Japanese industrial joint ventures; plant closings, particularly in the sunset states of the Northeast and Midwest; and the mobility of capital to the sunbelt states of the South and Southwest, to the Far East, and to the Third World. A brief comment on these matters is in order.

The United States in International Trade

The position of the United States in international trade and finance deteriorated significantly in the 1980s, beginning with the first administration of President Ronald Reagan (1981-84). Although at the beginning of that quadrennium the external trade in goods and services was substantially in balance, by the end of 1984 the U.S. trade deficit amounted to more than $123 billion, and the federal budget deficit topped $200 billion. The trade deficit peaked at $152.1 billion in 1987, and has fallen steadily since then. But some analysts warn that in the early 1990s the trade deficit will expand as the U.S. economy resumes growth at the same time other major overseas economies are faltering and a stronger dollar makes American-made goods more expensive. If left unchanged, the policy of the administrations of Ronald Reagan and George Bush of tying control of deficits principally to the engine of economic growth is likely to result in higher trade and federal budget deficits. This augurs deep concern, not least of all for the industrial labor sector.

The Loss of Jobs

At least two million jobs were lost in the period from 1981 to 1984 in the export sector of U.S. industry, and a substantial part of the production of American-based multinational firms was transferred abroad. In the third quarter of 1984 growth in domestic demand outpaced growth in the gross national product by a ratio of 3:1, a robust 5.7% and a sluggish 1.9%, respectively. The imported goods needed to meet much of that demand provided a further stimulus to imports. By the middle of the decade, it appeared that jobs would continue to be lost in the export sector of U.S. industry and that imported goods would play a growing role in meeting domestic demand. Downsizing of the U.S. automobile industry in particular has continued to exact a heavy toll on its domestic work force.

The Trade Deficit

The United States emerged at the end of the first Reagan administration as a leading debtor in the international community after borrowing at least $100 billion annually to finance its huge trade deficit. Because domestic savings will probably be inadequate to finance private investment and to rectify imbalances in international trade and the federal budget, foreign sources will be needed to help finance total demand. Many Americans fear that dependence on those sources to supply and fund a

substantial part of total demand will exacerbate the deficits and imperil
U.S. economic stability. The issue has recently begun to arouse other
anxieties as well. For example, there is growing concern in the United
States about the future availability of foreign investment resources,
especially from Germany and other countries in the European Economic
Community and from Japan. By early 1991, a combination of factors had
turned Germany from a capital exporter into a capital importer: a
declining trade surplus; the need to make large payments for the Persian
Gulf War; and the government's heavy borrowing on the world's financial
markets to pay for rebuilding eastern Germany, the onetime Communist
state that had recently unified with West Germany. Moreover, various
countries in the European Economic Community had begun to voice
interest in underwriting the economic reconstruction of post-Cold War
Eastern Europe and the Soviet Union. (Following the Soviet Union's
dissolution in the spring of 1992, interest in economic reconstruction was
redirected by a U.S.-led coalition of Western nations principally to Russia,
the most important of the fifteen successor states carved out of the old
Soviet state.) By early 1992, evidence was mounting also of a likely
decline in Japanese investment in the United States. Faced with a
deepening recession at home, Japan was expected to redirect investment
resources to its domestic economy. Together, these developments augur
a sharp drop in foreign resources available for investment in the U.S.
economy.

Borrowing and Interest Rates

Dependence on borrowing at home and abroad has worked to keep
U.S. interest rates high. This condition has aroused several fears: that a
large pool of mobile international funds will be drawn into dollar assets,
causing the dollar to be greatly overvalued in the international economy;
that American exports will continue to be priced out of world markets; and
that, in effect, the United States will persist in heavily taxing its own
exports while subsidizing imports through fluctuations in the exchange
rate. Among the principal losers will be American industrial labor,
particularly in the export sector.

Relations Between the United States and Japan

The United States and Japan are closely linked as military allies and
trading partners, but their relationship has become increasingly strained.
Militarily, the United States continues to press its Asian ally for a

significant increase in outlays, despite Japanese constitutional restrictions and their unwritten rule that limits the annual military appropriation to a maximum 1% of the gross national product. The United States contends that the economic prosperity of Japan is facilitated by the costly security shield America provides its ally. For trade, the relationship continues to favor Japan. The annual U.S. trade deficit with its Asian ally exceeded $40 billion by the beginning of the 1990s—by which time overall foreign investment in the U.S. economy had surpassed by a considerable amount American investment overseas. Many American economists and politicians regard these imbalances in United States-Japanese trade and the pattern of international investment as proof that the United States is no longer competitive in world markets and that it has mortgaged its future by becoming a net debtor nation.

Faced with growing U.S. protectionist sentiment, Japan has cautiously agreed to work at closing the trade gap. Besides adopting voluntary quotas for key exports, the Japanese have begun to transfer some of their industrial production to the United States (utilizing American labor and management personnel) and to lower their own protectionist barriers against the import of American goods and services. If broadened, these concessions may grant significant relief to American industry—and its work force—in both the domestic economy and the export sector. One other apparent concession, however, may have an offsetting effect. New and anticipated joint ventures for the manufacture of such items as automobiles, computers, photographic equipment, airplanes, machine tools, and robots are being organized according to a division of labor that favors Japanese workers over their American counterparts (Reich, 1984, pp. 19-23). Responsibility for product design, assembly, and marketing is assigned principally to the American partner; the Japanese dominate the production process and therefore command the bulk of the joint-venture work force. Automation of the assembly function over time can be expected to reduce still further the input of American labor. In sum, the establishment of joint ventures as part of a larger strategy to correct the imbalance in United States-Japanese trade, an innovation in corporate bilateralism, may impose a considerable hardship on American industrial labor.

American Labor and Reindustrialization

For most industrial workers in the United States, the arcana of deficits, high interest rates, overheated currencies, and transnational corporate alliances are best understood in terms of their overall impact on the lives of individuals and of communities. Few workers are unaware that over the past decade millions of jobs have been drained from the older U.S. industrial cities and towns, from the Northeast and Midwest, and also increasingly from smokestack communities elsewhere in America.[1] The process has been discernible in work-force reductions and in permanent plant contractions and closings. As the line of dispirited jobless—and often unemployable—industrial workers has lengthened, their communities across America have come to suffer a corresponding diminution of economic security.

Some critics hold that this development has its roots in a larger strategy for deindustrializing the United States through domestic corporate mergers, plant closings, community abandonment, and by scrapping basic industry (Bluestone and Harrison, 1982). From their ranks comes the call for an ambitious countervailing radicalism to reindustrialize America, which includes an industrial democracy strategy to promote worker and community ownership of industry, with workers and community owners exercising direct, permanent control over management (Bluestone and Harrison, 1982, pp. 193-264). In this view, workers and their communities can ill afford to assume that only unprofitable industries will contract and expire, that there will always be private investors to rescue profitable or potentially profitable industries faced with either contingency, and that a class of peripatetic high-level managers can operate industries more efficiently and more profitably than local workers and managers (Whyte et al., 1983, pp. 56-58).

The search for a radical solution based on a kind of reindustrial democratic philosophy evokes the old clarion call for a participatory democracy that weighs against institutional gigantism in modern life. Such a proposed solution warrants particular consideration in those older industrial areas of the United States—the Northeast and the Midwest—where the question of reindustrialization is high on the public agenda. Accordingly, what follows is a brief survey of various instances of applied industrial democracy in the United States and abroad, identifying some implications for reindustrialization in the U.S. case.

WORKER OWNERSHIP AND LABOR-MANAGEMENT COOPERATION: INDUSTRIAL DEMOCRACY IN THE UNITED STATES

Various strategies have been adopted in the United States to foster industrial democracy. In this section, two basic approaches are highlighted: worker ownership and labor-management cooperation.

Worker Ownership

There is a well-documented, if not well-known, tradition in American society of worker and, to a lesser extent, municipal ownership of industry (Carnoy and Shearer, 1980; Stave, ed., 1975). Before the Civil War, it was not uncommon for a few workers to join together as the owners of some light industry. In the last quarter of the nineteenth century, organized labor in the United States began to show interest in worker ownership. In the 1880s the Knights of Labor, for example, founded more than 100 cooperatives in mining, shoe manufacturing, and other industries. At their initiative, a central organ, the General Cooperative Board, was created to educate members in the arcana of management and finance and to promote the cooperative idea among artisans, farmers, and shopkeepers (Rayback, 1966, p. 160). But the notion that ordinary workers should have control over their workplace *and* their companies was destined to be undercut by the philosophy of Taylorism in American industry.

In recent years, there has been a revival of interest in worker ownership. Some have been drawn to it principally as a means of preventing plant closings, with their harsh effects on individuals and communities. Others look to worker ownership to realize a more just capitalism. For example, in the 1960s, to promote economic equity and industrial peace as barriers to socialism, San Francisco attorney Louis O. Kelso formulated a rudimentary scheme based on the idea of an employee stock option plan (ESOP)—a concept that has attracted interest abroad, for example, in Costa Rica, Thailand, and Zimbabwe (Kelso and Hetter, 1967; Goldmark et al., 1982). Kelso calculated that employee-shareholders who received dividend checks and a retirement income from company stock would have a deeper attachment to their companies and would, moreover, exert a greater effort to enhance productivity. By 1973, the ESOP idea's strong advocate in government, Senator Russell Long (D-La.), was working hard as chairman of the Senate Finance Committee to promote ESOPs through revision of the federal tax code. By 1980, there were as many as 3,000 such plans in the United States, and the number continues to grow (U.S. Congress, 1976, pp. 1-62; U.S. Senate, 1980, pp. iii-vii, 1-27).

At this juncture it is important to distinguish between *worker participation in corporate ownership* (via ESOP shareholding) and *worker participation in corporate management*. Closely examined, ESOPs are less instruments of worker control than plans for deferred compensation. They operate as follows: A company creates an employee stock option trust, and banks lend it money to buy company stock and other assets. The company makes payments to the trust to retire debt. As loans are repaid, the trust allocates to employees company stock that is vested in the names of the employee-shareholders for a prescribed period of time—usually a decade—based on a formula which takes into account wages and length of service. Upon retirement, workers receive their share of stock. From a tax perspective, the arrangement benefits all the principals. Companies can take deductions for cash dividends paid to the ESOP, and banks are rewarded by not having to pay income taxes on half the interest they collect on loans to ESOPs.

The federal tax code has been revised over the years to enhance the attractiveness of ESOPs. For example, the "leveraged ESOP" allows interest *and* principal to be deducted where the trust borrows from banks, collateralizing loans with company assets, stock, and credit. In a new twist unanticipated by the U.S. Congress, management in large industrial companies can reorganize as a "leveraged ESOP" in order to head off unwelcome corporate takeovers (*New York Times*, January 2, 1985, p. D1). In such an event, the position of management is likely to be strengthened at the expense of employees in the newly created ESOP. Employee-shareholders who fear that the takeover will result in a decreased work force are often more concerned with their own job security than with profiting from a stock sale. They do not sell their shares and are then expected to affirm their gratitude for the failed takeover by deepening their attachment to the company and its triumphant management.

But, following Louis O. Kelso, if ESOPs grant industrial workers a piece of the corporation, they do not guarantee employee-shareholders a key role in the management function (Kelso and Hetter, 1967, pp. 82-92). There are now only a few ESOP companies in which the workers own a majority of the voting stock. Among the more than 7,000 partially or wholly employee-owned companies in the United States (some 3,000 of which, as we have seen, are ESOPs), probably no more than 500 grant to low-level workers a key role in the management process (*New York Times*, December 30, 1985, p. IV3). Worker participation in management is usually limited to activities on the shopfloor, with control of the decision-making process for product design, manufacture, and marketing generally held tightly by higher-level, professional managers. The power and privileges of management in ESOP companies are further enhanced by the propensity of trustees to exercise workers' voting rights without prior consultation. Because many years are likely to pass before workers acquire majority ownership of an ESOP company, they are expected to wield little power and influence in management affairs (Simmons and Mares, 1983, pp. 116-135). In some cases management has refrained from embracing the ESOP option, despite its lucrative tax aspect, where there is fear of the workers' growing strength.

There are other serious drawbacks in the ESOP approach to industrial democracy and worker participation. First, financing is not easily available to buy out companies for the purpose of transforming them into

ESOPs. The problem is especially acute where government and the private sector are reluctant to make grants or loans to failing companies (*New York Times*, January 2, 1985, p. D1; U.S. Congress, 1978, E3325-E3328). Second, still feeling alienated from management despite their shareholder status, workers in ESOP companies may want to reap a quick profit by selling out to private investors. The impulse to sell is apt to be strong among those workers who are nearing retirement age, who are confident that the new owners will not effect a sharp reduction in the work force, or who are reluctant to forego wage and fringe benefits in order to reinvest profits in needed plant modernization. Selling off ESOP companies is a further check on the development of a worker-manager ethos in the industrial sector. And it is a risky course of action. The sale to private investors of companies whose profitability has been restored under worker ownership may promote the very condition—plant closings—which originally impelled workers to become corporate owners. Third, feeling themselves threatened by a new form of industrial organization favoring labor-management cooperation over the old system of adversarial relationships, trade unions tend to regard ESOPs with skepticism or outright hostility. These traditional representatives of labor are also likely to fear that the new arrangement will cause workers to lose the hard-won benefits of collective bargaining (Bluestone and Harrison, 1982, p. 261). Relations may consequently deteriorate within ESOP companies in the triangular network formed of workers, management, and trade unions. Finally, there is the considerable risk to workers—especially older ones—where pension funds are used as the principal source of capital to finance an ESOP buy out. The bankruptcy of an ESOP company is liable to cause great hardship for retired workers unprotected by a pension plan.

Labor-Management Cooperation

It can fairly be said of industrial democracy in contemporary America that opportunity and adversity, not principle, are the mothers of invention because of many recent decisions that led to the establishment of ESOPs. The primary goal has usually been to improve the financial condition of a company, to increase the productivity of its workers, to avert plant closings, or to repulse a hostile buy out. In devising strategies for worker ownership based on ESOPs, the principals have rarely been motivated to secure for industrial workers a key role in corporate decision making.

As with ESOPs, the approach to industrial democracy based on institutions of labor-management cooperation has not often achieved for workers a place next to upper management in the corridors of corporate power. Here, too, the emphasis has been essentially pragmatic, seeking primarily to improve the quality of labor-management relations as part of the search for industrial peace and/or to arrest industrial decline with its baleful effect on local communities. If dealing with adversity in industrial and community life through labor-management cooperation has not given ordinary workers a leading role in organizational decision making, it has in some cases at least enabled them to widen their scope of participation. One such case centers on factory workers in Jamestown, a small manufacturing city near the western border of New York State (Whyte et al., 1983, pp. 6-54; Simmons and Mares, 1983, pp. 80-95).

The Jamestown Area Labor-Management Committee (JALMC) was created in the early 1970s to help vitalize that community by arresting the erosion of its industrial base, particularly in furniture manufacturing and metal works. The committee was organized through the cooperation of labor, management, and a progressive city administration headed by Mayor Stanley Lundine (now lieutenant governor of New York State). Their goals were to save jobs threatened by plant closings; to establish problem-solving projects at the plant level based on the cooperation of labor and management, with the assistance of professional staff members of JALMC; to train union and management personnel to eventually take over the facilitating role of JALMC in their own company or in other local companies; to organize training programs throughout the Jamestown area and enlarge the base of skills for local industry; and to develop joint projects with other community organizations, including the public school system, the public junior college, and the county development agency. It was agreed from the outset that JALMC would preempt neither the collective bargaining role of the unions nor the mediation role of federal and state agencies. Moreover, it was stressed that the committee would be essentially facilitative, with JALMC doing its work through personal contacts, persuasion, and mobilization of requisite financing (Whyte et al., 1983, p. 8). The committee received strong encouragement along these lines from its various consultants, who included Eric Trist, a leading behavioral scientist and founder of the Tavistock Work Research Institute in London, and William F. Whyte, a distinguished sociologist, as well as some of his colleagues at the New York State School for Industrial and Labor Relations at Cornell University. By the end of the 1970s, JALMC had managed by trial and error to become institutionalized in the Jamestown area on the base of permanent labor-management committees in various plants. It had established an impressive record of helping to build trust in a community known for its poor labor-management relations, and it had enlarged the job base in companies the committee had assisted. Over time, management in those companies came increasingly to include its workers in decision making on such matters as shop-floor procedures and plant design (Whyte et al., 1983, pp. 6-54). The Jamestown approach to institutionalizing labor-management cooperation has been adopted by several communities throughout the United States (Simmons and Mares, 1983, p. 95).

CROSS-CULTURAL PERSPECTIVES ON INDUSTRIAL DEMOCRACY

Proponents of industrial democracy in the United States have long been attentive to kindred developments abroad. In the nearly half century after the Second World War, European initiatives have strengthened that conception, particularly in the industrial sector of the economy.[2] Among the most important—and influential—initiatives have been those in Sweden, Spain, and Yugoslavia. They merit examination here.

Sweden

Implementation of diverse programs for industrial democracy in Sweden over the past few decades reflects the play of forces in the workplace and throughout society. Together these forces marked an historic irony. Just when liberal social values were coming to dominate important spheres of life (e.g., education, the family, and a state increasingly tied to a welfare ethos), industrial management was promoting even more aggressively the values of efficiency and hard work to outproduce international competitors. As pressure mounted to increase productivity so, too, did the level of personal stress (Bjork, 1975, p. 17). Gaining their voice through the trade unions and a socialist government in power, workers responded by protesting against an industrial order that appeared to them to be incompatible with the new liberalization in Swedish society. As absenteeism and job turnover both escalated (the latter exacerbated by a law that protected workers from losing their rights with transfer between companies, and by another law that sharply reduced the pool of foreign labor), Swedish industry felt compelled to seek relief with a strategy of industrial democracy. Throughout the country, hundreds of programs were established, some based on new labor-management committees, others on reorganization of the workplace to enhance job satisfaction without sacrificing the value of worker efficiency in the prevailing system of capitalist production (Ritzer, 1972, pp. 399-407).

The automobile industry helped spearhead this development. Volvo, for example, reorganized several of its plants to promote the semi-autonomy of worker groups based on the tradition of skilled craftsmanship. These groups were empowered to set their own work pace and to determine the schedule for coffee breaks. Organized on fewer than a dozen workers, each group was made responsible for its own quality control, for maintaining an inventory of tools, and for processing the raw materials.

Newer Volvo plants, like the one at Kalmar, were designed to promote job satisfaction as a concomitant of worker efficiency. Constructed without a traditional assembly line and illuminated partly by the sun's rays, Volvo/Kalmar underlined the need for an environment in which autonomous and semi-autonomous groups would be able to function in unaccustomed comfort. Light and color held sway in the plant, with the noise level reduced significantly. In place of an assembly line, there was an electrically driven carrier system. Each car in production was given its separate carrier, controlled either by a central computer or by the workers themselves. Each work group moved the carrier through its area on the shop floor either by setting the timing of the carrier to resemble the movement of a traditional assembly line (allowing each worker to attend to his own repetitive task) or by adjusting the carrier to stop in the work area or to move through it at a slow pace (allowing the whole group to work together on a car). So long as they met their hourly quota for production, the Kalmar work groups could decide on task assignments and coffee break schedules. Saab, another leading manufacturer of automobiles in Sweden, has experimented with similar programs based on the principle of industrial democracy.

In sum, the Swedish automobile industry evinces a mixed character, with its traditional assembly line and its innovative work regimens. In other Swedish industries, many companies with plants organized on assembly-line production have introduced labor-management committees to deal essentially with shop-floor activities. Companies such as Volvo and Saab provide in individual plants the alternatives of assembly-line-like production and democratization of the work place. They emphasize giving workers the opportunity to organize their production on either the traditional or the non-traditional mode, or on a combination of the two. While there is some evidence of increased job satisfaction among Swedish workers using this more flexible approach, discontent continues to be voiced over the monotony that is intrinsic in the industrial workplace. Finally, it should be noted that democratization has not been extended to the upper reaches of corporate management. Shop-floor innovations in Swedish industry have come by a top-down process, allowing management to retain control over key decisions relating to design, manufacture, and marketing of product.

Spain

The exemplar of industrial democracy based on voluntary cooperatives using the technical methods of modern industry can be found in Spain, in the small Basque city of Mondragón (Thomas and Logan, 1982; Johnson and Whyte, 1977, pp. 18-30; Whyte and Whyte, 1988; Simmons and Mares, 1983, pp. 136-44). As with any commercial partnership, the members of the cooperative movement in Mondragón use their own resources to provide part of the business capital in which they retain full ownership rights. Within quite strict limits, additional funds can be obtained for investment purposes from the movement's own savings bank, the *Caja Laboral Popular*. (The *Caja*, which exists principally to help finance cooperatives, receives its funds from the savings deposits of the population in the Basque region.)

Most of the workers employed by a cooperative in Mondragón are members of that cooperative. They have equal rights in the organization, including the right to participate in meetings of the workers' assembly and to elect the supervisory board of the enterprise. The board, in turn, appoints the management. Wage differentials for the members of a cooperative are set according to occupational skills and job responsibilities. Wage rates for manual laborers are related to the rates of local trade unions in private industry. Wages are paid in advance. At the conclusion of each accounting period the members divide up any surplus revenue that may have accumulated over costs. Costs are calculated on wage advances, depreciation, and taxes. A part of the surplus is expended as interest on the members' capital. Most of the interest, which is paid at a minimum annual rate of 6%, can be drawn out by the members in cash. What remains of the surplus is then allocated as follows: 10% is paid to the members in proportion to their earnings; about 30% is held back as reserve and social funds; and the balance is added to the members' capital accounts in proportion to their earnings. Capital accounts are periodically revalued consistent with inflation. Only upon their retirement can the members withdraw funds from these accounts. In sharp contrast with the system of ESOP companies in the United States, the Mondragón system virtually ensures that its cooperative enterprises will not be sold off to private investors. As we shall see, the successful growth of Mondragón enterprises builds pressure not to sell those units, but to have them spin off other cooperatives to function efficiently on a smaller scale.

The Mondragón system was conceived by a Roman Catholic priest, José María Arizmendi, who settled in the city in 1941. Even before his death in 1976, Father Arizmendi was able to institutionalize the cooperative movement he had founded on the key Basque values of democratic association, hard work and thrift, and craftsmanship—stressing, in the process, the need in all cooperative movements to balance the interests of their members as owners and as workers. What sets Mondragón apart from other capitalist enterprises is its roots in an inspiring ideology and in Basque nationalism. The ideology of cooperation works together with local nationalism to provide an abundant supply of workers and management personnel. Able managers are willing to work for less in Mondragón than their counterparts earn in the private sector.

As part of its extensive institutional framework, the cooperative movement in Mondragón has spawned an array of support services. The movement has its own technical school and a polytechnic institute with university-level courses. There is an institute for research and development to advise the individual cooperatives on innovations in products and in manufacturing processes. The Management Services Division in the *Caja Laboral Popular* advises all new cooperatives on development planning; existing cooperatives often solicit advice from the division on how to improve their performance. Near the end of the 1970s, the Management Services Division in the *Caja* had more than 100 economists, engineers, attorneys, and other technical experts on its full-time staff. All together, these support services play a key role in launching new cooperatives, supplying them with a large pool of skilled workers, managers, and technicians, arranging for finance, and advising on product design, manufacture, and marketing.

Mondragón launched its first industrial cooperative in 1956, with five employees. Nearly three decades later, at least 87 cooperatives had 18,000 employees and gross annual sales amounting to $1.7 billion. The largest cooperative, Ulgor, manufacturing household durables, employed nearly 4,000 people in 1979. In the mid-1980s, Ulgor led Spain in the production of refrigerators and stoves. Other cooperatives manufacture such items as construction materials, electronic equipment, and foundry products. Mondragón is an extraordinarily dynamic system, having succeeded through the 1960s and 1970s in creating annually about three new cooperatives. (By the end of the latter decade, it had suffered only one failure, a fishermen's cooperative.) Eight hundred new jobs were created annually in the period from 1961 to 1976. The cooperative movement has had a robust return on capital, with a five-year average of 18%. The Basque region's great confidence in the movement is evidenced by the fact that by 1978 the *Caja Laboral Popular* had more than 300,000 depositor accounts and assets of $2.1 billion.

For almost two decades following the movement's establishment in Mondragón, the *Caja* was content merely to respond to proposals to create new enterprises, either by arranging for them to be spun off existing enterprises or by helping to finance new ones. But with the rapid growth of its assets, the cooperative bank felt compelled to adopt a more aggressive program for developing new enterprises, some more capital-intensive than their predecessors and requiring higher levels of skill and training. The drive to increase the number of enterprises has met several critical needs. By identifying and promoting new areas for productive investment, the *Caja* has carved out for itself a key role in the social and economic development of the entire Basque region.[3] By helping to finance more capital-intensive enterprises, the *Caja* has strongly encouraged skilled workers and technicians to remain in the region. Finally, the Mondragón system has demonstrated an admirable flexibility in responding to worker pressure to correct some of the Taylorist attributes particularly of the larger industrial cooperatives. The correctives include creating many new cooperatives in other than the assembly-line mode, with employment rolls close to a few hundred workers for each new unit; restructuring work patterns in existing enterprises to enhance job satisfaction; and revising the wage rate system. While the largest cooperative, Ulgor, has spun off a half-dozen cooperatives of modest size, this giant organization has yet to restructure itself as other than an unpopular traditional assembly-line industry.

Yugoslavia

Until its recent disintegration (see below and note 17), Socialist Yugoslavia represented a singular case of industrial democracy. Where institutions embodying that principle do exist, they are apt to be found at random in capitalist economies, as islands in a sea of enterprises organized on the authoritarian lines of Taylorist scientific management. In Socialist Yugoslavia, by contrast, the notion of industrial democracy was included in the concept of democratic self-management, usually vaguely defined.[4] Industrial democracy was, in effect, democratic self-management in the industrial sector.

Because democratic self-management was for four decades down to the end of the 1980s at the core of the official Marxist ideology, whose repository was until then the ruling Communist League in the one-party Yugoslav state, that concept was the basis on which economic and political life formally turned. (Multipartyism reigns today. Various parties contend within each of what were Yugoslavia's six constituent republics. In two of the leading republics, Croatia and Slovenia, popular elections held in 1991 brought anti-Marxist, secessionist political parties to power, auguring the dissolution of the Yugoslav Federation. See note 17.)

In Socialist Yugoslavia, almost all the industrial and service sectors along with nearly 20% of agriculture were nominally controlled by institutions of democratic self-management. Together with an array of sociopolitical organizations and communities of interest, the institutions of democratic self-management in the economic sphere were, in turn, linked through a delegate system to the organs of government at the *opstina* (commune), municipal, republic, and federal levels.[5]

Economic enterprises in Socialist Yugoslavia were called "organizations of associated labor," not "cooperatives," because ordinarily the members of a cooperative retained individual rights over their investment of capital in the organization.[6] (As we have seen, Mondragón is a prime example of a cooperative system.) In contrast, all enterprises in Yugoslavia that employed more than a few workers were, by law, socially owned. As such, they operated as institutions of democratic self-management.

The notion of democratic self-management derived from Marxist texts that antedated Yugoslav socialism and from the society's own historical experience. The partisan resistance movement led by Marshal Josip Broz Tito during the Second World War had perforce to lay the groundwork for its national and social revolution along Marxist lines against the backdrop of the anti-fascist struggle against the German and Italian invaders. Of necessity, the resistance movement had to pursue its multifarious goals with a highly decentralized, mobile organization that stressed initiative-taking and self-reliance. After surviving the war years, those values were then subordinated for a brief time to the Stalinist values of centralized party and state control, nationalization of the industrial and service sectors, and collectivization of agriculture. Over several decades following the break with Stalin's Cominform in 1948, Yugoslavia evolved by stages to a democratic self-management society. The process was fueled partly by the need to explain the expulsion from the Soviet bloc and to frame a distinctive Marxist socialism for an economically underdeveloped country cleaved deeply along the cross cutting lines of nationality, region, and religion.[7] In short, democratic self-management was imposed on Yugoslavia by a political leadership that wanted simultaneously to promote economic modernization within a heterogeneous society marked by zones of uneven development and to legitimize both the ruling Marxist ideology and the various key groups in the party, the state organization, and the economic and cultural spheres that had come to dominate public life. The commitment to democratic self-management was also reinforced by political strains in the Yugoslav Federation, among factions tied to competing national and regional interests. In time, the ruling Titoist coterie sought to regulate the factional conflict by devolving party and state power to the republic, municipal, and commune levels. Central authority was further weakened by instituting at the center of both party and state the principle that collective leadership was based on rotation.[8] It was hoped that divisive tendencies in Yugoslav society could be checked by a combination of devolution, collective leadership, and democratic self-management—all the while achieving economic progress on a wide front, and especially in the industrial sector.

By law, Yugoslav industrial workers had full management rights, including the right to allocate the net income of their enterprises either to themselves or to collective consumption or savings.[9] Workers were no longer obliged to pay interest on capital investment in their enterprises. In effect, they were able to use without charge the inherited capital of the enterprises, which was augmented by reinvested income and by loans made initially by the government and then increasingly by the socially owned banks. In theory, management in Yugoslavia resembled that found in the Mondragón cooperatives, with great decision-making authority lodged in workers' councils in the areas of production and marketing and in the selection of senior management personnel. In fact, decision making in those key areas was dominated by management boards and enterprise directors, whose real power derived from the alliances they struck with the management of banks and with party and government officials at the commune, municipal, and republic levels (see note 5). As a consequence, decisions relating to the industrial economy, including income-distribution, were affected by the political need for the wealthy republics to transfer part of their resources to less-developed areas in the south and by the autarkic tendencies that marked economic decision making at the republic and even the commune levels.[10] The principle of a unified market economy in Yugoslavia was more often honored in the breach.[11]

The Yugoslav case differed from that of Mondragón, moreover, in that workers in the former made no initial contribution to the equity of their enterprises, nor were they required to pay an official fee for job entry. (Corruption in the form of illegal fees played an important role in Socialist Yugoslavia, where the official unemployment rate exceeded 15%. Often, similar fees were also paid to secure an apartment through the enterprises in which workers were employed.)[12] Because society was deemed to own most of the economic resources in the country, workers enjoyed some part of their enterprises' savings just so long as they were employed by them. They ceased to derive benefits from enterprise savings upon their retirement, death, or transfer to another enterprise.

Despite the great human and financial resources that had been invested in operating (and trying to export) the Yugoslav system of democratic self-management, it continued to suffer widespread declining vitality.[13] The postwar drive to create a modern industrial society had left—mostly private—agriculture to stagnate.[14] Food imports increased, exacerbating the strain on limited hard-currency reserves.[15] As alienation spread, worker productivity decreased and absenteeism increased. Economic crimes abounded in industrial plants, where many workers stole expensive tools and materials for use in their "second jobs" in the grey market as private mechanics and artisans. Also, erosion of labor discipline was evidenced in numerous illegal strikes and in the many free riders in the workplace.[16] A large body of empirical research by Yugoslav and other scholars documented the growing cynicism among workers about democratic self-management institutions. Workers' councils were widely perceived as unable to deal with the vagaries of economic decision making when management hoarded vital information. Worker delegates at the commune, municipal, and republic levels of government tended to be perceived by their blue collar colleagues as self-interested political opportunists.

The deepening malaise in the industrial work force and among the general population in Socialist Yugoslavia was fueled also by key economic factors. Nearly two decades ago the thriving economy was bolstered by foreign credits. But by the end of the 1980s it was reeling from an official inflation rate of 2,000% and a hard-currency debt of nearly $20 billion. Over the past few years, the export trade continued to falter even while the dinar was plummeting against the dollar. The economic recession in Western Europe caused thousands of Yugoslav "guest workers" to return home to an uncertain future. The growing number of returnees threatened Yugoslavia with a sharp decline in hard-currency remittances. Political instability and ethnic violence in the country undermined foreign tourism, especially along the Adriatic coast, imperilling yet another important source of hard-currency earnings. Various economic reforms undertaken at the turn of the decade failed to arrest Yugoslavia's downward slide. Many Yugoslavs projected their own flagging spirit onto a society faced with mounting problems, at once economic and political, domestic and international. (With the end of the Cold War, nonaligned Yugoslavia was no longer on the knife's edge in the Balkans between East and West. As a result, it could not count on continuing political and economic support from the United States and its Western allies.) As early as the middle of the 1980s, severe strains were already operating on the legitimacy of Yugoslav socialism. Those strains pointed to a deepening social crisis that was destined, against the backdrop of the Communist world in turmoil in the period from 1989 to 1991, to bring Yugoslavia to the brink of dissolution or, perhaps, to set it on the road to transformation of its socialist system of rule with a new legitimacy to underpin it (Magid, 1991, *passim*).[17]

INDUSTRIAL DEMOCRACY IN A STRATEGY FOR REINDUSTRIALIZATION

In assessing the role that industrial democracy might play in some larger strategy for reindustrialization in the United States, it is well to recall the evolution over two centuries of our dominant modes of production. Before the Civil War, American industry was organized on a relatively small scale, with its base in skill-intensive craft activities. In the next half century, the primacy of that mode of production was effectively challenged by the rise of large-scale, mass-production factories. But in establishing their own economic ascendancy, assembly-line industries never did manage to sweep away entirely the ideology of craft production based on skilled craftsmanship. Nor were they able to wholly displace the organizational foundation for that ideology. Indeed, the older tradition survived alongside its aggressive rival down to the contemporary period. By the 1970s the metalworking industry in the United States was still operating mostly in that tradition. And notwithstanding its vaunted gigantism organized on assembly-line production, 20% of the steel industry's output was based on mini-mills. The vitality of the older tradition is also evident in the spread of high-technology industries throughout the United States. High-technology industries rely on a craft-based, skill-intensive work force. Encouraged by innovations in computer technology and by the general inability of mass-production companies to adapt swiftly to changing currents in manufacture and trade, the newcomers organized on a smaller scale have found their niche in an American economy more and more demanding of specialized product and service.[18]

The historical record yields these important lessons—modes of production will vary according to social needs tied to technological innovation and, in the process of change, old and new modes will likely fuse with each other, interpenetrate, or coexist, thereby avoiding a head-on clash that would otherwise culminate in displacement. Greater flexibility must underpin a strategy for reindustrialization that is intended to avoid displacement. Taking the long view, it is clear that the system of mass-production assembly line industry rooted in Taylorist scientific management need not define modern industrial organization. It is, rather, one way to conceive such organization. Evidence of the greater value of a mixed approach can be found in the experience of Volvo and Saab in Sweden, of the Mondragón cooperatives in Spain, and of democratic self-management in Socialist Yugoslavia. Whatever success the two Swedish industrial giants and the Basque cooperatives have had with their own variants of industrial democracy may be ascribed substantially to obviating the numbing effects of a Taylorist monolithism, that is, they anchored their industrial organization in a process of choosing from among alternative modes of production. Democratic self-management and economic development in Yugoslavia, by contrast, had both foundered principally on a rigid institutionalism tightly held by the imperatives of ideology and political power. The constricting character of the Yugoslav system can perhaps best be conveyed by noting this difference with Mondragón: Whereas the Basque cooperative movement had grown by creating more specialized cooperatives of small scale, Yugoslav industry had courted stultification by emphasizing gigantism around the enlargement of existing enterprises. Mondragón's efforts have been crowned by an impressive rate of job development and by increasing efficiency, productivity, and job satisfaction in the workplace.

Reindustrialization based partly at least on a growing base of small-scale, capital- and skill-intensive industries appears, on the record of Mondragón and high-technology enterprises in the United States, to hold out the promise that major objectives of industrial democracy will be achieved—greater autonomy in the workplace along with enhanced job satisfaction. It is reasonable to expect that in those industries requiring ever-higher levels of skill and training and a more self-regulating work regimen, a kind of self-correcting mechanism will improve the overall quality of work life. For the large body of shop-level workers who will likely remain in, or enter, mass-production industries, the experiences of Volvo and Saab in Sweden and of the Jamestown Area Labor-Management Committee in western New York State indicate that careful redesign of repetitive work regimens and of physical plants can elevate job satisfaction and the quality of work. It should also be noted that over the years many workers in Yugoslavia's mostly non-high-technology industrial sector advocated reforming the system of democratic self-management to provide for their own greater control over workplace activities.

But here a caveat is in order. Any decision about modes of production in a particular industrial plant, old, new, or redesigned, should take into account the preferences and capabilities of workers. Replacing relatively simple repetitive work with the complexity and individual responsibility that inevitably attends industrial workplace democratization will doubtless be more attractive to some workers than to others. Mismatching worker preferences and capabilities with modes of industrial production is liable to reduce job satisfaction and worker efficiency.

Two items in the industrial democracy agenda merit particular comment: worker participation in corporate ownership and worker participation in corporate management. As previously noted, they have grown disproportionately in the United States. Worker ownership has increased with the spread of employee stock option plans, but upper management has retained its virtual monopoly over decision making for product design, manufacture, and marketing. Given industrial management's ease of mobility, the risks associated with ESOPs appear to have been far greater for labor than for its superiors. And compounding their burden, workers concerned with job security have often had to accept a shrunken paycheck as ESOP employee-shareholders. Small wonder that many such workers and their advocates have bristled over the arrangement, suspecting that ESOPs were designed more to discipline labor than to promote either worker ownership or power-sharing with management.[19]

Neither the cases of Volvo and Saab in Sweden nor the Yugoslav system of democratic self-management signals a way for American industrial workers—who may wish to do so—to enter the halls of corporate decision making. In the experience of Mondragón, however, we encounter a basis for cautious optimism. Basque cooperative workers own their enterprises, and they wield influence on management decisions. Management at Mondragón finds itself increasingly pressured by workers to increase the material rewards of ownership if not to establish a duopoly of power. While rooted in the culture of Basque society, the cooperative system there might usefully be adapted in several of its key aspects to conditions elsewhere.

Worker cooperatives organized as part of a reindustrialization strategy particularly for U.S. enterprises of small scale would vitalize the principle of industrial democracy as they joined together with other small companies to spearhead the process of job development. Realistically, however, it is well to recall that Mondragón has succeeded partly because it has managed over several decades to strengthen the identification of cooperative members with their enterprises and because it has pioneered an array of supportive institutions—a bank, a research and development facility, and educational and training centers from which the Basque cooperative movement continues to draw creative energy and material assistance.[20] In recent years in the United States, there has been some discussion in private and in political circles of the possible benefits of launching a cooperative movement within the industrial sector—with its own energizing institutions, including a chartered bank. With or without that innovation, it is a healthy sign indeed that those who would frame a strategy for reindustrialization in the United States recognize that its success is conditional, among other things, on a pluralism of organizational forms and functions shaped always by trial and error.

NOTES

Reprinted with minor revisions from *Reindustrializing New York State: Strategies, Implications, Challenges*, by Morton Schoolman and Alvin Magid, eds., by permission of the State University of New York Press. © 1986 State

University of New York Press.

1. With regard to the American South, see, for example, *New York Times*, December 22, 1984, p. 8; December 27, 1984, p. A11. The anxieties of American workers over the issue of job security have been further exacerbated by negotiations between the United States, Canada, and Mexico over the North American Free Trade Agreement.

2. Attention has been focused especially on Western Europe, the birthplace of the Industrial Revolution and the spawning ground for an antidotal notion of participatory democracy. See the opening paragraph of this chapter, including references.

3. Profitability is not the principal factor in decisions regarding the establishment of new cooperatives. Greater weight attaches to the interests and needs of the members and to the long-term implications of investment decisions for regional development (Johnson and Whyte, 1977, p. 28).

4. The problem of conceptual ambiguity in the Yugoslav system of democratic self-management is underlined in Novosel, 1982, pp. 209-224. The evolution of democratic self-management in the industrial sector is examined in International Labour Office, 1962; *International Institute for Labour Studies Review*, 1972, pp. 129-72; and Pasic, Grozdanic, and Radevic, 1982.

5. The Socialist Alliance of Working People and the Veterans' Association were the two leading sociopolitical organizations. Communities of interest were based on schools, medical facilities, and art, culture, and research institutes. The Yugoslav Federation included more than 500 communes, six republics (Slovenia, Croatia, Serbia, Bosnia-Hercegovina, Montenegro, and Macedonia), and two autonomous regions within the Serbian Republic (Kosovo bordering on Albania, and Vojvodina).

6. The status of labor in the Yugoslav system is outlined in great detail in *The Associated Labour Act*, 1977.

7. The political development of Yugoslavia in the postwar era is surveyed in Johnson, 1972; Denitch, 1976; and Burg, 1983. For a useful overview of the factors of nationality, region, and religion in Yugoslavia, see Joncic ca. 1982.

8. Two executive groups formed the apex of the party and state hierarchies at the federal level in Yugoslavia. Each group had members drawn from the six republics and two autonomous regions in the Yugoslav Federation. There was a rotating presidency in each group.

9. Taxes were levied on economic organizations and the workers in order to support a wide array of social services and also government administration at the various levels.

10. The more developed areas are Slovenia and Croatia (along with the autonomous region of Vojvodina, a prosperous agricultural area within the Serbian Republic). The less-developed areas are the autonomous region of Kosovo within the Serbian Republic, Macedonia, Montenegro, and Bosnia-Hercegovina.

11. The absence of a unified market economy was underlined in the report and recommendations of the Kraigher Commission established to propose a long-term economic stabilization program for Yugoslavia. See Dokumenti Komisije, 1983, pp. 281-344.

12. The preoccupation many urban-dwellers had with the matter of securing adequate housing in a tight market is examined in Magid, 1991, *passim*.

13. Yugoslavia, in both the bilateral and multilateral aspects of its foreign policy of nonalignment, sought to promote the idea of democratic self-management. Many academicians and research institutes were also involved in that activity. See, for example, *Workers' Self-Management and Participation in Decision-Making as a Factor of Social Change and Economic Progress in Developing Countries, 1981.*

14. At the end of the Second World War, only 30% of the population of Yugoslavia lived in cities and large towns. By the end of the 1980s, only 30% of the population lived in the countryside. Farmsteads organized on a legal maximum of 10 hectares were often tended by elderly peasants, their sons having moved away to the cities and towns. Where relatively young family members continued to live on farms, they were apt to be part-time farmers engaged in full-time factory or commercial work. The Kraigher Commission (see note 11) stressed the need to vitalize private agriculture in Yugoslavia as part of a comprehensive strategy aimed at rural development.

15. Petroleum imports also soaked up a major part of the hard-currency reserves.

16. Most strikes were of short duration, a few hours or a few days. Strikers' demands were usually met in order to resume factory operations.

17. See Magid, 1991, pp. 45-54. In June 1991, two republics in the Yugoslav Federation, Slovenia and Croatia, each declared its sovereign independence, precipitating bloody clashes between Yugoslav army units and territorial forces in the two breakaway republics, and an escalation of intercommunal fighting in Croatia; backed up by Serbia's political leadership, Croatia's Serbian minority asserted its right to secede from an independent Croatia and annex itself to the Serbian Republic. With these developments, political conflict intensified on several fronts—between the federal government and authorities in Slovenia and Croatia, between the Yugoslav army dominated by Serbian officers and the Yugoslav government, between the European Community favoring a peaceful resolution of the Yugoslav issue and rival interests in Yugoslavia. (European governments feared that the destabilizing effects of the Yugoslav crisis might spread to neighboring countries, sending a flood of refugees to the West.) Eventually the European Community intervened to arrange what would prove to be a fragile three-month ceasefire throughout the country. By the summer of 1991, Yugoslavia was in turmoil. Its multinational army, which stood alone after President Josip Broz Tito's death in 1980 as the symbol of national unity, had suffered a sharp decline in public esteem for its role in the debacle. All-out civil

war was a distinct possibility. In the ensuing months Yugoslavia continued to unravel. By early 1992, Slovenia and Croatia made good their claims to sovereign independence: The European Community extended formal recognition and the United States followed suit. Then Macedonia and Bosnia-Hercegovina each opted for independence, petitioning the international community to extend formal recognition. (At the time of this writing, in early January 1993, such recognition has been extended only to Bosnia-Hercegovina. Fearing Slavic irredentism on its northern border with Macedonia, Greece has managed to block its NATO allies from formally recognizing independent Macedonia.) With these developments, Yugoslavia was reduced to a rump state based on Serbia (which included the former autonomous regions Kosovo and Vojvodina) and Montenegro. Bent on ending the intercommunal violence in Croatia and checking its spread to neighboring Bosnia-Hercegovina, in the winter of 1992 the United Nations moved the first contingent of a projected 14,000-member multinational peace-keeping force into Yugoslavia. The gravity of the situation in Yugoslavia could be seen in the fact that this was the largest military force ever mobilized by the U.N. for a peacekeeping mission. (In less than a year, the U.N. force grew to 23,000.) Notwithstanding, by the end of 1992, Bosnia's Serbs, Croats, and Muslims found themselves engulfed in war. Backed up respectively by Serbia and Croatia, the Bosnian Serbs and Croats grabbed for themselves about 95% of the territory of independent Bosnia-Hercegovina—leaving the rest for Bosnia's Muslims, who, numbering almost 2 million, constituted the largest ethnic group (about 44% of the pre-war population of 4.4 million) in the new state. (Before the war, Serbs and Croats comprised 31% and 25%, respectively, of the popula-tion of Bosnia-Hercegovina. By the end of 1992, Bosnian Serbs controlled almost 70% of the territory of Bosnia-Hercegovina.) Fears were now raised around the world that the war would soon spread to Kosovo, where ethnic Albanians (mostly Muslims) comprising 90% of the population of 2 million chafed under harsh Serbian rule, and to multiethnic Macedonia. In the event this might happen, neighboring Greece, Bulgaria, Albania, and Turkey might be drawn into the fray, fanning a more general conflagration in Balkan Europe. These developments and dark prospects had already wreaked havoc on the economy of what had been Socialist Yugoslavia—and especially on Serbia's economy. The collapse of the Yugoslav economy, coupled with the stringent economic sanctions imposed on Serbia as an aggressor state by the United Nations, had left the Serbian economy in shambles: By the end of 1992, 60% of Serbia's work force was idled, and its annual inflation rate was nearly 10,000%. By then, the institutionalism of democratic self-management had also fallen victim to Yugoslavia's and Serbia's fate. Almost nothing once healthy and viable in that institutionalism had managed to survive the assault on state, society, and economy in Yugoslavia.

    18. The changing pattern of production modes in the United States is examined in Piore and Sabel, 1984.

    19. See, for example, the cases of the Weirton (W. Va.) Steel Corporation

and the Rath Packing Company of Cedar Rapids, Iowa, in *New York Times*, January 6, 1985, p. III4; *New York Times*, January 13, 1985, p. I18; and *New York Times*, February 15, 1985, p. 16.

20. One indicator of this can be found in the low incidence of serious labor conflicts and strikes. With only a few exceptions, such conflicts and strikes have occurred in Ulgor, the giant industrial cooperative with a work regimen still based largely on the Taylorist philosophy. For example, upper management is appointed by the workers and it, in turn, appoints supervisory personnel. Many of these lower-level supervisors continue to exercise their responsibilities in an unpopular authoritarian manner. See Johnson and Whyte, 1977, p. 25.

Seven

The Future of Cooperativism in Central America: Elements for Discussion

Marielos Rojas Viquez

INTRODUCTION

For more than a decade, Central America has suffered from poor social, economic, and political conditions. Policies aimed at restoring financial stability have only increased problems in the economic and social spheres, and structural adjustment strategies do not seem to be leading to sustained economic growth or social transformations. Structural adjustment has substituted humanistic principles for speculative and monetarist ones. It has promoted the separation of the State from the management of the economy and stimulated privatization of important service and production sectors. This has occurred even in strategic areas in which key national resources are now vulnerable to absorption by transnational capital. The reduction of the role of the state, together with a decrease in social benefits and protection of domestic markets, has left national producers and many needy sectors totally unprotected, creating the basis for the free operation of transnational corporations.

This ominous development and the new world order brought about by the unexpected changes during 1990 and 1991 have forced Central American nations to seek alternative negotiated solutions. The search for a new model of development is imperative—in particular one that considers the social as well as economic transformations which are necessary to promote widespread development. In this regard, social participation in the processes of national capital formation and national consensus is particularly important. To accomplish this, it is necessary to strengthen and integrate the various social sectors of the economy. It is in this context that this chapter on cooperativism in Central America will seek to discuss (1) the historical experience of the cooperative movement in Central

America, (2) its current importance, and, (3) the problems it faces as it attempts to consolidate national and regional cooperativism.

HISTORICAL BACKGROUND OF COOPERATIVISM IN CENTRAL AMERICA

Attempts to create cooperatives in Central America date to the end of the nineteenth century. The first cooperatives did not appear, however, until the first decades of this century: 1923 in Costa Rica, 1914 in El Salvador, 1926 in Nicaragua, and 1930 in Honduras. A legal framework to regulate these organizations, which was inspired by successful foreign models, was forged during those early years, with popular sectors excluded from the process.[1] Such legislation appeared before the emergence, many years later, of a strong cooperative movement and is illustrative of the crucial role played by governments in promoting cooperativism in Central America.

In each Central American republic, state intervention in the cooperative movement was facilitated by the specific creation of institutions whose mandate was to promote and control cooperatives and other agencies dealing with them.[2] The first campaigns in support of cooperativism took place during the 1940s and coincided with increased democratization, including the creation of democratic governments in Guatemala in 1944 and 1954, political changes in Costa Rica in 1948, and the growth of state intervention in El Salvador.

The growth of cooperatives in Central America was also related to international events, such as the Alliance for Progress. The Alliance for Progress played a decisive role in the formation of savings and loans institutions and farming cooperatives. Likewise, farming cooperatives appeared in response to growing interest in agrarian reform in Latin American as part of the strategy to pacify the increasing social conflicts in rural areas. These circumstances led to the appearance of institutions in 1961 and 1966 whose objective was to integrate the various cooperative movements throughout the region.

Cooperativism in Central America began to thrive toward the end of the 1960s and the beginning of the 1970s, especially in Costa Rica, Guatemala, Honduras, and Panama. In Nicaragua and El Salvador, cooperativism did not gain strength until the 1980s (see Table 7.1). In each of these countries cooperativism was a response to both internal and external social and political factors. It was not, however, until the 1970s and early 1980s that, with some exceptions, cooperativism experienced accelerated growth at the regional level. The number of cooperatives in existence increased from 1,623 in 1973 to 5,851 in 1983 (see Table 7.2),

Table 7.1
Number of Cooperatives and Associated Members in Central America, by Country, 1952-1988

Year	1952		1963		1973		1983		1985		1986		1988	
Country	Coop.	Assoc.	Coop.	Assoc.	Coop.	Assoc.	Coop.	Assoc.	Coop.	Assoc.	Coop.	Assoc.	Coop.	Assoc.
Costa Rica	20	2,556	67	13,654	269	76,858	407	203,375	464	268,260	510	239,100	451	269,720
El Salvador	37	9,903	79	14,422	138	17,201	1,142	NA	663	99,400	663	99,400[2]	694	28,672[4]
Guatemala	43	8,026	40	3,439	512	55,552	814	174,872	895	209,441	941	210,846	1,008	218,595
Honduras	7	479	98	6,471	258	36,681	892[1]	130,555[1]	1,141	141,456	1,202	151,452	965	151,547
Nicaragua	11	NA	43	7,915	184	17,614	3,475	60,044	3,445	75,301	3,475[2]	75,301[2]	3,106[3]	72,200[3]
Panama	13	461	61	5631	282	40,103	263	77,102	NA	NA	332	94,112	3,412	100,105
Total	131	21,425	388	53,532	1,623	244,011	5,851	642,948	6,608	793,858	7,213	870,211	6,566	844,839

Notes: [1]Corresponds to the year 1984. [2]Corresponds to the year 1985. [3]Corresponds to the year 1987. [4]Founding members. NA: Data not available.

Source: Marielos Rojas Víquez, "Anuario del Cooperativismo en Costa Rica," Instituto de Investigaciones Sociales, Universidad de Costa Rica, 1990.

Table 7.2
Number of Cooperatives by Economic Activity and Country, 1990

Economic Activity	(1) Costa Rica	(2) El Salvador	(3) Guate-mala	(4) Honduras	(5) Nicara-gua	(6) Panama	Total
Agriculture	112	1,494	439	388	3,363	90	5,886
Banking and Credit	140	352	164	187	73	169	1,085
Consumption	78	69	119	16	60	19	361
Forestry	1	0	0	29		1	31
Industry	38	38	0	22	195	1	294
Fishery	13		3	4	17	3	40
Multiple Services	29		3	0	22		54
Transport	62	51	25	51	118	25	332
Housing	12	0	49	35	8	17	121
Other[3]	0	17	0	34	0	4	55
Total	485[1]	2,021[2]	802[1]	766[2]	3,856[2]	329[1]	8,259
Percent	5.8	5.8	9.7	9.3	46.7	4.0	100.0

Notes: [1]Corresponds to active cooperatives. [2]Corresponds to recorded cooperatives. [3]Corresponds to cooperatives classified as mixed, some work related, other student related.

Source: Derived from the following: J. Leopoldo Ríos Marroquín and Jonatan Salgado, "Situación Actual del Cooperativísmo en Centroamérica, Guatemala," Diciembre 1990, manuscript; Pedro Juan Hernández Romero, "La Situación Actual del Cooperativísmo en El Salvador," January 1991, manuscript; Marielos Rojas Viquez, "Una Visión Actual del Cooperativísmo en Costa Rica," 1990, in press; Javier Molina, "El Cooperativísmo en Nicaragua, 1980-1990," December 1990, manuscript; CCC-CA, "Panorámica del Cooperativísmo en Guatemala, Honduras, Costa Rica, Panamá, Puerto Rico, y República Dominicana," 1990, manuscript; Instituto Hondureño de Cooperativas, CHC y POCOOPCA, "Primer Censo Cooperativo Nacional," Honduras, Junio 1991.

an increase of 72.3%. It is striking how this growth coincided with the severe economic crisis in Central America. We are left to question whether such growth was fueled by the programs of social compensation developed for the neediest sectors of the Central American population as a response to structural adjustment policies.

In 1952, there were only 131 cooperatives and 21,425 associates in Central America. By 1988, this figure reached 6,566 cooperatives and 1 million associates. In the farming sector alone, there were 6,000 cooperatives and approximately 270,000 rural families associated with them by 1989 (Rojas Viquez, 1990). This astounding growth is best appreciated in Table 7.1. However, as has been pointed out in international forums, the central goal of cooperativism in Central America, namely, social and economic development, has not been achieved. In many countries the cooperative sectors are facing great difficulties and are at risk of dissolution. For example, cooperativism shrank in Costa Rica, Honduras, and Nicaragua in the second half of the 1980s. The total number of cooperatives in those nations went from 7,213 in 1986 to 6,566 in 1988.

It is important to stress that both in the past, as well as the present, regional and international organizations have sought to consolidate cooperativism in the region. Although considerable human and economic resources were invested toward this goal, the results are less than encouraging. It appears that the investments made by these organizations did not match the real needs of the cooperative movement. Instead, resources were directed to the creation of costly infrastructure personnel services, particularly salaries for technical specialists. It is commonly known that these activities have been increasingly frequent during the past two years, thus diverting resources from the development and strengthening of the basic organization—the cooperatives themselves.

Central American cooperativism has developed differently in each country. In some cases, political regimes have restricted the growth of these organizations; in extreme circumstances they have resorted to political repression. In other cases, cooperatives have become an alternative organization for small producers and entrepreneurs, many of whom see in them an opportunity to confront threats posed by transnational capital. Finally, in some countries the state has considered cooperatives as important contributors to economic development inasmuch as they serve as instruments of mediation of social problems, especially during times of economic and social crises.

The previous observations lead us to conclude that the Central American cooperative movement is (1) relatively young and (2) largely a product of government and international circumstances—not a direct initiative of the popular sectors. This does not imply that the movement has not played an important role as a social force with its own interests, but, as will be shown later, the circumstances of its promotion have led to many problems. Another conclusion is that the development strategies followed by much of the cooperative movement have been formulated more at the international than at the regional level. Likewise, these strategies have a short-term character and are geared more toward social goals than entrepreneurial ones.

CHARACTERISTICS OF CENTRAL AMERICAN COOPERATIVISM IN 1990

Currently, there are a total of 8,492 cooperatives in Central America, with 987,000 people associated with them (see Tables 7.2 and 7.3). Most are concentrated in Nicaragua (46.7%) and El Salvador (24.5%). Although the majority of the cooperatives are not in Costa Rica or Guatemala, the bulk of the membership is—28.5% of total membership is in Costa Rica and 25% in Guatemala. Thus, cooperatives in these two countries are larger in terms of member size. In addition, there are fifty-nine cooperative organizations, such as unions, federations, consortiums, and seven confederations (e.g., Banco Nacional de Desarrollo Agrario [Honduras], Instituto Nacional de Transformación Agraria [Guatemala], Instituto Nacional del Café [El Salvador], Empresa Nacional de Algodón [Nicaragua], Instituto Mixto de Ayuda Social [Costa Rica], Ministerio de Agricultura y Ganadería [Panama]).

Central American cooperativism is primarily an agricultural enterprise, with 72% of all cooperatives falling within this sector. However, the primary sector encompasses only 32% of total membership in cooperatives (see Tables 7.3 and 7.4). On the other hand, the tertiary sector comprises only 24.3% of all cooperatives, but has 66% of all cooperative membership associated with it. Thus, it is noteworthy that the largest cooperatives, by membership size, are located in the tertiary sector, particularly in service cooperatives such as savings and loans institutions.

The farming cooperatives contribute an important percentage of total agricultural production in all countries, with the exception of Guatemala and Panama. Their impact on production is especially important in coffee, sugar cane, rice, corn, beans, cotton, onions, potatoes, sesame, milk, and meat. On a smaller scale, cooperatives produce African palm, tomatoes, cucumbers, melons, tobacco, wheat, bananas, ornamental plants, and fruits (see Table 7.5). During the past few years, cooperatives have attempted to expand into non-traditional export crops, which is part of a general trend for Central American export agriculture. Some farming cooperatives are also involved in selling materials and agricultural equipment.   The cooperatives also make noteworthy contributions to the

Table 7.3

Number of Members of Cooperatives by Economic Activity and Country, 1990

Economic Activity	(1) Costa Rica	(2) El Salvador	(3) Guatemala	(4) Honduras	(5) Nicaragua	(6) Panama	Total
Agriculture	49,302	71,709	56,167	19,351	88,085	25,906	310,520
Banking and Credit	154,478	16,949	157,348	89,703	15,162	70,246	503,886
Consumption	14,593	2,908	18,399	506	3,640	2,311	42,357
Forestry	13	--	--	2,123	--	45	2,181
Industry	7,282	1,239	--	725	6,416	54	15,716
Fishery	395	--	82	101	359	92	1,029
Multiple Services	42,040	--	93	--	1,204	--	43,357
Transport	5,136	1,906	1,849	1,980	5,703	2,463	19,047
Housing	1,134	0	6,848	4,491	2,089	2,816	17,378
Other[3]	--	461	--	5,907	--	103	6,471
Total	274,373[1]	95,172[2]	240,786[1]	124,887[2]	122,668[2]	104,036[1]	961,922
Percent	28.5	10.0	25.0	13.0	12.7	10.8	100.0

Notes: [1]Corresponds to active cooperatives. [2]Corresponds to recorded cooperatives. [3]Corresponds to cooperatives classified as mixed, some work related, other student related.

Source: Derived from the following: J. Leopoldo Ríos Marroquín and Jonatan Salgado, "Situación Actual del Cooperativísmo en Centroamérica, Guatemala," Diciembre 1990, manuscript; Pedro Juan Hernández Romero, "La Situación Actual del Cooperativísmo en El Salvador," January 1991, manuscript; Marielos Rojas Viquez, "Una Visión Actual del Cooperativísmo en Costa Rica," 1990, in press; Javier Molina, "El Cooperativísmo en Nicaragua, 1980-1990," December 1990, manuscript; CCC-CA, "Panorámica del Cooperativísmo en Guatemala, Honduras, Costa Rica, Panamá, Puerto Rico, y República Dominicana," 1990, manuscript; Instituto Hondureño de Cooperativas, CHC y POCOOPCA, "Primer Censo Cooperativo Nacional," Honduras, Junio 1991.

Table 7.4
Number of Cooperatives and Associated Members in Central America, by Country and Economic Sector, 1990

Sector Country	Primary Sector		Secondary Sector		Tertiary Sector		Total	
	Coop.	Assoc.	Coop.	Assoc.	Coop.	Assoc.	Coop.	Assoc.
Costa Rica	126	49,710	38	7,282	321	217,381	485	274,373
El Salvador	1,494	71,709	38	1,239	489	22,224	2,021	95,172
Guatemala	442	56,249	0	0	360	184,537	802	240,786
Honduras	421	21,575	22	725	323	102,587	766	124,887
Nicaragua	3,380	88,444	195	6,416	281	27,808	3,856	122,668
Panama	94	26,043	1	54	234	77,939	329	104,036
Total	5,957	313,730	294	15,716	2,008	632,476	8,259	961,922
Percent	72.1	32.6	3.5	1.6	24.3	65.7	100.0	100.0

Source: Derived from the following: J. Leopoldo Ríos Marroquín and Jonatan Salgado, "Situación Actual del Cooperativismo en Centroamérica, Guatemala," Diciembre 1990, manuscript; Pedro Juan Hernández Romero, "La Situación Actual del Cooperativismo en El Salvador," January 1991, manuscript; Marielos Rojas Viquez, "Una Visión Actual del Cooperativismo en Costa Rica," 1990, in press; Javier Molina, "El Cooperativismo en Nicaragua, 1980-1990," December 1990, manuscript; CCC-CA, "Panorámica del Cooperativismo en Guatemala, Honduras, Costa Rica, Panamá, Puerto Rico, y República Dominicana," 1990, manuscript; Instituto Hondureño de Cooperativas, CHC y POCOOPCA, "Primer Censo Cooperativo Nacional," Honduras, Junio 1991.

Table 7.5
Percentage Contribution of Cooperatives to Total National Product, by Country and Principal Product

Product	(1) Costa Rica 1988	(2) El Salvador 1986-87	(4) Honduras 1988	(5) Nicaragua 1987-88
Coffee	38.8	13.1	86	41
Sugar Cane	20.0	39.1	NA	12
Cocoa	6.0	0	0	0
Onions	79.6	0	NA	0
Potatoes	48.0	0	NA	0
Rice	NA	26.3	32	15
Corn	NA	25.8	12	45
Beans	NA	21.8	6	66
Sorghum	NA	13.6	5	16
Cotton	0	0	0	16
Sesame	0	0	NA	85
Milk	41.6	0	0	NA
Meat	36.3	0	0	NA

NA: Not available.

Source: Derived from the following: J. Leopoldo Ríos Marroquín and Jonatan Salgado, "Situación Actual del Cooperativismo en Centroamérica, Guatemala," Diciembre 1990, manuscript; Pedro Juan Hernández Romero, "La Situación Actual del Cooperativismo en El Salvador," January 1991, manuscript; Marielos Rojas Viquez, "Una Visión Actual del Cooperativismo en Costa Rica," 1990, in press; Javier Molina, "El Cooperativismo en Nicaragua, 1980-1990," December 1990, manuscript; CCC-CA, "Panorámica del Cooperativismo en Guatemala, Honduras, Costa Rica, Panamá, Puerto Rico, y República Dominicana," 1990, manuscript; Instituto Hondureño de Cooperativas, CHC y POCOOPCA, "Primer Censo Cooperativo Nacional" Honduras, Junio 1991.

production of basic grains in almost all of Central America. Data for Costa Rica were unavailable, but research has shown that cooperatives are indeed important in the production of basic grains. This indicates the important involvement of cooperatives in the basic food security of these nations.

Another important characteristic of cooperativism is the involvement of women, who have become progressively integrated in the movement. In Panama, for instance, women represent 40% of the total membership of the cooperatives (Barrios, 1990). In Guatemala they represent 20% (Ríos and Salgado, 1990), in El Salvador 21.9% (Molina, 1990), and in Costa Rica 25.3% (Rojas Viquez, 1991). Even though these percentages are not very high, they are important in other ways. For example, in countries such as Costa Rica, Nicaragua, and El Salvador, cooperatives make significant efforts to include women at the base level and to promote them to decision-making posts, in both the cooperatives themselves, and in cooperative organizations.

CURRENT PROBLEMS OF CENTRAL AMERICAN COOPERATIVISM

Cooperatives face a number of problems throughout the region. The problems can be traced to two general factors. The first factor is derived from the historical development of cooperatives, while the second relates to the problems caused by recent structural adjustment policies.

The historical development of cooperativism in Central America has been largely determined by state intervention. The predominant view was that cooperativism was an instrument to pacify social conflict generated by the economic and social structure of society, receiving attention primarily at times of crisis. This may have contributed to giving cooperativism a socially oriented, instead of an entrepreneurial-oriented character. Paternalistic relations with the state resulted in cooperativism's dependence on government and international financial support. Obviously, this historical factor has limited the evolution of the cooperative movement as an independent sector of the economy, capable of advancing with its own resources. This, in turn, has generated a series of problems that are not insurmountable, but nonetheless complex.

At the global level, cooperativism has not accumulated sufficient experience in medium- and short-term strategy planning, since cooperatives have, by and large, focused on the short-term planning horizon. The development of inter-cooperative and intersector integration based on sound economic analysis of the regional markets has been deficient. There have been only limited efforts to integrate cooperatives with other social organizations in order to overcome the challenges facing national producers, workers, and other sectors of the Central American nations. Furthermore, at the micro level, cooperatives face problems such as limited business experience; competitive weakness (except for some cooperatives, which have achieved a high level of development and efficient administration and accounting systems); obsolescence of legal regulations; inadequate planning of productive projects; underdeveloped linkages with suppliers and producers; limited technology leading to low productivity; and the inability to integrate into the agrarian and economic structures of their countries.

Structural adjustment policies have also created new problems for the cooperatives, and simultaneously posed new challenges. These problems include limited access to credit because of increased costs; price uncertainty because of liberalization of markets; subdivision of cultivated land into small and unproductive plots (Honduras, El Salvador); and increased competition from transnational producers with the elimination of domestic protection. These problems threaten the short-term survival of many cooperatives, especially farming cooperatives, and large-scale collapse would affect thousands of families in Central America. This is reflected in the adverse impact on the region's food security, since the production of basic grains by the cooperatives is significant.

To summarize, the political, social, and economic consequences of structural adjustment could weaken the foundation that sustains the cooperative sector. There is no doubt that cooperatives, despite the complexity of the problems they face, still benefit approximately 1 million Central Americans, and significantly contribute to the national economies of the region. This contribution could easily be expanded if sectoral economic, political, and social strategies were to be redefined and reoriented, accounting for the dramatic economic changes of the past decade and the current, difficult political and economic situation.

SOME IDEAS ON CONSOLIDATING THE COOPERATIVE MOVEMENT

If consolidated, cooperativism could be placed on a firmer economic base. To successfully achieve this, it would entail coordinating simultaneously three factors: a comprehensive development strategy, a revitalized process of regional integration, and, a set of coordinated national policies.

The development of a strategy to consolidate the cooperative movement is a priority for the survival of the sector in the current context of widespread structural adjustment. The areas that require particular attention are those that strengthen the business capability of the enterprises to enhance economic efficiency and those that strengthen and integrate the organizations at the sectoral level. To achieve this, a comprehensive analysis is required of the current political, social, and economic milieu in Central America. This would help determine the present viability of the cooperative movement, the obstacles it currently faces, and the prospects for new opportunities for insertion into national and regional economic structures.

At the micro-enterprise level, studies should focus on the internal problems, needs and interests of the cooperative, in order to define the requirements for business consolidation, organization, and integration. A well-known need is the training of staff and the creation of assistance programs leading to improvements in managerial and productive aspects of the enterprises. Training should also encompass the development of the "human potential" of the cooperative's associates. In addition, training projects should incorporate the effective use of domestic and environmentally sensitive labor-intensive technologies. Likewise, cooperativism could provide for the development of a widespread scientific, technical, and domestic base, supported by the cultural and social environment and based on the rational use and knowledge of local ecosystems.

Another priority is the development of intercooperative integration schemes, both at the local and regional level. Despite the few examples found at the national level, cooperative consortia could form the basis for integration. This and other forms of integration would help cooperativism and protect national producers from the threat posed by transnational capital in Central America. Integration would also open new channels in international markets.

An important challenge facing Central American cooperativism is its active participation in the integration of the social sector, which is represented by cooperatives and workers and farmers associations, as well as neighborhood organizations, organized families, students, and other new channels of expression of grass-roots organizations. Cooperativism transmits many different messages, not all of which are consistent. The movement should aspire to present unified alternatives to the current body of structural adjustment initiatives. The alternatives presented by cooperativism should highlight local and regional needs and play a fundamental role in the implementation of national or regional pacts. This would, in turn, increase the likelihood of reaching true national consensus as an expression of real democracy.

NOTES

1. Guatemala adopted the "Ley de Sociedades Cooperativas No. 630." In 1904, El Salvador introduced a section in the Commerce Code dealing with cooperative corporations. In 1924, Honduras promoted cooperatives in its constitution of 1924. Panama introduced, in 1916, two sections on cooperatives in its Commerce Code.

2. In Guatemala this institution was the INACOP, created in 1978. In Costa Rica it was the INFOCOOP (1963); in El Salvador INSAFOCOOP (1969); in Honduras DIFOCOOP (1953), substituted later by IHDECOOP (1988); and in Panama IPACOOP (1980). In Nicaragua this role is played by several different institutions.

Eight

The Future Role of Multinational Enterprise and Foreign Direct Investment

Walter Goldstein

Twenty years ago there was a heated dispute over the growth of multinational corporations (MNCs) and their deployment of foreign direct investment (FDI). Academic critics and representatives from the less-developed countries (LDCs) at the United Nations alleged that MNCs had invaded the sovereignty of nation states and thus crippled their economic prospects. Conservative opponents demurred, claiming the MNC was the world's best hope to stimulate economic growth.[1] A special center was formed at the U.N. to study the issue; and the Organization for Economic Cooperation and Development (OECD), along with various business groups, tried to resolve the arguments by proposing codes of "good conduct" for MNC managers.

A cottage industry emerged in leading universities and business schools to write about FDI and the MNCs. It is now a mature, post-cyclical industry. The aim of most academic commentaries is to explain if not justify the contributions made by global corporations—or "cosmocorps." Financial analysts and management consultants today extol the economies of scale and the advantages of vertical integration that were achieved by world-renowned MNCs. Not all MNCs were big or successful, they add. But it is apparent that the top 1,000 global firms have helped revolutionize the conduct of international trade.[2]

Experts hold that one-third of the $4.5 trillion total of world trade is now directed through intra-firm commerce. The lead once set by American MNCs has been challenged by cosmocorps of Japanese and European origin. The marketing and price leadership of IBM, GE Citibank, or Coca Cola had once appeared invincible. Now they face aggressive competition from Mitsubishi and Deutsche Bank. State-owned MNCs such as Airbus Industrie and Petrobras have became major players in offshore markets, too. Many have negotiated joint-venture pacts with the command economies of Eastern Europe and the Third World.[3]

Criticism of the MNCs in the Third World became muted for two compelling reasons. First, there was no alternative source of investment capital once the worldwide debt crunch took hold in the 1980s. As syndicated loans and aid to the LDCs declined, they had no choice but to rely on the MNCs to bring in new investment. Loans from the World Bank fell in 1990 to $23 billion, but after debt interest was paid, a balance of only $6.4 billion a year remained. In 1988 the net inflow of FDI into the LDCs was $25 billion—while $120 billion (or 80% of FDI) went to the wealthy nations.[4]

Second, the growth of world trade has slowed to 1.5% a year. Protectionism and retrenchment have spread to many countries, and LDCs lost much of their access to the markets of the wealthy G-7 industrial leaders: the United States, the United Kingdom, France, Germany, Italy, Canada and Japan. A recent study by GATT (General Agreement on Tariffs and Trade) showed that 284 discriminatory restraints were exercised by the rich nations to limit the market access of LDCs and that further restraints were likely to appear in the 1990s.[5]

Real gross national product (GNP) growth in the LDCs slumped from 4.3% a year in 1988 to 2.2% in 1990, and their terms of trade declined. A few managed to buck the trend. LDCs in East Asia, such as Taiwan and South Korea, moved forward from a 5% stake of global GNP to 20% between 1965 and 1988, while most countries in Africa and Latin America faced zero growth or a sharp decline in real income. Naturally, the MNCs' spreading investments were greeted with acclaim rather than criticism.

The statistical evidence is dramatic. Between 1970 and 1990 world industrial output increased by 200%, export trade by 300%, but FDI flows by 500%. In the growth spurt of 1985-1990 FDI flows increased three times faster than the growth of conventional trade; and, the FDI financed by parent MNCs across the world rose threefold. Eighty percent of this cornucopia of corporate wealth went to rich rather than poor countries. West-West trade was driven by the spread of MNC activity. Some 35,000 parent MNCs created over 170,000 affiliate companies in host states. The asset value of the 100 largest MNCs amounted to $3 trillion in 1990, a sum greater than the GNP of Japan and twice the outstanding external debt owed by 120 LDC regimes. Nearly 75% of the FDI going to LDCs came from three nations—the United States, the United Kingdom, and Japan.[6]

The significance of FDI cannot be underestimated. International trade is today the key concern of every nation state regardless of its industrial wealth or political ideology. As security anxieties in the Cold War relaxed and fears of military conflict diminished, rich and poor nations realized anew that they were tied to Ricardo's dictates of comparative advantage. They could either compete in export markets or stagnate. A few sought relief by resorting to trade warfare. Some won temporary gains by devaluing their currency or increasing the money supply. Others tried to shelter key industries or angry farmers. Economic nationalism asserted itself everywhere and GATT rules were too often ignored.

The urgent quest for FDI came to change the debate over the MNC. Conventional trade growth slackened but intra-firm trade rose in importance. Protectionist regimes in Eastern Europe and Latin America slouched into poverty and autarky while the fabled Four Tigers of East Asia became wealthy world traders. South Korea, Taiwan, Hong Kong, and Singapore opened their economies to FDI and flourished; Japanese and American firms brought them capital, production lines, and skill training. The MNCs' aim was to lower production costs, realize economies of scale, and create "offshore export platforms" to enlarge their share of global markets.

Nowhere in all of Africa or Latin America was there a match for East Asia's export prosperity or its ability to attract MNC affiliates. A major exception appeared in the 500-odd *maquiladoras* that were constructed in the tariff-free zone along the U. S. border with Mexico. Japanese and American MNCs took advantage of loopholes in U. S. tariff laws to manufacture cheap components and finished goods in these sweatshops and export them to the United States at almost zero duty. [7]

Critics in the 1970s warned that the MNCs would exploit the defenseless work force and capital weakness of the host states. They pointed to the political bribes and illegal payments made by MNCs to corrupt regimes, or to the oligopoly rigging of commodities and oil markets. The MNC was not an ''engine of growth'' they argued, but, a monstrous agent of ''free trade imperialism.''[8]

The polemical assault on the MNC was gradually pushed aside in the 1980s. MNC activity intensified in banking, oil, manufacturing, and the numerous service sector industries that move world trade. As the MNCs diversified their operations across the globe, they paid more attention to their public relations and their political image. None cared to repeat the crude mistakes perpetrated by Anaconda Copper in Chile or Aramco in the Arabian Gulf.

Attacks on MNCs at the U.N. General Assembly or at UNCTAD diminished. A few LDCs learned how to build MNCs of their own. Others discovered that rewarding contracts could be negotiated with the most obdurate of incoming MNCs, making it easier to tax the foreigners' profits or making it more painful for them to jump ship and flee to another Third World territory. In some cases, the host state even extracted a sizeable piece of equity in the MNCs affiliates or it forced them to pay vast revenue advances for "services rendered."

It is likely that MNCs will extend their international production and trade arrangements in coming years. Instead of denouncing their imperialist designs, the LDCs will probably reach a modus operandi with these "malefactors of wealth." Negotiations between states and companies have become more sophisticated in recent years and so, too, has the academic literature. Angry confrontation and polemical dispute have been replaced by econometric calculation and diplomatic finesse. This does not mean that Marxist critics and laissez-faire theorists will be ignored or that cost accountants and management analysts will alone be heard. But it is likely that international capital movements and development economics will be appraised in a new light, along with novel forms of organization by the MNCs.[9]

EXTERNAL REQUIREMENTS FOR FDI

The success of MNC operations can be explained at two different levels. First, MNCs demonstrated a unique capacity to respond to rapid change in the external business world. Second, they adjusted to internal requirements for change: They brought flexibility rather than bureaucratic inertia into their expanding organization and financial transactions, and they pursued global economies of scale. The academic literature today puts a major stress not on the MNCs' reach for power and corporate expansion, but on its sensitivity to external change. No political or commercial agency has succeeded as well as the MNC in adjusting to the threats and challenges of the world order. Arguably, it will gain further strength as the century ends.[10]

Business conditions have abruptly changed since the oil shocks of the 1970s and the surging decade of growth in the 1980s. In the 1990s trade expansion has slowed, an imbalance of supply over demand has appeared, and there has been a wide resort to protectionism. Free trade axioms are wearing thin. Strategies of managed trade and the distorting ploys of non-tariff barriers are now acceptable. MNCs have learned how to cope with a harsh external environment by liquidating resources overnight or by rushing assets from one market to another as conditions change.

Some of the worst threats have appeared in the credit market. Long-term interest rates fell and real prices stabilized in the 100 years of peace from 1815 to 1914, and world trade increased by a factor of twenty five. Exchange and interest rates had been relatively stable during the twenty five years of fixed currency rates following the Bretton Woods agreement of 1946 and again world trade flourished. But after the dollar was cut loose in 1971, currencies became volatile, the cost of credit mounted, current accounts went into deficit, and export trade fell. Prospects for monetary stability and trade expansion in the 1990s do not look encouraging.

The mix of tight money policies in the industrial world and of snowballing debt among the LDCs could take a terrible toll. Many of the leading G-7 countries have switched their policy priorities from promoting GNP growth to the suppression of inflation at the cost of prolonging the 1990s' recession. New lending to the LDCs has ceased and their capital accounts are exhausted. Collectively, they pay $50 billion a year more in debt service to the rich world than they receive in extended or bridging loans; and all other forms of concessional aid or soft-loan grants have been cut.[11]

The continuing access to credit enjoyed by the MNCs was important both to their own operations and to the host states in which they established offshore plants. While smaller firms and state-run industries found the cost of credit exorbitant, most MNCs were adequately funded. Many banks had to shorten their lines of credit or loan portfolios, or demand greater collateral. But MNCs with global assets and diversified cash flow could borrow anywhere in the world. If necessary they could resort to internal and subtle modes of transfer pricing to shuttle needed funds between currencies or overseas affiliates.

It is important to distinguish between the MNCs' flow of short-term or liquid funds and the capital they place in fixed and direct investment. The former can be used for currency hedging or transient needs; the latter are sunk into assembly lines or to buyout foreign companies. Enormous sums of portfolio funding cross the exchanges every day, driven by fluctuations in spot currency or interest rates. In times of panic, such as the Wall Street crash of October 1987, nearly $2 trillion a day moved across the world by telex. The Japanese put hundreds of billions of dollars into U. S. T-bills when interest spreads widened between the yen and the dollar. They later lost one-third of their principle. Three years before, as the dollar peaked, dollars flowed the other way—to the European Community (EC). Both flows were rapidly reversed as currency and credit rates fell.[12]

Long-term capital is not nearly as volatile as short-term capital, but it is equally tied to market forecasts. Toyota, Honda, and Mazda built expensive ''transplant'' operations in the United States with funds that were drawn from their export earnings or raised anew on the Tokyo market. They drew on the overvalued dollar or on their inflated real estate holdings in Japan to lower their credit costs. They also hedged forward against the dollar, while accumulating investment resources overseas, until 1993 when the dollar plummeted and the yen soared.

In a similar manner the American MNCs spreading across Mexico found that they could leverage hard currency credit at home to fund operating costs for their *maquiladora* plant. This reversed a basic trend. In the 1960s and 1970s the United States and the United Kingdom were the largest sources of FDI. Suddenly, in the 1980s, they became recipients of major inflows of FDI. As their interest rate spreads widened and their external debts rose, $30 billion of FDI flowed into the two ex-creditor countries.[13]

A second trend surfaced as credit markets tightened in the 1990s. Prices changed on the supply and the demand side of the MNCs' operations. Production costs mounted along with the price of credit, profit margins shrank, and assembly lines were moved from one country to another. Supply-side calculations forced MNCs to trim their variable and fixed costs; Mercedes and BMW moved from Germany to South Carolina to enjoy transfer pricing advantages and lower costs. Demand-side schedules changed, too. As purchasing power declined worldwide, consumer spending shifted, and product-line sales fell. Japanese MNCs deployed production and sales from the U.S. to the Pacific rim. Ford Europe moved production from wholly owned subsidiaries in France to those in Mexico or East Asia. Volkswagen closed its assembly lines in West Germany and opened a new plant in Czechoslovakia. Holland America Line left its home country for good to locate its parent headquarters in the cheap currency zone of Miami.

It appears that a major trend in world trade in the next decade will be seen in the internationalization of production and distribution. In the contest between states and markets there will be a greater emphasis on the mobility of assets and less concern with the regulatory attempts of nation states. The cross-national division of labor and the flow of FDI will pursue market opportunities rather than political loyalties.[14] As market opportunities change and credit flows reverse course, the MNCs will have to move fast. If they improve their mobile deployments and market targeting, they will become dominant actors on the world scene. If they can shift FDI with dispatch, they will alter the GNP prospects of both rich and poor states.

INTERNAL REQUIREMENTS OF THE MNC

The academic literature sets out taxonomies that list the characteristics of the MNC and the determinants of the FDI which it deploys. There is no need to survey the literature in detail, but it would be useful to identify a core concern—the list of benefits that MNCs supposedly bring to LDCs:

1. By importing investment capital- and firm-specific technology,

MNCs can boost employment, skills, aggregate GNP, export revenues, and the debt-servicing ability of LDCs.

2. The skilled training of the LDC work force can enhance the value-added performance of the MNCs' local suppliers, contractors, and customers.

3. MNCs frequently aim to export to third countries rather than to swamp local markets; this can boost export earnings and arrest the LDCs' dreaded slide into currency inflation and import-substitution policies. By building cost-competitive and exporting plants, MNCs can deter LDCs from protecting inefficient industries.

4. MNCs sometimes create enclaves of wealth and privileged work in the LDCs. But many do not. Wise firms worry about host country welfare needs as well as their short-term financial goals. They set out to win political support from the host community as well as to improve their global market share.

MNCs vary widely in their characteristics. Companies in extractive or high-tech sectors (such as oil, electronics, or engineering) perform in a different manner than the MNCs engaged in such standardized or labor-intensive manufacture as food processing, automobiles, and textiles. Similarly, MNCs located in high-income countries tend to specialize in sophisticated labor or in the deployment of expensive research and development (R & D). In poorer economies, workers complain that they have to do the dirty or unrewarding tasks that MNCs shift downwards among their worldwide networks. It was once claimed that MNCs practiced economic apartheid by locating skilled work in the North and low rewards in the South. The complaint is not so widely heard today. MNCs have created millions of jobs, many with rapid learning curves, especially along the Pacific rim.[15]

A distinction is drawn in most taxonomy listings to separate three types of MNC behavior. The first itemizes firm-specific determinants, such as the MNCs' asset size, its market share, and its access to capital. The second focuses on locational factors that are driven by transport costs, trade barriers, or its preference for niche rather than mass markets. The third category highlights key policy issues, such as the willingness to share equity ownership or repatriate dividends from host to home countries.

The firm-specific determinants of MNC behavior are of great significance. The MNC parent headquarters must choose whether to invest in patented technology and keep it at home (as many pharmaceutical companies do), or alternatively to limit their capital exposure by diversifying investments overseas and joint venturing with host country suppliers. If an MNC aims for sharper product differentiation, it will focus on the revenue curve of a niche market (as do fashion products or sports cars), rather than the volume earnings of a mass automobile market. By contrast, if the MNC chooses to standardize its product lines, it will build multiplant operations overseas. Parent headquarters have to keep changing their priorities between realizing economies of scale, or the "economic rent" found in oligopoly industries, or between the slow product life cycle of specialized development rather than the fast turnover in a mass market.

The parent headquarters must also choose how best to raise capital and harvest market opportunities. If both goals are assured, it will construct a network of affiliates linked at legal "arm's-length" distance, as the richer banks or IBM can afford. But, if it has to cross-subsidize product lines or move funds between its far-flung subsidiaries, it will turn from arm's-length dealings to complex movements of funds or to covert forms of transfer pricing. These stratagems are not illegal. Management decisions and recruitment will build on the chosen trend. If political visibility and caution matter, local MNC officers will be recruited and "good citizenship" rules will be followed. But if global authority or patented R & D must be safeguarded, top managers will be sent from the home country to manipulate cash flows and guard the store.[16]

The second category of behavior lists the locational decisions that MNCs make. Production and transport costs figure prominently and so do product and pricing strategy. If a mass market must be captured quickly, so that the "economic rent" of a product lifecycle can be maximized, the MNC will integrate its operations vertically to save time and expense. If the strategy is to preserve a unique patent or process, it would be better to opt for a horizontal integration of sales and pursue a larger market share instead of a rapid return on investment.

Locational choices largely depend on the size of the markets at home, in the host nation, or in third countries. In the case of Holland or Switzerland, their home market is small and the rich markets of America or Europe beckon; so their MNC affiliates have built production plants in low wage nations, like Mexico or Spain, close to the point of sale. Their products can then slip under U.S. or EC tariff barriers at a low or zero duty, thus avoiding non-tariff barriers and quota restrictions and undercutting competition from rival MNC suppliers.

Locational choices are partly determined by fixed costs and wage levels. A vertically integrated company will provide substantial employment in low-wage countries to handle labor intensive operations; only a few skilled staff need then be hired at high incomes at home. Petroleum MNCs learned to hire offshore staff for oil refineries from cheap labor pools in the LDCs. They built refineries in the Caribbean so that U.S. wage and environmental controls could be sidestepped. Their vertical integration was strictly organized along cost lines. A similar pattern was designed by automobile MNCs. They built their offshore "transplants" wherever local taxes, wages, or environmental conditions were either lax or subsidized by host countries.[17]

Transfer pricing strategy is an important influence on location choice. The ability to link affiliate management at less than arm's-length distance is crucial if components, R & D license fees, investment funds, and other intra-company transfers are to be conducted out of public view. Affiliates are often implanted in tax-haven countries to channel fees or dividends beyond the reach of governments that seek to regulate capital flows or harvest tax revenues. Many of the most renowned MNCs register offices in such tax havens as the Cayman Islands, the Netherlands Antilles, or Liechtenstein. Many route their repatriation of dividends or their sales invoices with clever geographical ruses. Obviously, these subterfuges are denied to non-MNC enterprises.

The third category of MNC options is concerned with policy preferences. Some choose to recruit management personnel at home rather than abroad; or they finance plant extensions with overseas capital issues; or they leverage bank debt through affiliate holding companies. The unique ability of the MNC is to move production or sales facilities from one currency zone or hot market to the next. But hidden from view is an element of factor mobility of even greater value. Skilled managers and engineers can be shuttled between affiliates, taking firm-specific technology or financial skills with them, thus creating a global scanning capability at world headquarters that non-MNCs could never hope to match.

The movement of human and financial resources is legal but hard to monitor. American ''guest managers'' used to be found at the headquarters of Ford Europe or IBM Japan, but most have now been sent home and few permanent expatriate officers are to be seen. American MNCs learned to decentralize key management by keeping flexible controls and minimizing local hostility. Japanese MNCs have not yet managed to devolve responsibility while maintaining a central control of financial and planning functions in the parent headquarters.[18]

Telecommunications and support costs have declined as a result of the information revolution. MNCs have learned how to upgrade their operations while diminishing their size. No longer do world class companies hire immense staff or concentrate power at the apex. Instead they foster local autonomy and networking between hundreds of overseas affiliates and parent headquarters at home. Japan's Kereitsu and South Korea's Chaebol have innovated by extending equally massive though less sensitive networks. The days of the legendary American conglomerates (like ITT or Gulf & Western) are gone. Their place has been taken by smaller diversified MNCs that switch from one product line to another as local market or interest rate conditions dictate. The U.S. regional (or Baby Bell) telephone companies became MNCs in their own right by selling financial services as well as equipment across Europe and by pioneering new modes of intra-firm control.[19]

The MNC is no longer accused of using its global size to dominate mass markets or create oligopoly conditions. Its critical strength lies not in its size, but in its ability to exploit factor mobility. MNCs have promptly reacted to changes on the supply and the demand side of their operations. MNCs in consumer electronics spotted a sudden demand for VCR and FAX equipment and they captured the world market before non-MNCs even geared up their assembly lines. Toyota and Honda outclassed non-MNCs such as Renault and Volkswagen by changing car models and building transplants across the United States. In many cases MNCs made more money with money—by shorting the currency markets or exploiting interest spreads—than by trying to dominate every market available to them.

Moreover the MNCs have known when to retreat and when to offer strategic concessions. Some of the larger host LDCs, such as India and Brazil, insisted on limiting MNC product or marketing schedules, or they demanded participation in the parent corporation's equity. Brazil chose to manufacture the cheapest computer models formerly made by IBM and left IBM to engineer only the most expensive models. India set tight rules on market shares and dividend repatriation by MNC insurance agents, chemical combines, and computer firms. Years later, however, it was obliged to scrap its laws limiting foreign ownership in order to bring IBM and Ford back to India. It also lured Mitsubishi into India by ceding it a considerable market share while skimming off much of its profit. Similar ventures are now being negotiated by MNCs in Latin America and Eastern Europe.[20]

It is important to add that MNCs have often failed. Some invested unwisely and had to scrap expensive offshore plants. Others were outsmarted by host country competitors who knew more about local conditions, or by small companies that chose to suboptimize in niche sales rather than in massive revenue returns. Some MNCs were falsely lured with investment or tax incentives that were offered as bribes to encourage their entry to a host country and later discovered their greed had misled them. Others found themselves caught in an "obsolescing contract." In many cases it had been easy for the MNCs to dictate terms when they first entered. But, as the years went by, when their sunk capital was securely locked in, the local regime squeezed them for more concessions. The MNC remained hostage to the host regime because they knew that they could not abandon their plant or revise their original entry bargain.

Many mistakes were made by MNCs in their early stages of development. MNC oil companies failed to predict the wave of expropriations and nationalization in the Persian Gulf in the 1970s, or the rising pressure to tighten environmental controls at home. Automobile producers failed to anticipate shifts in consumer preference or in quality standards. Never before have leading firms lost as much money, or as quickly, as IBM, Renault, Chrysler, Fiat, and General Motors. Once-mighty companies such as Anaconda Copper, Getty, and RCA surrendered their overseas operations, and their legendary names disappeared from the "Fortune 500." State-run MNCs in the banking, insurance, and business-service sectors fared badly, too. Their distinction was to lose vast sums of the public's money in their out-of-state activities.

Despite these setbacks the MNC has become accepted as a dynamic and indispensable actor in the world trade system. It is no longer an object of scorn or political vilification in most economies. It is courted by left- and right-wing regimes for the valuable funds, the technology, and skilled jobs that it can bring to their people. It may not enjoy a benign reputation, but it is sufficiently well trusted to function efficiently. Ever since the collapse of the Soviet empire the MNC has been viewed as a critical agent of capital and growth. It must now choose if it will extend rapidly into Eastern Europe and the Third World.[21]

THE MNC ROLE AND DEVELOPMENT STRATEGY

For all of its new power, the MNC is still governed by the priorities of the host economies that it chooses to enter. When American or Japanese MNCs flocked into the EC trade bloc they encountered local resistance from the twelve-nation market. Although the EC's considerable purchasing power attracted the leading MNCs, they met a series of protectionist defenses and exclusionary tactics that took them by surprise. Some EC nations were tightly protectionist—such as France and Italy, where Japanese cars were allowed only 2% of the domestic market. Most of Europe's governments awarded their "national champions" rich public subsidies to counter foreign MNCs. The four-nation Airbus Industrie and the French computer and Dutch electronics firms were kept afloat with public funds. Overseas MNCs realized they had to compete with the national champions that had been specifically funded to beat back their competition.[22]

A different form of rivalry appeared in the three bloc markets of the industrial world. As the recession took hold, merchandise and current account balances slipped into the red in most of the G-7 nations. Threats were issued between Japan's yen bloc and the dollar bloc, and between both of them and the EC bloc, to raise tariffs and quotas, or to devalue their currencies. The aim was to stifle or under price export competition. As the fight over farm subsidies climaxed, the Uruguay Round of the GATT talks ground to a halt. That impasse threatened the MNCs bent on trading in manufacturing and service-sector accounts.

Running through the arguments over tariff wars and managed trade was a reality that was difficult to grasp. For a start there was the persistent trade deficit of $46 billion between the United States and Japan. It fueled a lasting political anger. It was not recognized that the value added by American MNCs operating inside Japan was actually greater than the sum of U.S. exports to Japan, and that the nagging trade deficit could be turned into a surplus if the MNCs' revenue streams were ever measured accurately. The same calculation could be made of MNC revenues raised within the United States or inside the EC bloc. Indeed, the U.S. trade deficit as a whole could be wiped out if the overseas sales of all its MNCs were to be counted into the U.S. global position.[23]

The hidden revenues of the MNCs were important for three reasons. First, the United States and the United Kingdom, the two largest creditors, had long survived as rentiers by living off their FDI in Europe and the Third World—while allowing their home-based export industries to weaken. Eventually, they were surpassed by Japan as an exporter of capital, and the flow of FDI worldwide began to escalate. As a result, foreign investment entering the United States and Britain balanced the outflow. Japan financed major transplant facilities in both countries and seized a major segment of their domestic markets. At the same time, the EC bought out numerous American companies in the U.S. market. It was clear that the intrafirm production of goods and services would soon become the decisive trend in world commerce.

Second, the MNCs' revenue streams gained in importance as the G-7 industrial countries resorted to deficit financing for their domestic and external budgets. The G-7 were driven to compete with MNCs in the credit and trading markets of an interdependent global economy; and the G-7 were not well armed. In a time of capital shortage the MNCs could access capital and leverage their credit in forward exchange markets. While the G-7 governments struggled to borrow from their own tax-resisting citizens, the MNCs played an ever-greater role in interstate affairs. The collapsing economies of Eastern Europe and the debt-laden nations of the Third World haggled for MNCs' funds and even the OECD nations argued with MNCs to leave their jobs and capital at home.

One of the primary tasks of the MNC was to develop the costly and global industries that an information-based economy urgently requires. It was vital to lure in MNCs, such as AT&T, Northern Telecom, or Siemens, that could deliver both the technology and the global structure to cope with telecommunications links, high-definition television, and fifth-generation computer capabilities. The EC aimed to subsidize its own production of semiconductor and electronic systems, but it largely failed. Like the rest of the world, it was forced into joint ventures with foreign MNCs to acquire costly technology and innovative R & D.[24]

Third, the MNCs enjoyed another advantage besides their global reach in capital and technology. They controlled access to world markets. Most governments hoped to run economic policy without foreign interference. But in the science-based and capital-intensive industries that specialized in exports and information, the MNCs played an indispensable role. There was no statist or inter-bloc agency that could replace them, and few states dared to shut out their competitive energies from their markets. Some of the MNCs made expensive mistakes, such as the Betamax that was launched by Sony before the VCR market was ready. But in the last resort a country as rich as Germany had to offer tax breaks to Mitsubishi to bring in a microchip plant, and IBM France became a national asset within the EC bloc.[25]

MNC PROMISES FOR THE THIRD WORLD

It is in this light that the contributions of the MNC to the development strategies of the Third World can be gauged. In the historic literature of Lenin and Hobson there was an assumption that imperialism was a mortal weakness of monopoly capitalism. Imperialist behavior was driven by two forces: the growing saturation of the home market and the labor economies that could be exploited in the weak and low-wage economies of the Western colonies.[26]

But the MNCs no longer fit that bill. They drew capital out of their home countries because the economies of scale in a global operation had become so valuable, and not because consumption or investment needs were exhausted. The capital they sent abroad was not invested in primary commodities or in the LDCs' labor-intensive sectors. On the contrary, their FDI funded software operations in India, component plants in South Korea or Malaysia, and data processing in Brazil. Investments in primary commodities, bauxite mines, banana plantations, and textile mills declined in significance. Instead the MNCs directed immense FDI flows into activity that drew on a small skilled workforce, firm-specific technology, and global links with a vertically or horizontally integrated production process.

The debate over the MNCs' contribution to LDCs development planning must be put into a contemporary focus. Most of the statist programs adopted by Third World economies have not succeeded. Many were badly managed by state bureaucrats, or they ignored the dictates of the market. In the 1960s there was a turn to import substitution strategies to boost industrial and agricultural growth. Everywhere they resulted in disaster and paralysis. The one-party regimes led by military juntas or corrupt centralizers wasted millions of lives and billions of dollars.

Attempts to construct regional cooperation blocs or free-trade pacts met with failure, too. The ASEAN and Andes pacts fell victim to internal strife and brutal competition; some members tried to lock out neighbors' imports, and others desperately bribed MNCs to finance exports, jobs, and capital. Foreign aid brought little of lasting value. It was either too limited or wrongly targeted to spur real growth; and aid provided a poor substitution for promoting export trade.[27]

Expanding trade was the pious hope of each LDC, but expansion was blocked by divisions in UNCTAD and by the refusal of the OECD bloc to negotiate a new trading order in North-South relations. In the past twenty years real income per capita in Africa and much of Latin America declined, development opportunities were lost, and debt burdens increased.

The argument of this chapter is that the MNC is in no way the only or even the best agent to alleviate the pressing human problems of the Third World. It is argued that too many LDC regimes have criminally wasted time and resources. Many resorted to central planning, forced nationalization, or an autarkic trust in import substitution. The miserable fate of Eastern Europe, Tanzania, North Korea, and Cuba suggests that state-run *dirigisme* might reward governing elites, but it puts a heavy brake on their national development. Many of these countries are now trying to open their markets or close their bureaucracies in order to stimulate GNP growth. It is notable that many socialist regimes turned in despair to solicit assistance from the once vilified MNCs.

There is another argument that is NOT advanced: that the MNC will provide a benign stimulus to growth and a valued contribution to world peace. On the contrary, as the nuclear confrontation and the ideological polarity of the Cold War fade into history, it is likely that there will be a renewal of trade wars, inter-bloc rivalries for credits and exports, and a deadly struggle between nationalist regimes and the FDI enclaves rooted within their economies. Radical regimes might expropriate foreign assets or call for a moratorium on debt servicing, but such measures could lead to chaotic consequences.

It is more probable that tariffs, quotas, a denial of entry into key industrial sectors, or a forced repatriating of dividends will become the weapons of twenty first-century warfare. Several LDCs today require that 90% of the MNCs' value-added work must be performed onsite or that it contain 80% of "domestic content;" or that MNC production capacity should be earmarked for export rather than local market sales. Governments have also tried to encourage competition between incoming MNCs in order to improve their bargaining advantages. Some threatened old and established affiliates, still tied to "obsolescing contracts," that new rivals will be admitted unless they bring more jobs. Others argued that a greater proportion of profits must be turned over to the host state.[28]

In the last resort it can be argued that powerful forces are churning up the international order. They will not be arbitrarily checked or reversed. The thrust toward global production and distribution is gathering strength in most manufacturing and business-service sectors. So, too, is a move to raise labor and capital productivity—either by achieving global economies of scale or curtailing unprofitable enterprises and wasteful employment.

This means that an international division of labor will inhibit statist intervention and that the comparative advantage won by FDI placements will become indispensable tools of world trade. These developments will also impose a ruthless discipline in development planning. Since nation states are charged with welfare responsibilities that contradict market forces, they fear that they will be left at the mercy of market forces. By contrast, MNCs could expand activities more freely, simply because they abide by the dictates and timing of the market. It must be granted that markets are imperfect and often rigged, and that MNCs are not always successful players. But they are simply too valuable to be replaced or suppresssed.

There is a Darwinian logic about the survival of MNCs in a world market. No one claims that the market alone should determine national rivalries or human welfare. But in the contest between states and markets there is a power that cannot be ignored. Centrally planned and laissez-faire states have railed alike against the economic growth that has been denied them—because they made wrong resource decisions or because they failed to match fast changes in the world's trade and technology. MNCs specialize in high risk and rapid change. Many fail. Some penalize host nations or their workers. But those that succeed are too complex to be replaced by political intervention, *dirigiste* regimes, or trade blocs; and the number of MNCs is likely to multiply as the world economy moves away from national units of operation to an internationalizing of capital, skills, and production planning. It may be that the next decade will emphasize competition between global companies rather than between foot-loose MNCs and protectionist nation states.

NOTES

1. For a critical review of the previous literature on MNC activities see Goodman, 1987 and Goldstein, 1965.

2. Contemporary listings of MNC activities are published by the United

Nations Center on Transnational Corporations (UNCTC). See the issue of the *CTC Reporter,* 1989 and 1988.

3. An encouraging view of the contribution of MNCs to East European and Third World development is often found in business journals. For example, the special issue on ''The Stateless Corporation'' in *Business Week,* May 14, 1990; or Reich, 1991.

4. Extensive data on FDI and trade flows appear in World Bank, 1991 and in *The Economist,* Dec. 22, 1990.

5. The contrast is drawn between the LDCs that removed trade barriers and the OECD nations that raised them in the latest GATT report. For a summary see *The Economist*, Sept. 21, 1991.

6. See the data tabulated in the *CTC Reporter,* 1989 and *The Economist*, August 24, 1991.

7. The spread of MNC affiliates and *maquiladora* plant is examined by Sigmund, 1980 and Drucker, 1974.

8. For a critique of the MNC see Barnet and Muller, 1979; Evans, 1978; and Strange, 1986, 1988.

9. On the range of behavior committed by MNCs in host countries see Moran, 1985 and Grosse, 1989.

10. For a selection of theoretical interpretations of MNC behavior see Rugman, 1982 and Dunning, 1988.

11. Current figures on debt or borrowing limits are difficult to track down. See for example two collections of Williamson, 1990a, 1990b and Goldstein, 1985.

12. See Bergsten and Islam, 1991.

13. The fast fluctuation in currency values and leverage is described in Solnik, 1991.

14. Emphasis on factor mobility and the unique skills of MNCs is noted in Vernon, 1972 and Casson, 1986.

15. A noted taxonomy of MNCs and interstate trading appears in Porter, 1991 and Ohmae, 1991.

16. On the techniques of transfer pricing and maintaining arm's-length relationships see Rugman, 1981 and Caves, 1983.

17. A long-standing classic on location theory is the work of Aharoni, 1966.

18. The first book of Porter (1980) looks at MNC preferences in specific countries and in industrial-sector competition.

19. For a wealth of anecdoctal data see Glickman and Woodward, 1989.

20. MNC experience in negotiating entry contracts is examined in Behrman and Grosse, 1990.

21. MNC techniques of problem solving in the Third World are investigated in Austin, 1990 and Molz, 1990.

22. On the difficulties faced by MNCs entering the EC bloc see Goldstein, 1992.

23. A revoluntionary calculation of the earnings of American MNCs in Japan has been set out in Julius, 1990.

24. The complex role and accounts of MNC in a new Europe are explored in Fielke, 1989.

25. EC industries and FDI are reviewed in Hufbauer, 1990.

26. On theories of imperialism see Barret-Brown, 1974 and Magdoff, 1969.

27. Belli, 1991 and Rubner, 1990.

28. A daring exercise in forecasting MNC expansion in world trade is committed by Reich, 1990.

Nine

Political Integration:
A Central American Option

Carlos A. Astiz

The mass media tell us that we have entered the age of privatization and integration. The regional superpower, in a reactive action, has reached an integration agreement with Canada and is now trying to draw Mexico into the process, while Chile is eagerly waiting offstage. The major South American countries have recently created yet another structure of commercial integration, the "Mercosur." Along the way one finds the Latin American Free Trade Area, the Andean Pact, and a variety of bilateral and trilateral agreements with narrower objectives. Regional organizations, such as the Latin American Economic System, have existed for a number of years with the goal of identifying communities of interests and generating joint policies in topics of regional relevancy such as the international debt.

These efforts, so far, have been unsuccessful. These failures were brought about by the political underpinnings found in any process of real supranational integration. The Latin American nation-states which participate in organizations such as LAFTA or the Andean Pact have at times been unwilling to acknowledge that the decision to integrate is at its core political. At other times, although the nature of integration was explicitly or implicitly accepted, prospective members failed to deal with it. Needless to say, if the political will is not present, the most favorable economic, geographic, and social conditions will not suffice to bring about integration. This proposition may convey a pessimistic outlook, inasmuch as the preponderance of Latin America's ruling elites has until now failed to address the issues that determine the success of integration processes. If the heart of the issue is not confronted, integration will not take place.

We are all aware of integration processes that have been successful outside Latin America. In some cases the regional community evolved into a federal, or even a unitary state: Not too long ago in terms of political evolution, Germany and Italy were collections of sovereign entities. Today the latter is a unitary state; the former is a federal state, currently made up of a well-integrated, and dominant, western portion that is in the process of incorporating the eastern portion. The artificial split now being erased was the price of the German defeat in the Second World War. The Swiss confederation provides us with another case of successful integration, in this case of distinctive communities. It could be argued, however, that these examples were "easy" cases, although a detailed review brings to the surface major religious, linguistic, and ideological differences between their respective components. The latest, and in some ways most successful, ongoing example of integration is the European Community, where one still finds national and regional differences that led to war not too long ago. These differences include levels of economic development, in addition to the sociological and ethnic divisions mentioned previously.

As Barbara Ward forecasted more than four decades ago, the world has entered an attitudinal stage that she labeled "the revolution of rising expectations."[1] If anything, this attitude has intensified with the passage of time. It is possible that the expectations and demands generated among the lower and middle classes will always run ahead of the capabilities of most nation-states to improve their lot. On the other hand, technological advancements have become so intense and dramatic that, given a conducive political framework, some less-developed countries could uplift their quality of life and scale of living so as to satisfy some of the demands being made by the bulk of their populations.

That these expectations are capable of being achieved has been demonstrated by the relative satisfaction, and simultaneous absence of militancy, of the lower- and middle-class migrants that have been moving to developed countries in search of ways to reach the goals identified by Ward. While the mass media are quick to call our attention to cases of dissatisfaction, we hear next to nothing about those who have succeeded in integrating into their new environments. In a sense, they have disappeared[2] into developed societies that delivered political stability, reasonable freedoms, effective satisfaction of basic needs, and fair opportunities for self-improvement and socioeconomic promotion.[3]

LACK OF COMPLEMENTARITY AS AN OBSTACLE TO REGIONAL INTEGRATION

The countries of Central America have a history of attempts at integration, including political integration.[4] Some of the institutions created during those attempts have continued to exist, although they have not performed the functions that their founders had in mind. This chapter does not propose to present a revisionist view of the institutional evolution of the Central American countries; it is necessary, however, to address the argument of "lack of complementarity," often mentioned in explaining failure to integrate.

The issue of complementarity or lack thereof is not as significant as its proponents would like us to believe, although there is no question that economic considerations are likely to "tow" the process of integration. Indeed, economic factors are some of the key components of the "revolution of rising expectations." However, the available data show that, on the whole, the economic situation of the Central American countries is not as diverse as it is generally believed. Significant differences in certain sectors of their economies appear to be balanced by similarities elsewhere. Tables 9.1 and 9.2 indicate the absolute amounts of international debt and their share of GNP and exports. The figures show that Panama and Nicaragua have been less affected than the other countries. But when weighted against total economic activity and coupled with external assistance, the effects of international indebtedness on the six countries do not seem to be radically different.

On the other hand, the information conveyed in Table 9.3 indicates that the terms of trade have improved somewhat for all the Central

Table 9.1
Public and Private International Debt in 1970 and 1986
(in millions of U.S. dollars)

	Public Debt		Private Debt		Total Debt
	1970	1986	1970	1986	1989
Costa Rica	134.0	3582.0	112.0	306.0	4468.0
El Salvador	88.0	1463.0	88.0	83.0	1851.0
Guatemala	106.0	2187.0	14.0	119.0	2601.0
Honduras	90.0	2342.0	19.0	125.0	3350.0
Nicaragua	147.0	5343.0	0.0	0.0	9205.0
Panama	194.0	3439.0	0.0	0.0	5800.0

Source: World Bank Development Indicators 1988 (World Game Projects Inc.) and 1991 (World Bank Publications).

Table 9.2
International Debt Service as a Percentage of the Gross Domestic Product and of Exports, 1970 and 1986

| | Percentage of GDP | | Percentage of Exports | | | |
	1970	1986	1970	1980	1986	1989
Costa Rica	2.9	9.5	10.0	29.0	26.3	19.2
El Salvador	1.0	4.7	3.7	7.5	18.0	16.6
Guatemala	1.4	3.9	7.4	7.9	23.4	19.0
Honduras	0.8	5.6	2.9	21.4	18.5	13.1
Nicaragua	3.0	1.2	10.5	21.5	12.9	8.6
Panama	3.1	3.0	7.7	11.5	7.6	0.1

Source: World Bank Development Indicators 1988 (World Game Projects Inc.) and 1991 (World Bank Publications).

American countries, but the improvement has been more significant for El Salvador, Costa Rica, and Guatemala. From 1965 to 1980 the economies of five of the countries generated average growth rates in the 5% to 6% range—the exception, Nicaragua, recorded an average growth rate of 2.6%. These are respectable performances, but do not reach the level of Latin American nations with large domestic markets, such as Brazil, which recorded an average yearly growth rate of 9% during the period from 1965 to 1980. The same table reflects the drastic reduction in economic growth witnessed throughout the developing world in the 1980s. Costa Rica and Panama succeeded in maintaining positive average rates of 1.3% and 2.6%, respectively, while the gross domestic products of El Salvador and Guatemala actually shrank in the same period. The negative outcome may not be unrelated to the consequences of guerrilla warfare and counterinsurgency activities.

The economic role of the state is not radically different in four of the countries under study. In Costa Rica, El Salvador, Honduras, and Panama, governmental activities claim approximately one quarter of the GDP. Nicaragua's public sector has controlled a much higher percentage (in excess of one-half of the GDP in 1985), a figure that reflects the policies of the Sandinista government. The success of the opposition in the last election will undoubtedly lead to a reduction in the share of the

Table 9.3
Average Growth Rate of the Gross Domestic Product, 1965-86, and Changes in the Terms of Trade, 1984 and 1986 (1980=100)

	GNP Growth Rate		Terms of Trade	
	1965-80	1980-86	1984	1986
Costa Rica	6.2	1.3	96.0	106.0
El Salvador	4.3	-1.0	99.0	114.0
Guatemala	5.9	-1.2	95.0	107.0
Honduras	4.2	0.6	97.0	103.0
Nicaragua	2.6	0.2	96.0	97.0
Panama	5.5	2.6	97.0	101.0

Source: World Bank Development Indicators 1988 (World Game Projects Inc.).

GDP extracted by the public sector. When we consider the political coalition that brought the Chamorro administration to power and the general trend toward "privatization," this share can be expected to return in the 1990s to its historical average immediately preceding the Sandinista overthrow of the Somoza regime—somewhere between 15% and 20% of the GDP.

Guatemala appears at the other end, with a governmental machinery that shows a very low extractive capability, consistently under 10% of the GDP. This low level of resources controlled by the government fits the political philosophy of the elite that has held power in Guatemala prior to 1944 and since 1954. Interestingly, the Arevalo and Arbenz administrations, variously identified as "populist" and "leftist," did not significantly modify the overall share of resources going to the government.

The area of income distribution, which is economically significant, as well as politically sensitive, shows less variation than knowledgeable individuals may have expected. Reliable income distribution data are difficult to come by, but it is widely accepted that the data circulated by international financial institutions, when available, are as good as can be obtained. Although all the Central American countries are members of the World Bank and the International Monetary Fund, only three have submitted income distribution data, which are reproduced in Table 9.4.

Table 9.4
Distribution of Income in Selected Countries Share of Gross Domestic
Product: 1970-1986

			Quintile		
	Lowest	Second	Third	Fourth	Highest
Costa Rica	3.3	8.7	13.3	19.8	54.8
El Salvador	5.5	10.0	14.8	22.4	47.3
Panama	2.0	5.2	11.0	20.0	61.8

Source: World Bank Development Indicators 1988 (World Game Projects
    Inc.).

The figures indicate a significant concentration of income in the top
twenty percent of the population of all three countries, with El Salvador
showing the lowest ratio between the extremes and Panama the highest.
Costa Rica is somewhere in between.

   If comparable data were available for the three missing countries,
Guatemala would probably present greater concentration at the top than
Panama; Nicaragua is likely to have the lowest ratio of the region; and
Honduras might place somewhere in between. But the important point
here is that, according to this data, the order of magnitudes between the
countries is not radically different. A recent study provides regional
percentages circa 1980 for five of the countries (Panama is not included).
It allocates 57.4% of the GDP to the wealthiest 20% of the population,
38.9% to the middle 60%, and 3.7% to the poorest one-fifth.[5] A somewhat
different set of Costa Rican statistical data confirms a significant transfer
of domestic income toward the wealthiest 20% of that country's inhabit-
ants during the past decade. The author of the study notes that the data
show "dangerous signs of income concentration."[6] The fact that income
concentration at the top has been a major feature of the political process
throughout Latin America in the 1980s does not diminish the importance
of this finding for Costa Rica.

THE ROLE OF SOVEREIGNTY AND REGIONAL INTEGRATION

Those among us who have engaged in political and legal studies have been presented with an obsolete meaning of sovereignty. Political leaders found it practical and convenient to accept the idea that all nation-states possess "absolute law-making and law-enforcing power." This view of sovereignty has for a long time flown in the face of actual political practice in federal systems and confederations, as well as in the international community. The concept fails to take into account the reality of "penetrated" political systems, of interdependence, and of dependency.[7] It also ignores the appearance in the past decades of enormous capital markets not subject to the control and effective jurisdiction of any one sovereign. How realistic, operational, and useful is the traditional concept of sovereignty when international agencies, such as the World Bank and the International Monetary Fund, as well as coalitions of banks, dictate the extraction and allocation of national resources and the policy choices that nation-states are expected to make? The report of a recent conference put it well:

Though sovereignty may be eroded and the currency of power changed, nation-states are not likely to disappear. But they and other institutions and groups will be compelled to learn to wield their more limited powers in a more ambiguous world. In this new world, individuals will have multiple loyalties which may be both complementary and conflicting and are often transnational. Institutions and groups will be more numerous and more diverse and less able to depend on the allegiance of the people comprising them. Classical sovereign power is obsolescent. . . . To be effective in this new era, nation-states, and other institutions as well, will be forced to adjust to a networking, partnering, and power sharing mode of operations. They will find themselves facilitating linkages, both internal and external. No longer figuratively placed at the top of a pyramid with unfetteredpower to command and control, governments must now operate as though they were a part of a circle, facilitating agreement and action, with capacity to enforce agreement only when substantial consensus has been achieved.[8]

On the face of it, the grant of authority to supra-national agencies is voluntary. After all, there have been nations that, in their dealings with international agencies, choose to retain their "sovereign rights." The consequences of these policies do not bode well for the peaceful progress of the "revolution of rising expectations." Perú under the Garcia administration is an example of this choice in the second half of the 1980s.[9] Those familiar with the results may be inclined to seek a better way.

A cursory review of the operation of the political systems of small developing nations of Latin America shows that, historically, actual implementation of their sovereign powers has been quite limited. All available evidence indicates that in the last decade of the twentieth century this implementation will be even more limited. To put it in a different light, small nations are faced with the unpleasant choice of either clinging to the traditional definition of sovereignty, or moving toward the implementation of demands encompassed by the revolution of rising expectations. The sooner this reality is recognized the more likely integration will be recognized as a realistic option. But regardless of the immediate reasons that justify integration, the political will to integrate has to include the recognition that national sovereignty is neither indivisible nor absolute. Political will, in turn, is a necessary condition of integration; its presence among a majority of the region's population is a necessary condition for effective common policies to be generated and implemented.

National sovereignty would have to be at least partially surrendered to regional international structures if the latter are to function effectively. Real integration requires that certain areas of heretofore national policy-making authority be transferred to supra-national organs where decisions may be made through majority votes. Once decisions are made, with or without the concurrence of every member, they are to be implemented and enforced in the territories of all members. This is what the nation-states that belong to the European Community have done. They have already reached a point where adjudications handed down by the supra-national courts that are part of the regional integration scheme are enforced in the territories of all members. European Community organs are in the process of committing themselves to region-wide use of a common currency, to the establishment of a community central bank, to the development of a common foreign policy, and to the organization of regional armed forces. This latest development is a curious outcome of the discontinuance of the Cold War and one of its unfortunate by-products, the internal strife in Yugoslavia.[10]

The elimination of legal and political barriers to integration is only one aspect of forward movement. The existence and identification of powerful positive factors are another necessary condition to move in that direction. The purpose here is not to belabor economic factors, such as the enlargement of the "domestic" market, increased competition, and the possibility of regional economies of scale. Complementarity among the countries under discussion has been reviewed earlier. Readers should be reminded that the European Community started as a narrow supra-national organization, originally responsible for streamlining the then-sick coal and steel industries of the countries that later became its original members. There was little complementarity and much overlap in that mandate. Coal mining and steel manufacturing had become economic drains. The needed adjustments and reforms were difficult to make under the national political environments. Sovereignty on those two industries was transferred to the supra-national European Coal and Steel Community in order to implement region-wide solutions separated, but not isolated, from the political systems of the member countries.[11] In this case, complementarity was not a major consideration, although it became significant when the Coal and Steel Community evolved into the European Community.

SOCIO-CULTURAL DIVERSITY AMONG MEMBERS

What one cannot fail to notice is the diversity of sociocultural components present in the original Coal and Steel Community, and more particularly in the present European Community. It is unnecessary to enumerate the historical, religious, linguistic, and ethnic diversity encompassed in the supra-national structures suggested as a potential model. Some member countries have fought long wars and have occupied and destroyed their present partners. The current members have been, and in certain areas still are, in competition with each other. More important, perhaps, significant interstate contradictions are generated by the internal distribution of power in some of the key actors. To mention just one example, farmers in France and the Netherlands carry a great deal of political weight, and their interests are considered paramount and entitled to national and regional response by French and Dutch ruling elites, regardless of party labels.

The political systems of other community members recognize the interests of different groups, such as urban dwellers, who seek low food prices and are not receptive to subsidizing the level of living of farmers in general, and of French and Dutch farmers in particular. This is a major conflict of interests among community members, and yet it has not prevented the organization from continuing its path toward greater political integration. It is not implied here that this particular issue has been permanently solved. French wine producers provided evidence to the contrary when Spain entered the European Community, and we have recently witnessed demonstrations by French farmers who were unhappy with the common agricultural policy currently in effect. On the other hand, subsidies to farmers through the existing price structure and through community support payments make consumers in general and national governments of those members whose farmers are not politically powerful equally unhappy.[12]

Let us look at the Central American countries in this context. The ethnic, cultural, linguistic, and religious background of the region's population is not nearly as diverse or as conflictive as that of the members of the European Community. The differences that exist in these categories are of degree, rather than of kind. Whatever diversities exist, they are found as much within nation-states as between them.[13] In fact, the concept of Central American integration can be traced to the immediate postindependence period, beginning with the formation of the United Provinces of Central America in 1824. It should be remembered that the constitution of the same year provided for a collegiate executive, evidently with the goal of ensuring representation of provincial interests in that branch.

This first effort at regional integration did not include what is today Panama, which was then part of Colombia. As we all know, the loose federation known as "The United Provinces of Central America" broke down fourteen years later and the component "provinces" became nation-states. One student of regional integration has labeled this effort nothing more than a "league of towns" and of regional ruling elites looking for collective security but, in the last analysis, unwilling to pay the political price demanded by it. Yet, this first attempt at integration planted in many minds the seed of its desirability. Twenty-four additional attempts at unity or integration followed, for an approximate average of one try every five years.[14] Professor Nye has pointed out that "in situations where nationalism in the sense of national consciousness is not profound, political elites might be particularly tempted to choose a highly nationalistic ideology and use the machinery of the state in a highly nationalistic way in an effort to increase national consciousness as a basis for their shaky authority—a process frequently called "nation-building."[15]

Some of the succeeding efforts at integration were implemented with the threat or actual use of force. The Guatemalan elite, supported by the largest regional territory and population, took the initiative to integrate Central America. At other times, El Salvador, Honduras, and Nicaragua agreed to join confederations, and Guatemala and Costa Rica were invited to join. The original motivation appears to have been the achievement of greater regional and internal security. In the nineteenth century the threats came from adventurers and pirates, rather than from traditional imperialism. A Salvadoran leader put it rather bluntly:

We could employ this time to unite ourselves toward the future, in order to be ready not only to maintain our territorial integrity, but also to insure domestic peace, the only foundation for our prosperity. I know that the current situation of the Central American Republics is bad, because they lack the means for a secure and dignified existence; and I say it: They are parodies and their governments are parodies. The Divine Providence has done much to protect us from piracy, and the miracles are self-evident. I am afraid that the Divine Providence will abandon us, and that we shall fall into the abysm.[16]

These efforts at regional integration do not appear to have been the total failure reported by many analysts.[17] Certain institutional foundations have been developed and accepted. The most important ones appear to be the Central American Common Market, the newly activated Central American Parliament, and the recently established Central American Foundation for Integration. On the other hand, the Organization of Central American States, established in 1951, seems to have achieved little in the forty years of its existence. Some of its members, however, have not given up: proposals to revitalize it are being floated from time to time.[18]

The Central American Common Market was established in 1960, with Costa Rica joining two years later. The actual operation of this organization places it somewhere between a free trade area and a custom union. During the first five years of operation the value of regional trade grew 400%, much faster than either world or Latin American trade; what is perhaps more significant, industrial goods shifted from less than 50% of total regional trade to 72%. Therefore, the early stage of the Central American Common Market was quite effective in achieving its limited goal of intensifying regional commerce. Writing of this period, Professor Nye gave credit for the progress made to the economic technocrats, while conveying a more guarded view of the labors of the foreign ministers and the "political" organs of the Common Market. He warned that "the political non-controversiality and low level of cost of the past may diminish in the future. . . . If a larger sense of political community, of common loyalties, does not grow at a rate commensurate with the politization of integration, the result may be stagnation. . . . a cumulative retrogression, or "spillback" until the institutions and tasks of integration are at a level that the prevailing sense of community, expectations, and interests can support.[19]

A number of subordinate agencies were established after the Central American Common Market was under way, with the goal of providing intellectual and technical support to its main institution. Some of these agencies generated needed information and trained civil servants; however, they did not intensify the sense of political community called for in the preceding forecast. Without it, the member countries were unwilling to go beyond the minimal surrender of sovereignty called for by the 1960 treaty.[20] It may be that this task has been reserved for the Central American Parliament, approved as part of the Esquipulas I agreement in May 1986. The regional legislature was formally created by a treaty dated October 2, 1987, signed by the presidents of Costa Rica, El Salvador, Guatemala,

Honduras, and Nicaragua, as an outcome of the Esquipulas II meeting.

The creation of the Central American Parliament, however, has forced supporters of regional integration to confront once more a substantial political obstacle—the existence in the region of governments that were not competitive or representative. This issue was raised when the president of Costa Rica, in his regional peace proposal of February 1987, called for free, pluralistic, and honest elections, including those to choose the members of the Central American Parliament.[21] The existence of competitive or representative systems that enjoy widespread legitimacy has been an essential requirement of the European Community; witness the admission of countries such as Spain, Portugal, and Greece only after the replacement of authoritarian regimes by administrations chosen in elections open to all parties.

In the past two years, however, opposition parties have won elections held in Costa Rica, Nicaragua, El Salvador, and Honduras. Some observers interpret these peaceful transfers of power as indications of a growing regional willingness to share political authority. At least one of the newly elected presidents has publicly expressed his perception of the current decade as a period of possible social and economic integration. In addition, Honduras, Guatemala, and El Salvador have already elected representatives to the Central American Parliament, which recently met for the first time. Nicaragua has postponed the election of its representatives until 1993. Costa Rica has not made a decision, apparently because it sees any type of political integration as a threat to its sovereignty. The reference to national sovereignty, however, appears to cover more pragmatic reasons. At least one Costa Rican newspaper judged the Central American Parliament "not feasible" on the grounds of regional political incompatibilities and the impossibility of conducting honest elections in Nicaragua. This last objection has been proved wrong by subsequent events. The newspaper concluded that Costa Rica will not benefit from the Central American Parliament and recommended that the country not participate.[22]

It would appear that this reluctance to open the door to what may become a politically effective regional organization is based on a particular perception of the political systems with which Costa Rica would have to integrate. Tables 9.5 to 9.8 provide sociopolitical data for the years 1980 and 1983 in the form of aggregate indices that combine diverse factors generally accepted as valid measuring data. As indicated in these tables, Costa Rica is clearly ahead in political participation, but Panama appears to match the former's performance in areas such as welfare, education, and health services. El Salvador and Guatemala are doing relatively well in the overall management of their economies. Finally, with the exception of Nicaragua in 1983, the Central American countries

Table 9.5
Aggregate Indices of Political Participation, Culture and Welfare: 1980

	Participation	Culture	Welfare
Costa Rica	26.0	16.0	10.0
El Salvador	12.0	17.0	9.0
Guatemala	12.0	7.0	5.0
Honduras	10.0	18.0	5.0
Nicaragua	9.0	15.0	7.0
Panama	9.0	15.0	10.0

Source: Indicators of World Social Development 1970-83 (World Game Institute).

did not seem to be too far apart in the allocation of resources to the military and security forces. Here again, it is reasonable to expect that, with the change in administrations in Nicaragua, we will see a further narrowing of the gap through relative reductions in military spending.

CONCLUSIONS

The sociopolitical data presented in Tables 9.5 to 9.8 convey an overall picture of regional similarities, rather than drastic differences. Clearly, the Central American countries are not homogeneous. However, those opposed to integration on the grounds of sociopolitical incompatibilities appear to be relying on memory and emotion, rather than on measurements of present-day reality, imperfect as they may be. In addition, an attractive and effective integration mechanism is likely to have the power to prescribe political entry requirements, similar to those developed by the European Community. In this sense, a successful process of integration may contribute to the expansion and continuity of competitive and representative systems in the nation-states of the region.

The English language has a useful phrase: "To hang together or to hang separately." The leaders of the countries that established MERCOSUR have invited Central America to participate in the efforts toward integration.[23] Although the agreement with the United States and Canada has not

Table 9.6
Aggregate Indices of Education, Health, Defense, and Economic Performance: 1980

	Education	Health	Defense	Economy
Costa Rica	19.0	17.0	18.0	10.0
El Salvador	5.0	10.0	14.0	11.0
Guatemala	3.0	8.0	17.0	12.0
Honduras	8.0	8.0	12.0	4.0
Nicaragua	9.0	9.0	9.0	1.0
Panama	16.0	15.0	17.0	6.0

Source: Indicators of World Social Development 1970-1983 (World Game Institute).

Table 9.7
Aggregate Indices of Political Participation, Culture and Welfare: 1983

	Participation	Culture	Welfare
Costa Rica	25.0	16.0	10.0
El Salvador	10.0	17.0	9.0
Guatemala	6.0	7.0	5.0
Honduras	15.0	18.0	5.0
Nicaragua	7.0	15.0	7.0
Panama	10.0	15.0	10.0

Source: Indicators of World Social Development 1970-1983 (World Game Institute).

Table 9.8
Aggregrate Indices of Education, Health, Defense, and Economic
Performance: 1983

	Education	Health	Defense	Economy
Costa Rica	15.0	18.0	17.0	0.0
El Salvador	5.0	9.0	12.0	7.0
Guatemala	3.0	8.0	14.0	11.0
Honduras	10.0	8.0	12.0	8.0
Nicaragua	12.0	9.0	3.0	-3.0
Panama	16.0	16.0	16.0	8.0

Source: Indicators of World Social   Development 1970-1983 (World
Game Institute).

been concluded, certain sectors in Mexico are beginning to behave as if
that process were fully under way.[24] The interest expressed by the European Community in political stability and their belief that it can be
achieved through integration cannot be ignored, particularly in view of
the growth in purchasing power expected to take place among the population of the member countries after 1993.[25] Finally, two public men with
diverse political philosophies, Octavio Paz and Senator Robert Kasten,
that are not likely to agree on very much, have voiced strong support for
the integration of Central America; they have suggested that their respective countries should deal with the region as a unit.[26] This is at the heart
of the view sponsored by the Central American Foundation for Integration, created in 1988 for the exclusive purpose of providing intellectual
leadership to the process.[27]

The citizens of the nation-states of Latin America do not have to
accept the views of outsiders, who may very well be motivated by their own
interests and perceptions. They do not have to follow the suggestions of
European diplomats, United States senators, Mexican writers, or South
American students of politics. They only have to follow the daily press to
know that two winds are blowing in today's world: (1) the disintegration
of political communities assembled by force, and (2) the establishment
and growth of supra-national organizations created with the consent of
their members, as an outcome of the political will of their populations.

With the United States and Russia acting in the international arena by mutual agreement, the developing countries will be faced with the practical necessity of operating as parts of regions. The smaller countries may find it necessary to associate with their neighbors in order to play an influential role if and when they join larger regional organizations. It is assumed that they expect to pursue their national interests vis-á-vis larger and more highly developed nations, which are themselves moving toward regional integration. The twenty-first century may not have a place for small and politically isolated countries, particularly if they do not possess state-of-the-art technologies.

NOTES

1. See Ward (1962), *passim*.

2. As opposed to the many members of the lower and middle classes who have been "disappearing" in developing countries as part of counterinsurgency operations.

3. It is not implied here that all migrants from less-developed countries have found satisfaction in the developed world, as recent events in Germany, France, and the United States indicate.

4. For a review of efforts in Central and South America see Mace, 1988.

5. Jauberth Rojas et al, 1991, p. 162.

6. Morales Hernández, 1989, p. 199.

7. For a detailed treatment of system penetration and the depreciation of sovereignty see Nowell, 1988, *passim*.

8. See the Stanley Foundation, 1992, pp. 11-12.

9. The refusal of the Garcia administration in the second half of the 1980s to implement the policies "recommended" by international lending agencies led to the isolation of Perú from sources of international credit and to the virtual bankruptcy of the country; the level of living decreased precipitously and the party in power was replaced at the next election. Although there were internal causes that contributed to the demise of the Garcia administration, such as the activities of the guerrilla organizations Shining Path and Tupac Amaru, the fact is that the winner of the last election has been implementing the policies suggested by the international lending agencies.

10. An effective integration mechanism, as the European Community is showing itself to be, must contain relatively easy procedures for its members to drop out; in addition, significant organizational adjustments must be subject to national ratification procedures, as indeed they are in the Community. Members must regularly have the opportunity to decide whether they can afford to continue with the integration scheme or abandon it. Denmark's decision in May 1992 to reject the European Community's latest amendments is an example of the

operation of this "escape procedure."

11. On the European Coal and Steel Community see Bowett, 1963, pp. 168-74; and Goodspeed, 1967, pp. 611-17.

12. For a solid analysis of this issue see Daltrop, 1986, pp. 172-79. For a review of the consequences of the common agricultural policy consult Hufbauer, 1990, pp. 27-29. There are indications that the European Community, negotiating as a whole, is strong enough to reach compromises that will negatively affect the interests of farmers without threatening the integrity of the regional organization.

13. An example of the ethnic differences within countries of the region can be found in Castro, 1988, pp. 115-24. Another case of domestic cleavages is discussed by Oliver, 1990.

14. See Karnes, 1961, *passim*.

15. Nye, 1968, p. 379.

16. Statement made by Gerardo Barrios, then president of El Salvador, as quoted in Garcia Laguardia, 1988, pp. 43-44.

17. For a negative view of Latin American integration and of its future, see Mace, *op. cit*.

18. Recent proposals to restructure the Organizations of Central American States, the political organ mentioned by Nye, have the same objective. See the announcement made by the foreign minister of Guatemala in *Prensa Libre* (Guatemala City), July 9, 1991, p. 2.

19. Nye, *op. cit*., pp. 421-22.

20. One such effort has been the Trifinio Plan, supported by Guatemala, El Salvador, and Honduras. See the declaration signed by these countries and published in *Panorama Centroamericano*, 20:i-ii, November 1989.

21. As reported by Garcia Laguardia, *op. cit*., pp. 75-76.

22. On the successes of opposition candidates and their significance, see *Presencia* (La Paz, Bolivia), March 1, 1990, p. 2. The election of members of the Central American Parliament appeared in *Central American Report*, May 24, 1991, p. 149. On Costa Rican sentiment toward this regional institution, see *La Nación* (San Jose), September 25, 1988, p. 16A. The Costa Rican government appears to have followed the newspaper's advise, according to Morales (1989), pp. 27-38.

23. This invitation, reported in *El Universal* (Caracas), April 5, 1991, p. 12, remains in effect. In the meantime, MERCOSUR has been progressing steadily in the institution-building arena, toward the development of a common international trade policy, and toward the elimination of regional disparities between its members, particularly between Argentina and Brazil. On the other hand, MERCOSUR is not succeeding in increasing the effectiveness of the national tax systems through regional sharing of data. See *La Nación* (Buenos Aires), May 23, 1992, p. 14.

24. *The New York Times*, October 22, 1991, p. D2.

25. See *Central America Report*, April 5, 1991, pp. 89-91; and *Estudios centroamericanos*, 44:233-37, March 1989.

26. For Kasten's view, see *Policy Review*, Spring 1989, pp. 72-75; for Paz' argument, see *The Washington Times*, March 5, 1990, pp. 1F and 4F.

27. See de la Ossa, 1988, pp. 54-59.

III

Recovery or Relapse:
Reflections on Central America
in the New World Order

Ten

Central American External Debt in the Context of Economic Globalization

Jorge González del Valle

INTRODUCTION

Despite the successful renegotiation of foreign debt undertaken in recent years by the highly indebted Central American nations of Costa Rica and Nicaragua, the debt problem still hangs over the Central American economies, slowing the full development of their potential. Repayment of the debt continues to have a negative impact on Central American public finances and trade balances. Thus, the bulk of export earnings must be spent in servicing the debt, providing little relief for the majority of the population and seriously limiting prospects for development with equity in the face of a stagnant economy.

Even though the international environment for debt renegotiation has improved significantly during the past two years, debtor nations must still undergo a cumbersome process of bilateral negotiations with different creditors. These creditors include financial organizations, government and government-sponsored institutions, commercial banks and private lenders. Not even those countries that accepted the risks of cross-conditionality (*condicionalidad crusada*) and invoked externally promoted programs of structural adjustment have obtained genuinely favorable outcomes from the negotiation process.

The current approach to debt renegotiation is not an efficient approach for tackling foreign debt problems. It seems unnecessary to use the psychological terrorism of the carrot and the stick, since debtor nations themselves often seek structural adjustment, sometimes without any real justification, and readily accept the terms of renegotiation offered by creditors. Moreover, it is erroneous to think that microeconomic-based solutions will necessarily resolve underlying macroeconomic problems which constitute, together with trade and international investment, the conceptual base of global economic integration. Employing these premises, an attempt will be made in this chapter to suggest alternative solutions, but first, a brief review will be presented of the current foreign debt situation in Central America and how it relates to the tendency toward the globalization of the economy.

CHARACTERISTICS OF CENTRAL AMERICAN FOREIGN DEBT

At the end of 1990, foreign debt for the five Central American nations was approximately $18 billion, 60% of which was owed by Costa Rica and Nicaragua. Despite efforts by all five nations to keep current on their payments, it is estimated that they are still behind in about one-fourth of their total payments. This makes it difficult for these nations to obtain new financing.

The Central American external debt situation deteriorated substantially during the 1980s—quadrupling in total. The most significant change occurred in the area of debt servicing. While in 1980 debt service required 12% of exports of goods and services, it currently requires 35%. This increase has meant an important reduction in the Central American nations' creditworthiness. Countries focusing their priorities on economic reactivation, which necessarily involves an increase in imports, have been forced into an involuntary moratorium on imports by the increase in the ratio of debt service to exports.

In some ways, the situation could have been even worse for the debtor nations. The amount of debt owed to official sources (both bilateral and multilateral) increased from 60% to 78% of total debt during the past decade. As we know, loans from official institutions are generally less expensive and more flexible in terms and grace periods than those obtained from commercial banks.

There has been a shift in the principal sources of international public lending. The Interamerican Development Bank (IDB) and the (BCIE) have become the two major multilateral lenders in Central America, leaving the World Bank and the International Monetary Fund (IMF) in a secondary position. Among the bilateral institutions, the United States is still the principal lender, but Mexico and Venezuela have become major sources of financing. A positive effect of this shuffling of financial institutions is an increase in opportunities for debtor nations to renegotiate their external debt. The Mexican and Venezuelan governments have launched well-known initiatives, on favorable terms, in order to reduce the debt Nicaragua owes them. They have also provided Honduras with transitory financing in order to facilitate debt renegotiation with other entities. Both the IDB and BCIE have introduced positive initiatives to restructure the debt of all five Central American nations.

In any case, the quadrupling of the public foreign debt led to a larger absolute debt with commercial banks, which represents a considerable financial burden on the Central American credit- worthiness. This situation was particularly severe during the world-wide recession of the 1980s, which brought instability in the balance of payments in all Central American nations. As mentioned previously, the difficulty of servicing the debt in the terms originally established brought about an involuntary moratorium. Under these circumstances, the negotiating position of debtor nations became very weak, and they were forced to seek help from international public institutions such as the World Bank and the International Monetary Fund. This was not the case for El Salvador and Guatemala, which were only slightly behind on their payments—they approached the World Bank and the International Monetary Fund for other reasons.

Generally, countries accepting structural adjustment policies (which bring a degree of uniformity to the global economy) find it less difficult to renegotiate their debt than countries that do not engage in structural adjustment. Until now, however, the benefits obtained by those countries engaging in structural adjustment have not been significant, nor has there been an improvement in their creditworthiness. Nonetheless, the well known IMF "conditionality" has become globalized following increasingly standardized patterns.

CONTRADICTIONS OF GLOBALIZATION

The situation just described is in stark contrast with improvements in the external debt position of many countries during the past few years, whether or not they have undergone structural adjustment. Before the first serious debt crisis materialized in Mexico in 1982, private and official creditors refused to renegotiate debt, despite the worsening worldwide economic recession. Since then, however, the creditor-debtor relationship has changed considerably, and has become much more rational and realistic.

At first, the debt crisis was believed to be a short-term problem of liquidity. However, as the economic recession worsened, creditors came to understand the complexity of the problem and to appreciate the difficulty that debtor nations faced in making payments. The first plans that took into consideration the interdependence between foreign trade and debt servicing appeared in 1985 and 1986. By 1990, it was openly acknowledged that without economic growth, larger trade volumes could not be expected, and without larger trade volumes, creditworthiness becomes a fundamental problem.

These are the basic issues that must form part of an integrated economic analysis of the debt issue. However, for many years, different financial interests influenced the policy-making of the dominant players in the world economy. For example, it was only after a slow evolution from the Baker Plan to the Brady Plan, and later the Bush Plan, before creditors had sufficient confidence to listen to the economic arguments of the debtor nations. But from the Latin American perspective, these arguments had been clear since the Quito Declaration of 1984. The Cartagena Agreement (1986-88) repeatedly made these same arguments, culminating in the Proposal for Latin America and the Caribbean of 1990.

During the renegotiation process, creditors insisted on two approaches. First, a case-by-case approach to debt renegotiation. Second, the imposition of conditionality under the supervision of the IMF. The Latin American proposals, on the other hand, incorporated ideas that distinguished between the different types of international debt. This approach banished conditionality to a secondary concern. Unfortunately, there was no true dialogue among those involved in these two positions and the financial position of the creditors ultimately prevailed.

One would expect that in a rational world the globalization of trade and international investment, together with the virtual universalization of supervised structural adjustment, would also make possible the exploration of global approaches to the foreign debt problem. In trade, for example, it makes no sense to assume that a country with limited creditworthiness increase its imports by eliminating tariff protections, nor does it make sense to expect an increase in foreign investment by removing financial barriers if restrictions on the balance of trade threaten the stability of the exchange rate and slow down the rate of economic growth.

What is necessary is a better understanding on the part of the international creditors of the economic causality in the less-developed nations. From this perspective the progress made through structural adjustment policies is quite mediocre. In many Latin American nations such policies have resulted in a worsening of socioeconomic conditions, with few gains made toward attaining the expected economic advantages.

DRAFT OF A GLOBALIZING PROPOSAL

During 1985 and 1986, this author had the opportunity to present some ideas to the Economic Secretariat for Latin America (SELA) and to the leadership of the Cartagena Agreement regarding a possible global mechanism to refinance Latin American foreign debt. The proposal was not well received by creditor nations at the time, but since 1988, the governors of the IMF (representing Japan and several members of the European Economic Community (EEC)) have presented similar plans. This has stimulated a better acceptance at the international level of the global approach to debt renegotiation.

The proposal was based on translating the well-known approach to consolidating national debt to the international sphere. The mechanism can be applied to any number of countries, but its advantages increase as the number of countries involved expands. The scheme can be applied only to Central America, or be extended to Latin America and the Caribbean. This chapter limits the proposal to Central America.

Goals of the Global Approach

The main goal of the proposal is the pooling of all external debt in arrears, as well as that debt which presents too heavy a burden on the creditworthiness of debtor nations. The process would achieve the following goals: (1) to reduce debt service to a more reasonable coefficient of the annual total of the export of goods and services—for instance, to no more than 15% per year, and (2) to consolidate payments into one financial entity, thereby eliminating the array of bilateral agreements that has to be renegotiated. For the five Central American nations, this would effect between $9 and $11 billion, or 51% to 61% of the total foreign debt. The terms of the remaining debt do not impose an excessive burden on these nations' creditworthiness.

The Institutional Framework

It would be necessary to create a Fiduciary Fund of Foreign Debt (FFDE), preferably administered by the IDB, although the World Bank or the IMF could administer it, in order to achieve the aforementioned goals. The institution in charge of administering the fiduciary fund could limit its role to financial mediation, although it could also guarantee all or part of the debt concentrated in the pool. Administration by the IDB would be preferable for three main reasons: (1) it is currently the main creditor of the Central American countries, (2) in recent years, its board of governor's has approved policies that increasingly involve it in the foreign debt problem, and (3) it is the international financial institution in which the Central American countries play a relatively greater, although far from dominant, role.

Operations of Consolidation

In order to avoid possible suspicions among the participants, the debt to be placed into the FFDE would have to be accepted by debtors, creditors, and the fiduciary institution. This would ensure that only "unpayable debt" would be placed in the fund, in order to reach the final goal of limiting annual debt services to 15% of the total exports of good and services. Debt accepted by the FFDE would be converted into bonds, which would be distributed between private and official creditors in exchange for the remaining balance. The original agreements would, therefore, be canceled. Both the principal and the interest of the bonds would be backed by debtor countries. Ideally, this guarantee would be collective, although limited to the total amount of debt each country transferred to the FFDE. Likewise, in an ideal setting the bonds would also be guaranteed by the fiduciary institution.

The terms, interest rates, and redemption of the bonds would be determined by the total amount issued, with the goal of limiting debt service to 15% of exports of goods and services, and the nominal cost of the debt. It would be highly desirable for the creditors (especially the commercial banks and the Paris Club) to agree to a reduction in interest rates in order to increase the likelihood of recovering their investment. This reduction, however, is not essential to the process, since whatever the debtor nations may lose in the nominal cost of the debt is compensated for by longer terms.

The bonds issued could be distributed either in series, with different terms and interest rates, or issued together, with standard terms and interest rates. Differences in interest rates by creditor would not present a problem, since bonds could be issued with a bonus or with a discount, depending on the nominal interest agreed upon with the FFDE. For many reasons, a single-bond issue would be preferable.

Sinking Fund

The sinking fund constitutes an essential piece of the proposed global mechanism, since it is the main incentive for private and official creditors to accept the swapping of debt for bonds. The fact that the fiduciary institution, and not the debtor nations, will manage the fund adds credibility to the bond issue. The consolidation of foreign debt would allow debtor nations to make annual payments not to exceed 15% of their good and services exports (at least for the debt administered by the FFDE). If the general program of redemption is adjusted to real conditions, temporary deficiencies in one country would be compensated by surplus income in the other nations, or in future years for the country in question.

Negotiation of Bonds in the Market

If the redemption mechanism were reinforced in the way just proposed, the bonds issued would have little difficulty finding a place in international markets. Private creditors would find them particularly appealing, since in recent years they have been forced to sell their credits in closed markets with steep discounts. Official creditors will most likely keep the bonds until their final redemption, especially if the FFDE spreads out the due dates.

One could go a step further by creating a secondary market, albeit limited, based on the sinking funds' own resources, which would exceed the redemption amounts in times of export bonanzas. There would also be surplus resources if, for instance, the FFDE pays interest annually or biannually, while redeeming the principal only every three to four years. Depending on the evolution of the FFDE operations, the consolidation of a secondary market for the bonds could attract new international financing for the Central American nations. In the long term, the FFDE could increase its functions and become a finance promoter with the collective backing of the five Central American nations.

ADVANTAGES OF A GLOBAL DEBT MECHANISM

One of the advantages of this mechanism proposed for global debt renegotiation is that it combines conventional financial instruments. It is more specific than the approaches of the president of France and the finance ministers of Japan and the Netherlands, but does not differ from them substantially. The following brief summary will show that it generates considerable benefits at a low, if any, cost.

First, since it is a selective, not an automatic, mechanism, it allows for balancing the interest of debtors and creditors. Only unpayable debt, owing to high interest rates or short terms, or debt in arrears, would be eligible for conversion into bonds. Second, both creditors and debtors would benefit from this proposal. Debtors would receive considerable relief in their creditworthiness, since debt service would be limited to a moderate coefficient of their exports. Creditors would also benefit, since their chances of collecting the debt will increase and, since, in general, lenders benefit from solvent and healthy international clients. Third, although desirable, it is not essential that creditors reduce interest rates as the guarantees on their credits increase, as long as they accept longer terms. The internationalization of their credits could allow them to trade the converted bonds in the market, thus potentially recovering their investments in shorter terms.

Using data from 1979 it is possible to determine that the conversion of Central American debt could be done by issuing bonds of 19 to 23 years maturity, considering that the total amount to be converted is from $9 to $11 billion. The annual interest rate would be 9% or 10%. In either case, annual amortization would not exceed 15% of the exports of goods and services of debtor nations. These figures should not alarm creditors, given that toward the end of 1990 the average term of all Central American debt was seventeen years and the average interest rate was 6.7%. Arrears constituted about 25% of the total.

There is no question that the consolidation of the worst segments of Central American debt, and its conversion into internationally guaranteed bonds presents advantages for both creditors and debtors. In any case, a global approach is a satisfactory solution to the current situation, which is plagued by mutual recriminations and criticisms, and exacerbated by frequent confrontations, financial crises, and the prolongation of involuntary moratoria.

It would also be naive to think that a global solution to the debt crisis is merely a technical problem. If this were the case the problem would have been solved a long time ago. The political will of creditor nations has still not matured sufficiently, and this is hampered by the commitment to conditionality. There is, however, still hope that the logic they prescribe will force an acknowledgment that economic globalization will not be possible without a true internationalization of the foreign debt problem.

CONCLUSIONS

Although our initial concern is with Central American foreign debt, we cannot isolate this problem from the general foreign debt situation in less-developed nations. After all, Central American foreign debt represents less than 4% of all Latin American and Caribbean foreign debt, and perhaps less than 3% of that of other underdeveloped nations. The characteristics of the problem, nevertheless, are similar in all cases.

The most complete example of economic globalization in recent history was the British Empire in the second half of the nineteenth century. Foreign debt played a crucial role at that time, through direct investment and through the promotion of loans in British sterling on a global scale. The colonization of Canada, Australia, India, eastern Africa, the Middle East, and the Caribbean was closely tied to financial dependency based on "British debt." Even in the newly born Latin

American republics this financial dependency has left profound scars.

It is well known that the two world wars allowed the United States to occupy the place unwillingly abandoned by Great Britain. The change in international creditors is still lamented in Panama, Cuba, Nicaragua, and the Dominican Republic. Economic and political dependency has become more severe and has meant a de facto globalization of trade, foreign investment, and monetary standards. The last hopes that the multilateralism advocated by Bretton Woods in 1945 would diminish bilateral economic dependency have long since vanished.

The creation of the IMF and the World Bank constituted the third, and more civilized, platform for economic globalization. It was more civilized because it was modeled after the reforms that followed the Great Depression of the 1930s. It was also visionary because it foresaw the transition toward a decolonized world, and a world less dependent on the political balance of areas of economic influence.

In retrospect, the biggest failures of Bretton Woods were its insistence on the gold standard, instead of creating a more stable monetary base, and its lack of tenacity in creating the International Organization of Trade following the formal collapse of the Havana Treaty. The first of these failures resulted in the arbitrary and violent termination of the international monetary standard in 1971. The second ended with the GATT agreements, which, far from regulating international free trade, have been the source of disputes that invariably have resulted in protectionism, discrimination, and unfair practices.

The fourth stage of economic globalization, which we see imposed at the present time, lacks a genuine multilateral foundation, and has been motivated more by politics than by a sincere interest in equality. It still suffers from conditions similar to those of a neocolonial scheme. First, the announced globalization appears to be an organization of economic blocks that could result in "captive markets" under the disguise of free trade. Second, the reemergence of areas of influence has taken on a clear geopolitical character. Third, the prolongation of the debt problem and its increased link to structural adjustment programs is a clear symptom of a trend toward economic control.

Therefore, there is little optimism toward the prospects for the prompt tackling of the foreign debt problem of the less- developed nations on a global scale. Inconsistencies in the global approach to trade and international finances and the case-by-case and bilateral approach to debt crisis are likely to be deliberate. A new international conference, as profound and open as Bretton Woods, will be required to tackle the ideological contradictions of economic globalization. Unfortunately, the powerful Group of Seven is not interested.

Nevertheless, three events could significantly change the current state of affairs. First, it is likely that structural adjustment policies will result in strong counteractions if promised economic benefits do not materialize. In this case, forced commercial and financial openings would have to be reconsidered. Second, if partial debt renegotiation cannot eliminate involuntary moratoria and fails to restore the creditworthiness of debtor nations, the World Bank and the IMF will have to take a different approach. Third, developments in eastern Europe could result in changes in the political and economic power of the European Economic Community, thus shifting solutions toward more interesting and pragmatic ways than those dominating our world today.

Eleven

Central America in the Global Economy

Alvaro de la Ossa

The new paradigm is to establish a real, true and coordinated insertion into the world around us, and not resign ourselves to the alternative of a relationship in which, almost in a colonial manner, the currently prevailing political and economic dependence is consolidated.

Central American Foundation for Integration

INTRODUCTION

Globalization is a major theme at present, and time is required to examine it fully. In this chapter, twelve sub-themes selected from previous research on this subject are discussed. However, this discussion does not include the impact on the Central American nations of the changes occurring in the formerly socialist nations. These changes are quite distinct from the reality of our nations, and the ramifications of such changes are not yet clear. We admire the movement towards freedom in these countries; in Central America much effort is still needed to promote freedom and democracy. In fact, in recent years we have been moving backwards. We hope that the aspirations of these newly formed states will be sustained within a system of economic organization which accounts for their needs for political liberty and not on a basis of subjugation to an economic discriminatory system as exists in our part of the world.

THE CONCEPT OF GLOBALIZATION

The world economy has experienced the development of domestic markets and the expansion of world trade. Likewise, as a result of processes of economic integration that began in 1948, the world economy saw commerce grow within trading blocks. We saw the creation of the Union of Banana Exporting Countries, the Organization of Petroleum Exporting Countries (OPEC), the consolidation of the European Common Market, the search for autarky within the socialist nations, and the development of standards for relations between poor and rich countries defined by the Potsdam and Yalta agreements. However, none of this was sufficient. Now we are witnessing the creation of megamarkets. This evolution is necessary for capitalism and its survival.

With time, it has been evident that the capitalist system accumulated its own weakness. December of 1971 is an example of this path, as well as the Black Monday of the stock market. Recessions have been successive and even overlapping at times, with some lasting longer than others. The new rules of the global economy are outlined within the confines of the economic crises of the 1980s.

In effect, many factors have converged to produce the current state of affairs. One of these factors was the need for common coexistence among the richest countries on earth. Those countries were obliged to avoid the modalities of internal politics, especially individual protectionist and defensive measures, that could set off a chain of repercussions that could destabilize the entire Western world as a geopolitical and economic unit. If not, capitalism would enter into a deep state of crisis. Beginning with the Helsinki Accords, the world's economic powers initiated a process of permanent consensus among themselves.

Another important element of globalization is the force exerted by technological change. Capitalism's frontier is located at the cutting edge of technology. A new technological revolution has arrived that has given capitalism new life and a new manner of functioning.

Consequently, in the context of rapidly changing technology and expanding markets and of coordinated international economic policies, we have entered the world of globalization. For those at the bottom of the economic hierarchy, this means a further step toward marginality. It is the globalization of the postindustrial world that further limits the real and potential growth of other countries.

THE NEW IMPERIAL CUPOLA

The world economy has passed through protectionism, product wars, competition for markets, reprisals, embargoes, and other unorthodox modalities—all under the basic notion that "anything goes." The effects have been devastating. Consequently, it became necessary to recognize the need for a consensus. Additionally, such a consensus was reached because of the recognition that it is impossible to go from a world of two powers to one under the existing rules and conditions of the eighties. In economic terms, the era of individual imperialism has passed. There is not only one superpower, but a power group that defines the terms of present and future coexistence. This is how the alliance, the coalition, and the multinational power is formed. This power is represented by joint and shared economic strength backed by the terrifying technology of arms.

ECONOMIC MANAGEMENT IN THE NEW GLOBAL ECONOMY

In order to manage world economic issues in the new international arena, each participant must bring the following to the bargaining table: (1) its own economic power, (2) its alliances with other developed or relatively more developed countries among the Third World nations (usually to expand markets, but now with greater emphasis on ensuring the use and control of nonrenewable resources), and (3) its respective sphere of influence. Consequently, the spheres of influence take on significance in the definition of the shares of power, even if only temporarily. At the same time, the possibility for redefinition of spheres of influence is opened. This process unleashes geographic power zones, resulting in the formation of new megablocs, such as those resulting from Lomé IV, the new Initiative for the Americas, and the Pacific Basin. In other words, for the moment, the periphery has come to play an important role in the policies of the core countries.

In order to delay increased marginalization, this temporary new role for the Third World might provide an advantage if acted on quickly. The marginalization is provoked by globalization and certainly comes from the consolidation of the following phenomena, which originated in the formation of global capitalism: (1) the permanent stagnation in trade of basic products, (2) the erosion of comparative advantage, (3) the infinite enlargement of the gap in technology between rich and poor countries, and (4) the increasing participation of industrialized countries in world commerce for strategic basic goods, directly or though their worldwide investments.

The Impact of Globalization on Latin America and the Caribbean

Partly as a result of the factors just mentioned, Latin America and the Caribbean are being transformed into a more clearly defined U.S. sphere of influence. "Classical" dependence was added to the Monroe Doctrine, onto which the "vertical" power of the sphere of influence is now being superimposed. A new type of dependence has been established that neither Dr. Prebisch nor the Economic Commission for Latin America (ECLA) could have imagined. Now, the equation not only includes technological dependence, or the endlessly widening commercial gap, but also financial control and direct political influence over the economy and public policy, regardless of social structure. In other words, traditional dependency has been transformed and mutated into another, more absolute type, which we could call "absolutist dependency."

Consequently, globalization for Central American countries implies an increment in dependency on the United States. The models of stabilization and adjustment that have been imposed since 1983, even though they were supported by domestic groups which stood to benefit from such change, were generated by this new focus on globalization. Under these models, industrialization is undermined; the state is used to direct public income to promote non-traditional exports (which in some cases are still agricultural in nature); and rates of infant mortality increase as do endemic and previously eradicated diseases. Obviously, there are other effects as well. In summary, the end result is the formation of a new agricultural model similar to that of the 1950s (perhaps even more despised for its consequences) but more diversified in terms of products and exporting agents.

Theoretical Alternatives: Some Conjectures

Central America must make a historic, end-of-the-century decision. Unfortunately, decisions are made by the current political leadership, who in Central America often have a more localized than universal vision. This is unfortunate because they represent very homogenous political groups who, in the last 30 years, have demonstrated a real failure to generate progressive thought. In summary, what exists is a clear lack of vision.

There are at least three theoretical future alternatives that can be distinguished: (1) acceptance of the new "absolutist dependency," (2) isolation as an alternative for survival, and (3) the game of participation on the turf of dependency, with diagonal relations among all kinds of third parties. The concept of "diagonal" relations refers here to relations by dependent countries within a sphere of influence of the developed countries, as distinct from the hegemonic country's respective zone of influence. Such is the case, for example, between Central American and the European Community.

Available Alternatives: Some Viable, Some Not

In practice, there are examples of tight or close relations with an influential bloc, in which some degree of internal autonomy exists. This is the case, for example, between Spain and the European Community, between Mexico and the North American group— it is hoped, and between the "tigers" of Asia and Japan. The countries that take such a path have a higher comparative degree of development, or much greater internal resources than do the Central American countries. For countries with small economies, one can observe some successful cases of liaison with their historically closest hegemonic bloc. The most outstanding example of this is the Lomé accord, with the recent surprising incorporation of Haiti and the Dominican Republic into that group. Nevertheless, the Caribbean countries of the Lomé group are not fully satisfied with this relationship.

In Central America, there are some domestic groups that, in one way or another, have expressed a preference for one of the liaison alternatives. Some have indicated interest in transforming their countries into new Puerto Ricos, including getting rid of bothersome nationalists.

Only a few still dream of ultra-isolationism, in order to preserve the religion, customs, and social hegemony of a few now-declining groups. These groups would prefer that their countries be aligned with blocs so as to retain control of agricultural production and commercial financing, but without the damaging environmental effects of industry. A few churches and chambers of commerce seek refuge in this archaic model, which is obviously impractical. There have been other politically impractical models of isolation, such as Chile until 1973, and Peru and Nicaragua in more recent years.

Among the alternatives available, it seems that the neoliberal model has begun to prevail. This model, which is well known and well supported from outside, substantively modifies the structure of Central American countries. Its hallmark is the absence of attention to social aspects. In the case of Central America, it eliminates what little economic equilibrium had existed before, producing a growing concentration of wealth in the hands of the few, and a progressive pauperization of the rest of the population. Consequently, it will crumble democracy throughout the region.

The Most Reasonable Alternative or the Norm of Common Sense

In spite of the aspirations of many groups, some of which have more power than one might imagine, the participation of Central America in this new world of trading blocs seems to be, according to common sense, closer to the third theoretical alternative: the game of participation in the turf of dependency. In other words, the most reasonable alternative for Central America seems to be found in a wide diversity and extensive range of distinctively styled dependencies. This includes informal behavior at the international level, including the rupture of formal pacts and other agreements.

This situation is clearly new, almost unheard of, and due to flexible commercial agreements and the availability of financing and technology for development. For example, pacts could be made with blocs (Europe under the Maastricht Treaty), with individual countries in blocs (e.g., Mexico, France, Germany), with countries that are not part of blocs (e.g., India, China) and/or with Japan. Relations with the United States could be redefined through a profound and serious comparison of the Caribbean Basin Initiative, the Initiative for the Americas, and NAFTA. With respect to the rest of Latin America, there are formal pacts already in existence with some countries, as well as sporadic or continuous relations with other Latin American and Caribbean countries without official agreements. For example, an agreement was signed with Mexico in Tuxtla Gutiérrez based on previous political understandings. Similar agreements are in process with Venezuela and Colombia.

The Absence of Common Sense

Unfortunately, the elements necessary for a diversified, external, regional policy continue to be out of reach. Many of the agreements are based on other needs and interests. The Caribbean Basin Initiative was created as a unilateral effort on the part of the United States, and ascribed to by Central Americans so as to have access to the U.S. market. The Initiative for the Americas has not been the object of consistent study and evaluation, either at the regional or national level. Central American governments have eagerly sought agreements taking into account the fast-track authorization given to the President of the United States, in order to incorporate themselves into a free trade zone still not fully defined by the United States itself.

With a pressured diplomatic style but lacking the necessary technical skill, messengers travel between Washington and their capitals to formalize these accords, even when they can still relying access the U.S.

market through the Caribbean Basin Initiative (CBI), which has been extended. One country in the region has even gone so far as to substantially modify their financial, monetary, and exchange rate policy, and accelerate tariff reductions in order to conform to the North American requirements for inclusion in these agreements, a prerequisite for free trade.

In other words, Central America is prepared to make concessions to the richest countries on earth, without a clear indication of what benefits they will receive. Moreover, this is occurring despite the fact that the Initiative for the Americas does not clearly recognize the differences in development between Central America and the United States of America.

The Tuxtla Gutiérrez agreement with Mexico was signed without prior study and without the ensured support of a unified and strong Central American negotiating position; the true impact of this agreement remains unknown. Research is not even being conducted at all on the impact of recent agreements with Venezuela and Colombia.

Central America has not even been able to develop a consensus about how to confront the rest of the world. In particular, no Central American common ground or any profound sentiment of joint participation can be detected with respect to the Presidential Declaration of Guadalajara. Additionally, Central American countries have solicited participation in the General Agreement on Tariffs and Trade (GATT), without jointly negotiating their admittance. They coordinated their participation in the Uruguay Round in a manner that their decisions were on individual national concerns and on the advice of financial consultants affiliated with organizations adhering to the neoliberal model.

An example of this state of affairs can be found in the support of the international coffee agreement by Central American countries. They collectively believed that reliance on "market forces" would be advantageous. Now they have had to accept the return of market regulations in light of the unfavorable consequences. They are now strapped with subsidizing coffee growers with scarce public funds, and hence, obliging society to pay for governmental error.

In other words, it seems that the art of negotiation is being mistaken for the substance and objectives of negotiation. It appears that there is no political will for reflecting on the past and for forming concrete positions which are distinguishable from those of the other negotiator. The electoral cycle seems to be determining the negotiating posture.

The political interests of the current politicians, which are homogenous in their vision of Central America's problems, lack common sense. That interest is not linked with the policy evaluations made of their technicians, even when made with independent financing and appropriate criteria. It seems that, given their low level of technical expertise, some of them, now more than ever, should be accustomed to take into account the impact of their policies on their populations. There must be some reason for which politicians and their main advisors are avoiding the most logical solutions. Can it be due to the well-acknowledged power of the most influential internal groups and the pressure they are applying to maintain their privileges? Can it be due to the profound political ambitions of some groups? Will this cause new levels of corruption? Will alternative methods be found to consolidate the acquisition of wealth through the new policies of export promotion? Will benefits for foreign businesses increase? Where is the common sense in the policies exercised by the international or bilateral financial bodies?

THE REAL LIMITATIONS TO JOINT ACTION

A substantive element required for the consolidation of a Central American political front—one that is diverse and flexible, and takes into account all areas of external relation—is a prior base for joint action. Regional integration may form the basis for this new initiative in joint external policies. However, it is still unclear whether the official commitments on regional integration, which has been under construction since the fall of the Sandinistas in Nicaragua are the most adequate. Currently, Central American integration is centered on policies of structural adjustment and promotion of exports geared to the global economy at almost any cost. In other words, these presidential accords still lack, among many other things, a consolidated external policy of widespread development. For this reason, integration alone as it stands will not provide solutions to the complex problems of economic development of these countries. Structural adjustment is not the same thing as development.

In addition to this process of cosmetic integration, there is a real lack of capacity and conviction for joint action because of real divisions among countries generated by wars; political changes during the 1970s; embargoes; the effects of the economic crises of the 1980s; the impact of adjustment policies; and differences in style and the intent of external financial organizations. These and other factors have generated changes in the prevailing economic structure, reducing prospects for creating understandings outside of neoliberal norms. In other words, the Central American countries are divided internally and separated externally.

The Real Scope of Economic Negotiations with Third Parties

In order to define the scope of action, the nature of negotiations, and the proposals for external relations, the current political structure of Central American countries must be modified. Once accomplished, it is necessary to derive a basic and realistic accord for joint Central American action. As past Central American integration efforts have demonstrated, a united Central American posture toward third parties is a more efficient manner to conduct external relations and produces better results in the great majority of cases. Possible joint actions include agreements for protection of industry and other activities that require a supporting framework prior to their full participation in the international market; agreements for transference, adoption, and development of technology (but of great breadth, especially during the period of adjustment and prior to the changes in policy toward the rest of the world); reorientation of conditionality, and of those "assistance" and other economic policies created by international financial institutions; and common solutions to crucial social problems.

On this last point, it is worth mentioning that it is difficult to conceive of a new development push in the region without a prior solution to serious social problems, exacerbated by the superimposed crises that have stricken Central America. This does not suggest a new political initiative based on charity. The point is that the present political economy ignores the dominant social reality of the region and therefore does not generate substantive solutions.

Readaptation of Cultural Relations

Man cannot live by efficiency alone. All of the agreements that Central American diplomats have signed with developed countries in the past have included cultural development assistance, if only for the sake of justifying their jobs. Through time, this aspect has been lost inasmuch as similar clauses are no longer included in agreements. Currently, the more developed countries "export" their culture to Central America, which Central Americans look to with astonishment. Nonetheless, the necessary level of transference or absorption of cultural development is never attained, although cultural exchange unites and facilitates development.

Therefore, Central America has always been left simply with the primacy of the economic—television is in charge of the rest. We become familiar with other countries through their media, which does them no favor and prejudices enormously the receivers of exported messages. Additionally, the GATT agreements ensure that such programs and videos are paid royalties and other surcharges to fatten the wallets of their producers. It is evident, then, that regarding culture, an enormous, unexplored area exists. Worsening cultural dependence must be transformed into cultural interdependence.

CONCLUSIONS

Although this analysis has been schematic, it seems evident that one can derive some reasonable conclusions from it. First, substantive changes must occur in the political position of Central American countries, in a manner that enables them to reflect on the past and consider the future as a national and regional issue, not as a perpetration of the current political "zoos" and the consolidation of measures to enrich the few. Democracy is not created from the top; it is destroyed from the top. Second, a profound change in economic focus is necessary. Adjustment is not development. Insertion in the international economy is an important element of development but not its only purpose. Central American countries need to adjust their political economies toward balanced development with justice and equity, which the general mode of macroeconomic policies do not take into account. Third, it is not possible to reduce commercial policy and economic relations to a bilateral level exclusively. Diversification of relations is the main goal for survival. A coordinated regional effort of a continental Latin American-Caribbean nature must form the political base for international relations. Finally, substantive reform in the productive capacity of the region based on technological capacity and real competition is necessary. Assistance must be centered on an improvement of the productive process, and not on subsidies that stimulate production at fictitiously lower costs.

This chapter ends as it began, with a reflection made by the Central American Foundation for Integration:

Now more than ever, we must make a last ditch effort to return to forms of mutual cooperation and defense of our interests, or we will transform ourselves, each day increasingly so, into divided geographical units, available and employable by third parties for their own ends, with the consent of the domestic groups they support.

Twelve

Understanding Economic Integration: Its Role and Reason in Central America

Dante Ramírez

Economic integration is a fact of life today in Central America. Enacted by individual countries in the region, this development has had an external impetus, independent of official policy. Economic integration in Central America mirrors a similar development spanning the globe and involving diverse forces and actors. In other words, besides being a voluntary project conceived by particular countries in different regions around the world, economic integration is in no small measure an externally generated current promoted by conditions obtaining in the international economy. On the one hand, economic integration is a product of growing worldwide interdependence; on the other, it derives from productive forces that require wider stages of action in order to create material abundance. The formation of international trade blocs underscores this trend.

The current debate on Central American integration is of more than academic or theoretical concern. It bears directly on the material well-being of the region. The destiny of our region is tied to the outcome of the debate. As with any human effort, regional integration may take different paths. Central American countries may choose to influence the functioning or trajectory of integration, or stand by passively—giving expression, in the latter case, to the fatalism typically displayed by peripheral countries accustomed to being penetrated and dominated by external forces.

Today, no one can afford to ignore or dismiss the issue of integration. At a minimum, studying the issue can be expected to raise social consciousness. This lends special importance to the Central American case, as its particularity bears on the larger issue of cooperation in the international system. Since integration's complex implications encompass all spheres of life in the region, the diverse forces and interests that are now organizing themselves to respond to the new regional integration initiative must not be allowed to solely control its future course of development.

The drive to achieve integration among the countries of Central America is taking place within a new order that is both continental and global. When such an initiative derives from military interests, these interests are apt to arouse suspicion—especially when, notwithstanding the growing gap between poor and rich countries, advocates of regional integration continue to spend billions wastefully on arms. This cannot promote peace and development. In the new international order, on the regional and global planes, increased outlays for the military cannot have a salutory effect either for peace or development.

For poor countries, such as those of Central America, there must be hope that a new world order will be premised on a just international economic system—one whose form and function will be created freely by all peoples on Earth. In that order, there must be full consciousness of interdependence among countries, of the value of such reciprocity, and of the need to eschew hegemonism in the resolution of international political disputes. If this is what George Bush, former president of the United States, was referring to when he noted the emergence of a new world order in the post-Cold War era, then the development is likely to follow a benign path. But if President Bush was referring to some alternative scheme, one in which great-power hegemony would continue to obtain, then the augury is of more tension and conflict around the world—a multipolar order hardly more benign than the bipolar order which it replaced.

Historically, foreign forces have intervened in and exploited Central America. Exploitation by countries outside the region has been the principal cause of Central America's continuing underdevelopment. In order for the people of the region to perceive a significant advantage in the new world order, this historical pattern of intervention and exploitation must be undone. Is this possible? Current political reality, which obliges Central America to play a subordinate role in the international division of labor, causes us to be pessimistic, for several reasons. First, Central America has no illusions about its weight in the international community. Second, it is not optimistic that the first-world countries will finally recognize that promoting sustained economic growth and development in the weak countries is more likely than any other strategy to promote strength and prosperity in the international system.

In the aftermath of the Second World War, when the United Nations and the international organs were established, the great powers reserved for themselves, as if by natural right, a decisive role in international affairs. Since then, the great powers have failed to act effectively to ameliorate the condition of the world's impoverished majority, in what we call the "Third World." Should that majority, including kindred elements in Central America, expect now that a new world order, one more equitable and benign than the old Cold War order, will emerge by the hand of political leaders in the leading countries which crafted the old script and which will probably want to craft the new one, too?

Our people continue to be underdeveloped, and the economic gap between the rich and poor countries continues to grow. All but a few social sectors in the countries of Central America continue to suffer impoverishment. Yesterday this asymmetry could be ascribed to differential capital resources; today the imbalance has more to do with unevenness in the distribution of technological knowledge and information. This seems to indicate that we are nowhere near the end of history. The augury of capital strengthened by technology is a pattern inimical to the interests of the world's underdeveloped and poor. Must this inevitably be the pattern in the next century and beyond? Are there no alternatives to the forced choice between opulence and misery in mankind's struggle to advance?

In summary, for countries such as those in Central America there must be a more just order. International economic justice is the key here. All states, rich and poor, large and small, must finally embrace Francois Perroux's caveat that economism "as the supreme regulator of relations among countries, is that which must be regulated by the demands of international norms."

Many hold to the view that placing ethics ahead of all other considerations in the relations among strong and weak countries is at best naive, despite the fact that there is ample evidence of moral considerations having influenced decisions in public life to abolish slavery and to improve the lot of women, children and prisoners. It should be stressed here that a call for ethics and morality in international life is not an argument for basing such life on piety or philanthropy. Rather, the wish is to stress the practical importance of principles of equity and reciprocal interest. The concern is principally with distributive morality. In this vein, Gunnar Myrdal's observation in his book *The State of the Future* is impressive: If we want to find a way to resolve the dilemma posed by the ties between national integration and international disintegration, we have to confront the necessity of rectifying our view of the problem; internationally, we have to try to harmonize, coordinate, and unify the structures of the national political economy. According to Myrdal, there must be an international economic disarmament that gradually eliminates the disintegrating effects of national economies, or of those that have risen from transnationalization. The fruits of this effort will be to guarantee stable markets and, consequently, higher production along with higher levels of gainful employment. The Letter of Rights and Economic

Obligations of States, approved some time ago by a great majority of countries over the opposition of the leading industrial powers, holds out the hope for an international order that approximates what is desirable. In this spirit, Jan Tinbergen, a Nobel laureate in economics, has underscored the need to lift the curtain of poverty that divides the world.

We must neither ignore the differences among the developed and underdeveloped countries, nor deny that these differences continue to fly in the face of the many proclamations calling for economic equality among nations. All countries together must seek to create a more equitable world, finally establishing an Age of Reason in international affairs.

Heretofore, the World Bank and the International Monetary Fund (IMF) have acted principally in the interests of the Western industrialized countries, and at the expense of the overwhelming majority of Third World countries. New thinking is needed to correct this inequity. A model for such thinking can be found in an old proposal to establish, under United Nations auspices, a Fund for Economic Promotion, which would be supported by an influential and well-endowed mechanism and which would serve the interests of poor countries just as the World Bank and IMF have served the interests of the rich ones.

While technical assistance to the developing world is approaching the saturation point, financial assistance is not even close to the prudent and conservative levels set by the United Nations. On reflection, it may be unnecessary to reach even those modest levels of financial assistance if international commercial organizations can be moved to pursue the course that the more affluent countries followed in the last stages of the Second World War, especially with regard to promoting price stability. A world based on more equitable distribution of economic resources is more likely to stimulate commerce than higher levels of economic aid.

The need to forgive the external debt of the poorest countries in the world and, concomitantly, to reduce the indebtedness of mid-level countries should also be stressed. In the latter case, debt payment must be compatibly scheduled with sustainable rates of growth. To continue to act otherwise is to underscore that at the end of the century and the millennium the leading industrial countries will still be caught up in the familiar colonizer syndrome, that they will persist in rejecting the key notion that interdependency and equity, not exploitation, must define the new international order.

It is essential today that the institutionalism of the United Nations be subjected to critical reevaluation. The U.N. system was created in another age, at the intersection of the end of the worst conflagration in human history and the beginning of the Cold War. The norms and practices of the U.N. continue to reflect the origins of the United Nations. It is time to reform the U.N. system to reflect the new international realities of economic interdependence and political multipolarism in a post-Cold War era no longer marked by confrontation between the U.S. and Soviet superpowers and their respective blocs.

While the United Nations and its specialized bodies do some positive work, there can be no doubt that by their actions and omissions the leading powers in particular continue to flaunt the original ideals of that great international institution. While it is probably true that the world would be even worse off without the United Nations, this concession should not dissuade us from the need to reconstitute a better United Nations in the interest of promoting a better world. It is time to effect a reorganization, particularly of the U.N.'s bureaucratic structures, in order to improve the condition of international life. Reform of the judicial-institutional scaffolding of the United Nations is one of the most important tasks of our time. A broadly representative international commission composed of members with the highest moral and intellectual qualifications should be charged with this task.

Similarly, reevaluation must be made of the purposes, roles, and structures of key regional organization, For example, the Organization of American States (OAS) and the Economic Commission for Latin America (ECLA). More often than not, the OAS has displayed impotence when having to deal with the great problems facing Latin America; too often it has appeared to be little more than an ornament in regional affairs. It is time to undertake a serious assessment of its effectiveness and worth within Latin America and the intersection between that region and its industrially advanced neighbors in North America. What will the OAS's role be in the hemisphere's future? For example, will it have any role to play vis-à-vis the emerging economic bloc comprising the three parties to the North American Free Trade Agreement—the United States, Canada, and Mexico? In the meantime, the countries of Latin America and the Caribbean must strengthen ECLA's role, allowing that organization to serve even more effectively as a permanent forum in which issues of common interest may be discussed and policy positions formulated for transmission back to governments in the region.

Clearly, the hour has arrived for settling on a program of regional integration among the Central American countries. Based on that development, it is hoped, all of Latin America will someday achieve an effective mechanism for an even more comprehensive regional integration in the great land mass between the Rio Grande and Tierra del Fuego, including the island countries and territories in the Caribbean basin. Latin America may want someday to take its cue from Europe, where, despite the mutiplicity of ethnic groupings, language forms, and national sensibilities, the continent continues to evolve toward a more integrative future. The constellation of economic and political forces in the international domain is apt to require of Central America and, by extension, Latin America, that programs of regional integration be undertaken in the interest of regional defense and advance. Regional integration may prove to be the most effective means by which small- and medium-sized countries influence the movement of economic and political forces on the international plane.

In Central America, the campaign for regional economic integration is being renewed, but with a different tone this time. Currently, the emphasis is on regionalism compatible with neoliberal economic philosophy. This tendency stresses the operation of market mechanisms rather than development planning under a strong central authority. Marketization, it is widely believed in Central America, will promote economic efficiency and growth within the wider context of global competition. In other words, in Central America we are trying to encourage on the regional interstate level a development that can be seen as taking hold already on the national level. Of course, this alternative model for development is marked by both strengths and weaknesses. It remains for us Central Americans to assess the model carefully in order to promote its strengths over its weaknesses. In any event, pressure is rapidly building throughout Central America to adopt a scheme for effective regional economic integration. While the date for its adoption is not yet ascertainable, it is clear that no country in the region wants to find itself outside the new framework, lagging behind.

As the international political economy continues to undergo fundamental change in the post-Cold War era, Central Americans will find themselves more and more pressured to tie their destiny to developments whose sweep will, at a minimum, be hemispheric, perhaps even global. In due course, we in Central America will come to believe that the world's larger, more developed economies will exert a locomotive effect upon development in our own region. But Central America will probably long have to live with the reality that its own regional integration cannot undo national borders or supplant national power. Regional integration in Central America must somehow accommodate itself to that crucial reality.

The development of each Central American country presents concrete and specific problems for which it is difficult to prescribe general remedies. Nonetheless, the process of integration must not only highlight commonalties across countries, but also serve to reduce those differences that tend to distance us from our neighbors. It is the latter factor that will benefit Central America in its relations with third parties that might intend to split the region. Moreover, we ascribe to the premise that the Central American republics will one day forge an economic union that will serve as a model for the Third World, providing a framework for effective negotiations with other blocs. It is important to keep in mind that the process of integration will only be effective if the various parties perceive a benefit from the union, for no nation will put forth the effort to integrate without receiving substantive benefits for that effort.

All previous attempts to achieve regional integration have foundered on the rock of measuring costs and benefits. Many of us Central Americans have sharply debated this point, since it was obvious that (1) those countries which registered negative balances in the operation of their system could be expected to seek compensation and (2) that this issue would cause suspicion to be cast on the process of integration itself. Indeed, this is what has occurred.

The models which Central Americans may wish to consider for adoption must take previous experience into account. A few further comments are in order here. First, it has to be recognized from the outset that economic integration among countries does not imply simply the liberalization and increase in exchange and factors of production. Above all, integration is a program with a vision of economic and/or political unity, a good example of which can be found in the case of the European Economic Community. The forms or modalities for alternative integration models may vary according to historical circumstances, but always there must be a shared interest, at a minimum, in integrating the commercial sector. In the Central American case, a key historical factor is widely known, that is, that the region was united under colonial rule and that since independence it has struggled to regain a lost unity. In this sense, the issue of integration in Central America has had a fundamental political dimension since the abolition of the federal pact in the first half of the nineteenth century.

The growing importance of transnational meetings at the presidential level in Central America is a good indicator of continuing interest in the question of regional integration. All of the conferees have recognized that in Central America the impulse to move forward on the path of integration is sharpened by the reality (1) that the region contains some of the least- developed and poorest countries in the Western Hemisphere and (2) that widespread underdevelopment and poverty have widened the gap between poor and rich sectors within each Central American country. The so-called social debt has grown more than the external debt, with a corollary inequity and lack of solidarity. This threatens each Central American country with political instability and political violence—a situation that can be ameliorated if regional economic integration is seen as an instrument of development and not merely as a guideline for development. No benefit is to be derived from integrating human misery, a point that must not be forgotten as we contemplate the future outlines of the post-Cold War international order. Strategies and action programs must be adopted to benefit the impoverished majority in Central America, and worldwide; at the regional level especially, integration must be regarded as instrumental to the attainment of that end. In these times, we have an opportunity to construct a scheme for regional economic integration that all Central Americans will perceive as promoting peace, work, and prosperity—a scheme which falls victim neither to arcane social doctrines nor to outside powers armed with the oppressive instruments of external assistance.

References

Adelman, Irma, and John Edward Taylor. 1990. "Is Structural Adjustment With a Human Face Possible? The Case of Mexico." *Journal of Development Studies*, Vol. 26, April, 387-407.

Aguilera, Gabriel y Romero, Jorge. 1981. *La Dialecta del Terror en Guatemala.* EDUCA: San José.

Aguilera, Gabriel y Romero, Jorge. 1989. "Centroamérica: Concertación y Conflicto; una Exploración." *Nueva Sociedad* (Venezuela), No. 102, July-August, 33-40.

Aharoni, Yair. 1966. *The Foreign Investment Decision.* Boston: Harvard Business School.

Albrecht, D. E., and S. H. Murdock. 1990. *The Sociology of U.S. Agriculture.* Iowa State University Press: Ames.

Ameringer, Charles D. 1982. *Democracy in Costa Rica.* New York: Praeger.

Anderson, Dennis, and Mark W. Leiserson. 1980. "Rural Nonfarm Employment in Developing Countries." *Economic Development and Cultural Change,* Vol. 28, No. 2, 227-48.

Arias, Salvador. 1989. *Seguridad or Inseguridad Alimentaria. Un Reto para la Región Centroamericana. Perspectiva para el año 2000.* San Salvador: UCA Editores.

Austin, James E. 1990. *Managing in Developing Countries.* New York: Free Press.

Avineri, Schlomo. 1987. "Sustaining Democracies in Regions of Crisis: The Israeli Experience." A Report of an International Conference, Sedom, Israel, January 8-10, 1987. Released by the National Democratic Institute for International Affairs, Washington, D.C.

Bacha, Edgmar, and Richard E. Feinberg. 1986. "The World Bank and

Structural Adjustment in Latin America." *World Development*, Vol. 14, March, 333-46.

Baldares, Manuel de Jesús. 1985. *La Distribución del Ingreso y los Sueldos en Costa Rica*. San José: Editorial Costa Rica.

Baloyra, Enrique, and Rafael López. 1982. *Iberoamérica en los Años 80: Perspectivas de Cambio Social y Político*. Madrid: Centro de Investigaciones Sociológicas - ICI.

Barnet, Richard J., and Ronald E. Muller. 1979. *Global Reach*. New York: Simon & Schuster.

Barret-Brown, Michael. 1974. *The Economics of Imperialism*. Baltimore: Penguin.

Barrios, Javier. 1990. *Diagnóstico Preliminar del Sistema Cooperativo de Panamá*. Monograph.

Behrman, Jack N., and Robert E. Grosse. 1990. *International Business and Government*. Charleston: South Carolina University Press.

Belli, Pedro. 1991. "Globalizing the Rest of the World." *Harvard Business Review*, Vol. 69, No. 4, July-August.

Bergsten, Fred, and Shafiqul Islam. 1991. *The U.S. as a Debtor Country*. Washington, D.C.: Institute for International Economics.

Berry, Albert. 1991. "Stabilization, Adjustment and Income Distribution in Latin America." University of Toronto, Monograph.

Bertrand, A. L., and F. L. Corty. 1962. *Rural Land Tenure in the United States: An Ecological Perspective*. Baton Rouge: Louisiana State University Press.

Bhagwati, Jagdish N. 1982. "W. Arthur Lewis: An Appreciation." In *The Theory and Experience of Economic Development*, ed. Mark Gersovitz, Carlos F. Diaz-Alejandro, Gustav Ranis, and Mark Rosenzweig. Boston: Allen & Unwin.

Binder, Frederick. 1974. *The Age of the Common School: 1830-1865*. New York: Wiley.

Bjork, Lars. 1975. "An Experiment in Work Satisfaction" *Scientific American*. March.

Blachman, Kenneth A. 1980. "Comparative Measurement of Political Democracy." *American Sociological Review*, Vol. 45, June 1980, 370-90.

Black, Jan Knippers. 1986. *The Dominican Republic: Politics and Development in an Unsovereign State*. Boston: Allen & Unwin.

Bluestone, Barry, and Bennett Harrison. 1982. *The Deindustrialization of America: Plant Closings, Community Abandonment, and the Dismantling of Basic Industry*. New York: Basic.

Blumberg, Paul. 1969. *Industrial Democracy*. New York: Schocken.

Bonanno, A. 1990. *Agrarian Policies and Agricultural Systems*. New York: Westview Press.

Booth, John A. 1984. "Representative Constitutional Democracy in Costa Rica: Adaptation to Crisis in the Turbulent 1980's." In *America: Crisis and Adaptation*. Albuquerque: University of New Mexico Press.

Booth, John A. 1989. "Costa Rica: the Roots of Democratic Stability." In *Democracy in Developing Countries*, eds., Larry Diamond et al. Colorado: Lynne Rienner.

Bowett, C. W. 1963. *The Law of International Institutions*. New York: Praeger.

Boyd, Derick A. C. 1988. *Economic Management, Income Distribution, and Poverty in Jamaica*. New York: Praeger.

Bulmer-Thomas, Victor. 1987. *The Political Economy of Central America Since 1920*. Cambridge: Cambridge University Press.

Bulmer-Thomas, Victor. 1988. *Studies in the Economics of Central America*. London: Macmillan.

Burg, Steven L. 1983. *Conflict and Cohesion in Socialist Yugoslavia: Political Decision-Making Since 1966*. Princeton, N.J.: Princeton University.

Carnoy, Martin, and Derek Shearer. 1980. *Economic Democracy*. White Plains, N.Y.: M. E. Sharpe.

Carter, M. 1984. "Identification of the Inverse Relationship Between Farm Size and Productivity: An Analysis of Peasant Agricultural Production." *Oxford Economic Papers*, 36, 131-45.

Carter, M., and D. Mesbah. 1992. "Posibilidades de Crecimiento Agrícola y Disminución de la Pobreza Rural A Traves de la Intervención en el Mercado de la Tierra." *Colección Estudios*, CIEPLAN 33.

Casson, Mark. 1986. *Multinationals and World Trade*. London: Allen & Unwin.

Castel, Charles. 1991. "Debt Crisis Adjustment Programs and Socioeconomic Structure in Latin America." Master's Essay. New York: The University at Albany, State University of New York.

Castro, Carlos. 1988. "Estado y Movilización Etnica en Panamá." *Estudios Sociales Centroamericanos*, September-December, 115-24.

Caves, Richard. 1983. *MNE and Economic Analysis*. Cambridge: Cambridge University Press.

Cearra-Hatton, Miguel. 1989. "La Economía Dominicana: Crisis y Reestructuración 1968-1988." Centro de Investigación Económica, April, mimeograph.

Céspedes, Victor Hugo, Alberto DiMare, and Runolfo Jiménez. 1985. *Costa Rica: Recuperación Sin Reactivación*. San José: Academia de Centroamerica.

Céspedes, Victor Hugo, Alberto DiMare, and Runolfo Jiménez. 1988. *Costa Rica: Estabilidad Sin Crecimiento*. San José: Academia de

Centroamerica.

Cochrane, W. 1979. *The Development of American Agriculture: A Historical Analysis*. Minneapolis: University of Minnesota Press.

Collier, David (ed.). 1979. *The New Authoritarianism in Latin America*. Princeton: Princeton University Press.

Comisión Económica para América Latina (CEPAL). 1979. *Centroamérica: Evolución Económica Desde la Posguerra*. Doc. CEPAL/Mex/ODE/34, México, diciembre.

Comisión Económica para América Latina (CEPAL). 1987. "Lineamientos Metodológicos para una Estrategia de Seguridad Alimentaria." LC/MEX/L.49. México, May.

Corradi, Juan. 1985. "La Cultura del Miedo en la Sociedad Civil: Reflexiones y Propuestas." In Isidoro Cheresky and Jacques Chonchol, ed., *Crisis y Transición de los Regimenes Autoritarios*. Buenos Aires: EUDEBA.

Daltrop, Anne. 1986. *Politics and the European Community*. London & New York: Longman, 2d ed.

de Janvry, A., and E. Sadoulet. 1983. "Social Articulation as a Condition for Equitable Growth." *Journal of Development Economics*, Vol. 13, 275-303.

de Janvry, A., and E. Sadoulet. 1989. "A Study in Resistance to Institutional Change: The Lost Game of Latin American Land Reform." *World Development*, Vol. 17, No. 9, 1397-1407.

Del Aguila, Juan Manuel. 1982. "The Limits of Reform Development in Contemporary Costa Rica." *Journal of Interamerican Studies and World Affairs*, Vol. 24, August, 355-74.

de la Ossa, Alvaro. 1988. "Fundación Centroamericana por la Integración."*Polémica*, May-August, 54-59.

de la Ossa, Alvaro, and E. Alonso. 1990. "Exportaciones No Tradicionales en Centroamerica." *Cuadernos De Ciencias Sociales*, FLACSO, San José, Costa Rica.

Denitch, Bogdan Denis. 1976. *The Legitimation of a Revolution: The Yugoslav Case*. New Haven, Conn.: Yale University.

Diamond, Larry, et al. 1989. *Democracy in Developing Countries: Latin America*. Colorado: Lynne Rienner.

Drazen, A., and Z. Eckstein. 1988. "On the Organization of Rural Markets and the Process of Economic Development." *The American Economic Review*, Vol. 78, No. 3, 431-43.

Drucker, Peter. 1974. "MNCs and Developing Countries." *Foreign Affairs*, Vol. 53, No. 1, October.

Duany, Jorge. 1990. *Los Dominicanos en Puerto Rico: Migración en la Semi-periferia*. Puerto Rico: Ediciones Huracán.

Dunning, John H. 1988. *Explaining International Production*. London:

Unwin Hyman.

Ebel, Roland H. 1972. "Governing the City-State: Notes on the Politics of Small Latin American Countries." *Journal of Interamerican Studies and World Affairs*, Vol. 14, 325-46.

Ebel, Roland H. 1982. "The Coming of the Post-Agricultural Society: An Exercise in Economic and Political Futurism." *Interamerican Economic Affairs*, Vol. 35, No. 4.

Edelman, Marc, and Joanne Kenen. 1983. "Recent Literature on Costa Rica's Economic Crisis." *Latin American Research Review*, Vol. 18, 166-80.

Edelman, Marc, and Joanne Kenen. 1989. *The Costa Rica Reader*. New York: Grove Weidenfeld.

Edwards, Sebastian. 1988. "Terms of Trade, Tariffs, and Labor Market Adjustment in Developing Countries." *The World Bank Economic Review*, Vol. 2, No. 2, May, 165-85.

Edwards, Sebastian, and Alejandra Cox Edwards. 1990. "Labor Market Distortionsand Structural Adjustments in Developing Countries." NBER Working Paper Series, No. 3346, May.

Edwards, Sebastian, and S. Van Wijnbergen. 1988. "Structural Adjustment and Disequilibrium." In *Handbook of Development Economics*, ed., H. Chenery and T. N. Srinivasan. New York: North-Holland.

Ellner, Steve. 1989. "Viraje en la Izquierda: Nuevos Rumbos, Nuevas Perspectivas." *Nueva Sociedad*. (Venezuela), No. 101, May-June, 77-91.

Evans, Peter. 1978. *Dependent Development*. Princeton, N.J.: Princeton University Press.

Fagen, Helio. 1982. Crisis Económica en Costa Rica: Un Análisis de Los Ultimos Veinte Años. San José: Editorial Nueva Década.

Feinberg, Richard. 1984. "Costa Rica: the End of the Fiesta." In *From Gunboats to Diplomacy*. Baltimore: Johns Hopkins University Press.

Fields, Gary S. 1975. "Rural-Urban Migration, Urban Unemployment and Underemployment, and Job-Search Activity in LDCs." *Journal of Development Economics*, Vol. 2, No. 2, June, 165-87.

Fielke, Norman S. 1989. "Europe in 1992." *New England Economic Review*, May-June.

Flynn, Patricia. 1985. "U.S. Military Moves in Costa Rica and Honduras." In *CENSA'S Strategic Reports*. Berkeley, Calif.: Center for the Study of the Americas.

García-Huidobro, Guillermo, et al. 1990. *La Deuda Social en Costa Rica*. San José: PREALC-OIT.

Garcia Laguardia, Jorge Mario. 1988. *La Frustrada Vocación Federal de*

la Región y el Proyecto de Parlamento Centroamericano. Central
America: Cuadernos de CEPAL, # 28, 43-44.

Gindling, Tim H. 1991. "Labor Market Segmentation and the Determination of Wages in the Public, Private-Formal, and Informal Sectors
in San José, Costa Rica." *Economic Development and Cultural
Change*, Vol. 39, No. 3, April, 585-606.

Gindling, Tim H., and R. A. Berry. 1991. "The Performance of the Labor
Market During Recession and Structural Adjustment: Costa Rica
in the 1980s." Unpublished manuscript.

Glickman, Norman J., and Douglas P. Woodward. 1989. *The New Competitors: How Foreign Investors are Changing the U.S. Economy*.
New York:Basic.

Goldmark, Susan, et al. 1982. *Capitalizing Workers: The Impact of
Employee Stock Option Plans in Selected Developing Countries*.
Washington, D.C.: Development Alternatives.

Goldstein, Walter. 1965. "The MNC and World Trade" In *The MNC and
Social Change*. ed. David E. Apter and Louis W. Goodman. New
York:Praeger.

Goldstein, Walter. 1985. "The Continuing World Debt Crisis." *International Tax and Business Lawyer*, Vol. 3, No. 1.

Goldstein, Walter. 1992. "EC92: 'Euro-stalling', The EC 1992."
Foreign Policy, No. 85, Winter, 129-47.

Goodman, Louis W. 1987. *Small Nations, Giant Firms*. New York:
Holmes and Meier.

Goodspeed, Stephen S. 1967. *The Nature and Function of International
Organization*. New York: Oxford University Press, 2d ed.

Griffith-Jones, Stephany, and Osvaldo Sunkel. 1989. *Debt and Development Crises in Latin America: The End of an Illusion*. New York:
Oxford University Press.

Grosse, Robert. 1989. *MNCs in Latin America*. London: Routledge.

Guendell, Ludwig, and Roy Rivero. 1987. "El Desarrollo de la Política
Social en Costa Rica: Crisis y Perspectivas." *Polémica*. San José:
No.2, segunda epoca, May-August, 51-64.

Gutiérrez Saxe, Miguel, and Jorge Vargas Cullell. 1986. *Costa Rica es el
Nombre del Juego: Un Analisis de la Crisis de 1984*. San José:
Instituto Costarricense de Estudios Sociales.

Harris, John R., and Michael P. Todaro. 1970. "Migration, Unemployment and Development: A Two- Sector Analysis." *American Economic Review*, Vol. 60, No. 1, March, 126-42.

Hayami, Yujiro, and Vernon W. Ruttan. 1985. *Agricultural Development:
An International Perspective*. Baltimore: Johns Hopkins University Press.

Herrick, Bruce, and Barclay Hudson. 1981. *Urban Poverty and Economic*

Development: A Case Study of Costa Rica. New York: St. Martin's Press.

Hopfensperger, Jean. 1986. "Costa Rica: Seeds of Terror." *The Progressive*, September, 24-27.

Hufbauer, Gary C. 1990. "An Overview" In *Europe 1992; an American Perspective*, ed. Gary C. Hufbauer. Washington, D.C.: The Brookings Institution.

Huntington, Samuel P. 1968. *Political Order in Changing Societies*. New Haven, Conn.: Yale University Press.

Huntington, Samuel P. 1988. "One Soul at a Time: Political Science and Political Reform." *American Political Science Review*, . Vol. 82, 3-8.

International Center for Public Enterprises in Developing Countries. 1981. *Workers' Self-Management and Participation in Decision-Making as a Factor of Social Change and Economic Progress in Developing Countries: National Reports Vol. II: Algeria, Guyana, India, and Tanzania*. Ljubljana, Slovenian Republic: International Center for Public Enterprises in Developing Countries.

International Labour Office. 1962. *Workers' Management in Yugoslavia*. Geneva: I.L.O.

International Labour Office. 1972. "Workers' Participation in Management: Country Studies Series, Yugoslavia No. 9." *International Institute for Labour Studies Review*, Vol. 9, 129-72.

Jauberth Rojas, H. Rodrigo, et al. 1991. *La Triangulación Centroamérica-México-EUA; ¿Una Oportunidad para el Desarrollo y la Paz?* San José, Costa Rica: Editorial Dei.

Johnson, Ana Gutiérrez, and William Foote Whyte. 1977. "The Mondragón System of Worker Production Cooperatives." *Industrial and Labor Relations Review*, Vol. 31, No. 1, 18-30.

Johnson, Ross. 1972. *The Transformation of Communist Ideology: The Yugoslav Case, 1945-1953*. Cambridge: Massachusetts Institute of Technology.

Joncic, Koca. 1982. *Narodnosti u Jugoslaviji (Nationalities in Yugoslavia)*. Belgrade: Jugoslovenska Stvarnost.

Julius, DeAnne. 1990. *Global Companies and Public Policy*. London: Pinter.

Karnes, Thomas L. 1961. *The Failure of Union: Central America, 1924-1960*. Raleigh: University of North Carolina Press.

Kelso, Louis O., and Patricia Hetter. 1967. *Two-Factor Theory: The Economics of Reality, How To Turn Eighty Million Workers into Capitalists on Borrowed Money*. New York: Random House.

Kirkendall, R. 1987. "A History of the Family Farm" In *Is There a Moral Obligation to Save the Family Farm?*, ed. G. Comstock. Ames,

Iowa: Iowa State University Press.

Kirkpatrick, Jeanne. 1979. "Dictatorships and Double Standards." *Commentary,* Vol 68, 34-45.

Komisije, Dokumenti. 1983. *Book 4: Zaklúnji Deo Dugorocnog Programa Ekonomske Stabilizacije.* Beograd: Centar Za Radnicko Samoupravljane.

Koo, A. 1968. *The Role of Land Reform in Economic Development.* New York: Praeger.

Koo, A. 1982. *Land Market Distortion and Tenure Reform.* Ames, Iowa: The Iowa State University Press.

Ladejinsky, W. 1966. "Agrarian Reform in Asia." Reading No. 86, In *Selected Reading to Accompany: Getting Agriculture Moving,* ed. R. Borton. New York: The Agricultural Development Council.

Lele, Uma. 1990. "Structural Adjustment, Agricultural Development and the Poor: Some Lessons from the Malawian Experience." *World Development,* Vol. 18, No. 9, 1207-19.

Lin, C. 1988. "East Asia and Latin America as Contrasting Models." *Economic Development and Cultural Change,* Vol. 36, No. 3, S153-S193.

Lindblom, Charles E. 1977. *Politics and Markets: The World's Political-Economic Systems.* New York: Basic.

Linz, Juan, and Alfred Stepan. 1978. *The Breakdown of Democratic Regimes.* Baltimore: Johns Hopkins University Press.

Lipset, Seymour Martin. 1989. "The Expansion of Democracy." *Vital Speeches of the Day.* January 10, 751.

Lizano, Eduardo, et al. 1989. "Crecimiento Económico y Deuda Externa: Consideraciones sobre el caso de Costa Rica." *Comentarios Sobre Asuntos Económicos,* No. 85. San José: Banco Central de Costa Rica.

Looney, Robert E. 1987. *The Jamaican Economy in the 1980s: Economic Decline and Structural Adjustment.* Boulder, Colorado: Westview Press.

López, Ramón. 1986. "Structural Models of the Farm Household that Allow for Interdependent Utility and Profit-Maximization Decisions." In *Agricultural Household Models: Extensions, Applications, and Policy,* ed. Inderjit Singh, Lyn Squire, and John Strauss. Baltimore: Johns Hopkins University Press.

Mace, Gordon. 1988. "Regional Integration in Latin America: A Long and Winding Road." *International Journal,* 43, Summer, 402-27.

Magdoff, Harry. 1969. *The Age of Imperialism.* New York: Monthly Review Press.

Magid, Alvin. 1991. *Private Lives/Public Surfaces: Grassroots Perspectives and the Legitimacy Question in Yugoslav Socialism.* New

York: East European Monographs/Columbia University Press.

Mann, Arthur J., and Carlos E. Sánchez. 1984. "Monetarism, Economic Reform and Socio-Economic Consequences: Argentina 1976-82." *International Journal of Social Economics*, Vol. 11, Nos. 3-4, 12-28.

Mann, Arthur J., and Carlos E. Sánchez. 1985. "Labor Market Responses to Southern Cone Stabilization Policies: The Cases of Argentina, Chile, and Uruguay." *Inter-American Economic Affairs*, Vol. 38, No. 4, 19-39.

Martínez, Juan Ramón. 1992. "Comentarios Preliminarios al Documento de Concertación de la Ley de Modernización Agrícola" *Diario la Tribuna*, January 9.

Melmed-Sanjak, Jolyne. 1991. "Cooperative Farm Viability and Flexible Institutional Choice: Inferences from the Experience of Agrarian Reform in Northern Honduras." SUNYA Discussion Paper No. 91-04.

Melmed-Sanjak, Jolyne, and Carlos E. Santiago. 1989. "Labor Demand in Non-Farm Small-Scale Production: Is the Household Production Model Relevant?" *Albany Discussion Paper Series*, No. 89-08.

Menjívar, Rafael, et al. 1986. *Centroamerica: La Democracia Como Experienca y Como Posibilidad*. San José: Documentos de ICADIS, May.

MIDEPLAN. 1990. "Evolución Socioeconómica de Costa Rica. 1975-1979." *El Desarrollo Social en el Largo Plazo*, San José, September.

Mill, John Stuart. 1905. *Considerations on Representative Government*. London: Routledge.

Molina, Javier. 1990. *El Coopertivismo en Nicaragua: 1980-1990*. Monograph.

Molz, Richard. 1990. "Privatization in Developing Countries." *Columbia Journal of World Business*, Vol. 25, No. 2, Spring/Summer, 17-24.

Morales, Abelardo. 1989. "Ajuste Estructural Vrs. Integración; los Vericuetos de la Política Regional de Costa Rica." *Polémica*, January-April, 27-38.

Morales Hernández, Francisco. 1989. "El Desafío Democrático Costarricense." In *Costa Rica: La Democracia Inconclusa*, ed. Manuel Rojas Bolaños et al. San José, Costa Rica: Editorial Dei.

Moran, Theodore. 1985. *MNCs*. Lexington, Mass.: Lexington.

Nabli, and Nugent, Jeffrey. 1989. "The New Institutional Economics and its Applicability to Development." *World Development*, Vol. 17, No. 9, 1333-47.

Nelson, Joan M. 1989. "Crisis Management, Economic Reform and Costa

Rican Democracy." In Barbara Stallings and Robert Kaufman, eds., *Debt and Democracy in Latin America*. Boulder, Colo.: Westview Press.

Neubauer, Deane E. 1967. "Some Conditions of Democracy." *American Political Science Review*, Vol. 81, December, 1002-1009.

Noé Pino, Hugo. 1988. "The Structural Roots of Crisis: Economic Growth and Decline in Honduras, 1950-1984." Diss., University of Texas at Austin.

Noé Pino, Hugo y Alcides Hernández. 1991. "La Economía Hondureña en los Años Ochenta y Perspectivas para los 90's." *Honduras: Crisis Económica y Procesos de Democratización Política*. Centro de Documentación de Honduras, Tegucigalpa.

Noé Pino, Hugo, and Mario Posas. 1991. "Honduras: los Actores Sociales y sus Proyectos." *Cuadernos CRIES*, No. 20, Managua.

Noé Pino, Hugo. 1991. "El Ajuste Estructural en Honduras." *Informe Especial*, CEDOH, Tegucigalpa, Honduras.

Noé Pino, Hugo. 1992. "Consideraciones Generales sobre el Ajuste Estructural en Honduras." Presentation at the VII Congreso Nacional de Economistas, Tegucigalpa, July 28-31.

North, Douglas. 1989. "Institutions and Economic Growth: An Historical Introduction" *World Development*, Vol. 17, No. 9, 1319-32.

Norton, Roger. 1992. "Perspectivos sobre las Políticas Macroeconómica y el Sector Agropecuario." Report prepared for the IICA. August.

Novosel, Pavao. 1982. "Komunikacija i Razvoj: Jedna jugoslavenska perspektiva (Communication and Development: A Yugoslav Perspective)." *Informatologia Yugoslavica*, Vol. 14, Nos. 3-4, 209-224.

Nowell, Gregg Patrick. 1988. *Realpolitik versus Transnational Rent-Seeking: French Mercantilism and the Development of the World Oil Cartel, 1860-1939*. Ph.D. diss., Massachussets Institute of Technology.

Nye, Jr., Joseph S. 1968. "Central American Regional Integration." In *International Regionalism: Readings*, ed. Joseph S. Nye, Jr. New York: Little, Brown & Co.

O'Donnell, Guillermo. 1973. *Modernization and Bureaucratic Authoritarianism*. Berkeley, Calif.: Institute for International Studies.

O'Donnell, Guillermo. 1978. "Reflections on the Patterns of Change in the Bureaucratic-Authoritarian State." *Latin American Research Review*, Vol. 13, 3-38.

O'Donnell, Guillermo, Philippe C. Schmitter, and Laurence Whitehead. 1986. *Transitions from Authoritarian Rule: Comparative Perspectives*. Baltimore: Johns Hopkins University Press.

Ohmae, Kenichi. 1991. *The Borderless World*. New York: Harper Business Press.

Oliver, James. 1990. "Commentary: Costa Rica's Atlantic Region: The Burden of the Banana Legacy." *Mesoamerica*, Vol. 9, Nos. 10-12, March.

Olsen, Mancur. 1963. "Rapid Growth as a Destabilizing Force." *Journal of Economic History*, Vol. 23, 529-52.

Owen, W. 1966. "The Double Development Squeeze in Agriculture." *The American Economic Review*, Vol. 66, No. 1, 43-70.

Parkin, Fred. 1978. *Orden Político y Desigualdades de Clase*. Madrid: Editorial Debate.

Pasic, Najdan, Stanislav Grozdanic, and Milorad Radevic. 1982. *Workers' Management in Yugoslavia: Recent Development and Trends*. Geneva: International Labour Office.

Pateman, Carole. 1970. *Participation and Democratic Theory* Cambridge: Cambridge University Press.

Paz Cafferate, Julio, et al. 1989. "El Sector Agropecuario en Honduras: Diagnóstico, Politicas y Recommendaciones." Chemonics International Consulting Division, Washington, D.C., February.

Peeler, John A. 1985. *Latin American Democracies: Colombia, Costa Rica, and Venezuela*. Chapel Hill: University of North Carolina Press.

Piore, Michael J., and Charles F. Sabel. 1984. *The Second Industrial Divide: Possibilities for Prosperity*. New York: Basic.

Porter, Michael. 1980. *Competitive Strategy*. New York: Free Press.

Porter, Michael. 1991. *The Competitive Advantage of Nations*. New York: Free Press.

Posas, Mario. 1979. "Política Estatal y Estructura Agraria en Honduras (1950-1978)." *Estudios Sociales Centroamericanos*, No. 19, San José de Costa Rica.

Putterman, L. 1983. "A Modified Collective Agriculture in Rural Growth-with-Equity: Reconsidering the Private Unimodal Approach." January, 77-100.

Pyatt, Graham, and Erik Thorbecke. 1976. *Planning Techniques for a Better Future*. Geneva: International Labour Office.

Ranis, Gustav. 1987. "Latin American Debt and Adjustment." *Journal of Development Economics*, Vol. 27, October, 189-99.

Rayback, Joseph. 1966. *A History of American Labor*. New York: Free Press.

Reding, Andrew. 1986. "Costa Rica: Democratic Model in Jeopardy." *World Policy Journal*, Vol. 3, 301-15.

Reich, Robert. 1990. *The Work of Nations: Preparing Ourselves for 21st Century Capitalism*. New York: Knopf.

Reich, Robert B. 1991. "Who is Them?" *Harvard Business Review*, Vol. 69, No. 2, March-April, 77-88.

Reuben, Sergio. 1988. *Ajuste Estructural en Costa Rica: Estudio Económico de Una Década*. San José: Editorial El Porvenir.

Rios, J. Leopoldo, and Jonatán Salgado. 1990. *Situación Actual del Cooperativismo en Centroamérica: Caso Guatemala*, monograph.

Ritzer, George. 1972. *Working: Conflict and Change*. Englewood Cliffs, N.J.: Prentice-Hall.

Rivera, Eugenio, et al. 1986. *Centroamérica: Política Económica y Crisis*. San José: DEI-ICADIS-UNA.

Riveros, Luis A., and Carlos E. Sánchez. 1990. "Argentina's Labor Markets in an Era of Adjustment." *World Bank Working Papers*, WPS 386, March.

Roach, John M. 1973. *Worker Participation: New Voices in Management*. New York: Conference Board.

Robbins, R. M. 1942. *Our Landed Heritage: The Public Domain, 1776-1970*. 2d ed. Lincoln and London: University of Nebraska Press.

Rodríguez, Ennio, et al. 1989. *De Cara al Nuevo Milenio*. San José: EUNED.

Rojas Viquez, Marielos. 1990. "Anuario del Cooperativismo en Costa Rica." Instituto de Investigaciones Sociales. San José: Universidad de Costa Rica.

Rojas Viquez, Marielos. 1991. *Una Visión Actual del Cooperativismo en Costa Rica*. San José, Costa Rica, Monograph.

Rourk, Phillip W. 1979. "Equitable Growth: The Case of Costa Rica." *Case Study in Development Assistance*, No. 6. USAID, Washington, D.C., July.

Rousseau, Jean-Jacques. 1968. *The Social Contract*. London: Penguin.

Rovira, Jorge. 1990. "Costa Rica: Partidos Políticos y Regimen Democrático." *Polémica* (San José), No. 11, segunda época, 44-60.

Ruben, Raúl. 1991. *El Problema Agrario en Honduras*. Centro de Documentación de Honduras. Tegucigalpa.

Rubner, Alex. 1990. *The Might of the MNCs*. Colorado: Praeger.

Rugman, Alan M. 1981. *Inside the Multinationals*. London: Croom Helm.

Rugman, Alan M. 1982. *New Theories of the MNE*. London: Croom Helm.

Santiago, Carlos E. 1989. "The Dynamics of Minimum Wage Policy in Economic Development: A Multiple Time Series Approach." *Economic Development and Cultural Change*, Vol. 38, No. 1, October.

Santiago, Carlos E., and Erik Thorbecke. 1988. "A Multisectoral Framework for the Analysis of Labor Mobility and Development in LDCs: An Application to Postwar Puerto Rico." *Economic*

Development and Cultural Change, Vol. 37, No. 1, October, 127-148.

Sauma, Pablo, and Juan Diego Trejos. 1990. *Evolución Reciente de la Distribución del Ingreso en Costa Rica*. Doc. No. 132, Instituto de Investigaciones Económicas de la Universidad de Costa Rica (IICE-UCR), June.

Schiller, B. 1989. *The Economics of Poverty & Discrimination*, 5th ed.

Schoolman, Morton, and Alvin Magid. 1986. *Reindustrializing New York State: Strategies, Implications, Challenges*. New York: State University of New York Press.

Schott, Jeffrey J. 1991. *Free Trade and U.S. Foreign Policy*. Washington, D.C.: Institute for International Economics.

Schultz, T. W. 1968. *Economic Growth and Agriculture*. New York: McGraw-Hill.

Seligson, Mitchell A., and Edward Muller. 1989. "Ordinary Elections in Extraoridinary Times: the Political Economy of Voting in Costa Rica." In *Elections and Democracy in Central America*, eds., John A. Booth and Mitchell Seligson. Chapel Hill: University of North Carolina Press.

Sethuraman, S. V. 1976. "The Urban Informal Sector: Concept, Measurement and Policy" *International Labour Review*, Vol. 114, July-August, 69-81.

Sheahan, John. 1987. *Patterns of Development in Latin America: Poverty, Repression, and Economic Strategy*. Princeton, N.J.: Princeton University Press.

Sigmund, Paul. 1980. *MNCs in Latin America*. Madison: University of Wisconsin Press.

Simmons, John, and William Mares. 1983. *Working Together*. New York: Knopf.

Singh, Inderjit, Lyn Squire, and John Strauss. 1986. *Agricultural Household Models: Extensions, Applications, and Policy*. Baltimore: Johns Hopkins University Press.

Smith, Arthur K., Jr. 1969. "Socioeconomic Development and Political Democracy: a Causal Analysis." *Midwest Journal of Political Science*, Vol. 13, 95-125.

Sobrado, Miguel, et al. 1988. *Quién Quiere la Guerra en Costa Rica: Un Análisis Documentado Sobre Hechos Ocurridos Entre 1982 a 1987*. San José: ICES-CRIES.

Sojo, Ana. 1990. "Las Politicas Sociales en Costa Rica." In *Los Años 90: Desarrollo Con Equidad?*, ed. Adolfo Gurrieri and Edelberto Torres-Rivas. San José: FLACSO-CEPAL.

Solnik, Bruno. 1991. *International Investments*. New York: Addison.

Stanley Foundation. 1992. *Changing Concepts of Sovereignty: Can the*

United Nations Keep Pace? Muscatine, Iowa: The Stanley Foundation.

Stave, Bruce M. 1975. *Socialism and the Cities*, ed. Port Washington, N.Y.: Kennikat.

Strange, Susan. 1986. *States and Markets*. New York: Basil Blackwell.

Strange, Susan. 1988. *Casino Capitalism*. New York: Basil Blackwell.

Taylor, Frederick Winslow. 1947. *Principles of Scientific Management*. New York: Harper and Row.

Terkel, Studs. 1974. *Working: People Talk About What They Do All Day and How They Feel About What They Do*. New York: Pantheon.

Thomas, H., and C. Logan. 1982. *Mondragón: An Economic Analysis*. London: Allen and Unwin.

Thorbecke, Erik. 1965. "The Role and Function of Agricultural Development in National Economic Growth." In *Economic Development and Agriculture*, ed. Erik Thorbecke. Ames, Iowa: Iowa State University Press.

Thorbecke, Erik. 1980. "Agriculture and Economic Development" *Social Research*, Vol. 47, 290-304.

Thorpe, Andy. 1992. "Caminos Políticos y Económicos hacia la Reactivación del Sector Agropecuario Hondureño: Una vez Entendido el Ajuste," draft.

Todaro, Michael P. 1969. "A Model of Labor Migration and Urban Unemployment in Less Developed Countries." *American Economic Review*, Vol. 59, No. 1, March, 139-48.

Torres-Rivas, Edelberto. 1980. "Vida y Muerte en Guatemala: Reflexiones Sobre la Crisis y la Violencia Política." *Foro Internacional* (Mexico), Vol. 20, April-June, 549-74.

Torres-Rivas, Edelberto. 1987. *Centroamerica: La Democracia Posible*. San José: EDUCA-FLACSO.

Torres-Rivas, Edelberto. 1988. "Centroamerica: Transiciones Autoritarias Hacia la Democracia." *Polémica* (San José), No. 4, segunda epoca, January-April, 1-13.

Torres-Rivas, Edelberto. 1989. *Interpretación del Desarrollo Social Centroamericano*. San José: 12a. edición, FLACSO.

Ulate, Annabelle, and Ennio Rodriguez. 1983. "Costa Rica en los Años 80: Un Caso de Estrangulamiento Externo. Antecedents y Perspectivas." In *Costa Rica Hoy: La Crisis Y Sus Perspectivas*, ed., Jorge Rovira. San José: EUNED.

United Nations Center on Transnational Corporations. 1988. *TNCs in World Developments*. New York: United Nations.

United Nations Center on Transnational Corporations. 1989. "FDI Flows in the Mid-1980s." *CTC Reporter*, No. 27, Spring.

United Nations Center on Transnational Corporations. 1989. "UNCTC's

Billion Dollar Club Database." *CTC Reporter*, No. 28, Autumn.

United States Agency for International Development-Honduras. 1990. Agricultural Sector Strategy Paper." Office of Agriculture and Rural Development. Tegucigalpa, Honduras, February.

United States Congress. 1976. "Broadening the Ownership of New Capital: ESOPs and Other Alternatives." Joint Economic Committee, 94th Congress, 2nd Session. Washington, D.C.: U.S. Government Printing Office.

United States Congress. 1978. "Employee-Community Ownership to Save Jobs When Firms Shut Down." *Congressional Record*, 95th Congress, 2nd Session.

United States Senate. 1980. "The Role of the Federal Government in Employee Ownership of Business." Select Committee on Small Business, 96th Congress, 2nd Session. Washington, D.C.: U.S. Government Printing Office.

Valdés, Alberto. 1986. "Impact of Trade and Macroeconomic Policies on Agricultural Growth: The South American Experience." In *Economic and Social Progress in Latin America*. Interamerican Development Bank, Washington, D.C.

Valenzuela, Arturo. 1978. *The Breakdown of Democratic Regimes: Chile*. Baltimore: Johns Hopkins University Press.

Vargas Cullell, Jorge. 1987. "La Militarizacion y la Reestructuración Nacional de Costa Rica." In *Centroamerica: La Guerra de Baja Intensidad*, eds., Raúl Vergara Meneses et al. San José: CRIES-DEI.

Vega Carballo, José Luis. 1982. *Poder Político y Democracia en Costa Rica*. San José: Editorial El Porvenir.

Vega Carballo, José Luis. 1983. "Podria Sobrevivir la Democracia Costaricense?" *Polémica* (San José), No. 12, November-December, 4-29.

Vega Carballo, José Luis. 1987. *Hacia Una Interpretación del Desarrollo Costaricense: Ensayo Sociológico*. San José: DEI.

Vega Carballo, José Luis, 1987. "Partidos, Desarrollo Politico y Conflicto Social en Honduras y Costa Rica: un Análisis Comparativo." *Polémica* (San José), No. 1, segunda epoca, 43-59.

Vega Carballo, José Luis. 1983. "Central American Modernization: a Choice of Bullets or Ballots." *Harvard International Review*. Vol. 6, 10-13.

Vega Carballo, José Luis. 1990. "Costa Rica: Conjunturas, Classes Sociales en Su História Reciente, 1930-1975." In *America Latina: Historia de Meio Seculo*, ed. Pablo Gonzez Casanova and José Luis Vega Carballo. Brasilia: Editora Universidade de Brasília.

Vernon, Raymond. 1972. *Storm Over the Multinationals*. Cambridge:

Harvard University Press.

Ward, Barbara. 1962. *The Rich Nations and the Poor Nations*. New York: Norton.

Whyte, William Foote, et al. 1983. *Worker Participation and Ownership: Cooperative Strategies for Strengthening Local Communities*. Ithaca, N.Y.: New York State School of Labor and Industrial Relations, Cornell University.

Whyte, William Foote, and Kathleen King Whyte. 1988. *Making Mondragón: The Growth and Dynamics of the Worker Cooperative Complex*. Ithaca, N.Y.: New York State School of Labor and Industrial Relations, Cornell University.

Williamson, John. 1990a. *Latin American Adjustment*. Washington, D.C.: Institute for International Economics.

Williamson, John. 1990b. *Progress of Policy Reform in Latin America*. Washington, D.C.: Institute for International Economics.

Wootton, Graham. 1967. *Workers, Unions, and the State*. New York: Schocken.

World Bank. 1991. *World Development Report*. Washington, D.C.: World Bank.

Worrell, DeLisle. 1990. "The Caribbean." In *Latin American Adjustment*, ed. John Williamson. Washington, D.C.: Institute for International Economics.

Index

Agrarian Reform Law of 1962
(Honduras), 81, 93
Agrarian Reform Law of 1975
(Honduras), 99n15
Agricultural Modernization Law
(Honduras), 76
Agriculture: collective, 71, 72, 82;
colonization projects, 81, 82;
commercial, 64, 69, 76;
cooperatives in, 130, 132, 134,
135; exports, 9, 47; family, 62,
66, 68, 73, 77n1; Honduran,
79-98; and income distribu-
tion, 71; modernization in, 9,
77n1; part-time, 70; plantation,
74; pricing structures, 87;
reform in, 8; subsistence, 68;
tenant, 74, 78n12
Agro-business, 28
Alliance for Progress, 32, 130
Andean Pact, 155, 161
Arizmendi, José María, 115
Astiz, Carlos, 11, 161-178
Austerity, 11
Autarky, 145
Authoritarianism, 3, 4, 18, 35;

military-oligarchic, 39n1
Automation, 107

Baker Plan, 184
BANAFOM. See National Bank of
Public Works (Honduras)
Banco Nacional de Desarrollo
Agrario (Honduras), 134
Blocs, trading, 3, 12, 196, 201
Bolivia, 44
Brady Plan, 184
Bretton Woods Agreement, 146,
189
Bureaucracy, 104; agrarian, 76;
Costa Rican, 31; cuts in, 30;
paternalistic, 31
Bush, George, 105, 184, 202

CACM. See Central American
Common Market
Caja Laboral Popular (Spain),
115, 116, 117
Capital: access to, 149; accounts,
147; accumulation, 64;
exports, 154; flight, 48;
foreign, 95; formation, 5, 22,

77n1, 82, 129; goods, 46;
human, 53, 75; investment,
148; long-term, 147; mobility, 104; productive, 64;
short-term, 147;
transnational, 133
Caribbean Basin Initiative,
196, 197
Cartagena Agreement, 184
Center-periphery relations, 32,
34
Central America: agrarian
policy, 70-73;
cooperativism in, 129-140;
economic integration in,
201-208; exploitation of,
202; external debt in, 181-
190; foreign intervention
in, 15; in global economy,
191-200; internationalization of, 15; political
integration, 161-176
Central American Common
Market, 6, 20, 22, 26, 80,
171
Central American Foundation
for Integration, 171, 175,
191
Central American Parliament,
171, 172
Central American Research
Institute, 88
Central Bank of Honduras, 80-
81
Centrism, 29-32
"Chicago Boys," 36
Chile, 44
Clientelism, 31, 34
Communism, 32
Compensation programs, 29;
social, 33
CONADI. See Honduran
Corporation of Investments

Consumer price index, 24, 39n3
Consumption, per capita, 23
Cooperativism, 10, 129-140;
characteristics of, 134-138;
in Mondragón (Spain) 115-
117, 118, 121, 122, 123;
problems in, 138-139
Corporations, multinational, 3,
10, 105, 129, 139, 143-157;
in globalization of production, 10-11; role in eco-
nomic restructuring, 10-11
Corruption, 35, 91
Cosmocorps. See Corporations,
multinational
Costa Rica: abolition of military, 17, 19; agrarian
sector, 22; autonomy of,
15; centrism in, 29-32;
civil war, 30; class structure, 20, 26; as constitutional democracy, 15;
consumer price index, 25,
39n3; cooperatives in, 130,
131, 132, 133, 134, 135, 136;
debt service, 164; economic
crisis, 7, 22-26, 48; economic
recovery in, 4; emergency
programs, 33, 34; employee
stock option plans (ESOPs)
in, 109; external debt in, 181,
182; foreign aid to, 33-35;
gross domestic product, 5,
20, 22, 164, 165; gross
national product, 47; growth
rate, 164; income distribution, 166; industrial sector,
22; international debt of,
163; isolationism in, 20;
opposition parties in, 172;
per capita consumption, 23;
per capita income, 4;
political stability in, 8;

political systems, 30-32;
public policies, 33-35;
social development of, 13-
38; socioeconomic evolu-
tion, 7; socioeconomic
indicators, 5; socio-occupational structure, 26, 27, 28,
29; state intervention, 164;
structural adjustment in, 14,
47-50; unemployment in, 24;
United States' relations
with, 19, 33, 39n1
"Coyotes," 91-92
Credit, access to, 9
Crime, organized, 34
Currency: common, 168;
devaluation, 47, 48, 50, 84,
89, 145, 153; exchange, 22;
fixed rates, 146; foreign,
21, 22; inflation, 149;
markets, 152; spot, 147
Current accounts: balances on,
44, 45; deficits in, 21, 35,
146

Debt: crises, 76; foreign, 33,
38; international, 163;
land, 64; in less developed
countries, 147; leveraged,
151; to official sources,
182; pooling, 185; private,
45; public, 23, 45; resched-
uling, 47, 48, 181, 184, 185;
servicing, 44, 45, 46, 147,
148, 156, 181, 182, 183, 186;
social, 207; swapping for
bonds, 186-187
Debt, external, 6, 8, 11, 12, 22,
43-47, 45, 84, 94, 181-190
Deindustrialization, 108
de la Ossa, Alvaro, 11-12, 191-
200
Democracy: Costa Rican, 16;

industrial, 9, 10, 103-123;
participatory, 103; "pro-
tected," 17, 32, 36; "re-
stricted," 17; survival of,
18
Demographic change, 49, 77n3
Denationalization, 48
Development: agrarian, 8;
agricultural, 61, 67;
commodity program, 67;
cultural, 199; dualistic, 53;
economic, 133; export
promotion, 43; industrial,
21; infrastructural, 67;
institutional, 62, 65, 69,
73, 75; socioeconomic, 32;
strategies, 6; and structural
inequities, 7
Developmentalism, 16
DGEC. See Dirección General
de Estadística y Censos
Dirección General de
Estadística y Censos, 24
Distribution-Preemption Act of
1841, 68
Dominican Republic: gross
national product, 47; labor
costs, 50; migration rates,
49, 50; real wages, 50;
structural adjustment in,
44, 47-50

ECLA. See Economic Commission for Latin America
Economic: austerity, 10; crises,
4, 22-26, 30, 48, 133; dependency, 189, 194; develop-
ment, 133; diversification,
80; globalization, 181-200;
growth, 31, 43; indicators,
45; integration, 5, 11, 192,
201-208; liberalization, 8, 43,
48, 79, 83, 86; management,

193; nationalism, 145;
recovery, 3; restructuring,
3; stabilization, 11; stagnation, 50
Economic Commission for
Latin America, 16, 24, 97-
98, 194, 205
Economic Secretariat for Latin
America, 184
Economy: agro-industrial, 31;
closed, 58; command, 144;
home, 34; industrial, 46;
informalization of, 34;
open, 58, 97; rural, 67; of
scale, 145, 146, 168; social
sectors, 129
Education, 24, 97; agricultural,
69; and agriculture, 62;
declining expenditures, 46;
demand for, 68; and farm
ownership, 68; land-grant
system, 69; public, 31, 73,
77n8; public land for, 68;
role in empowerment, 66-
67; rural, 65
El Salvador, 20; civil war in, 3;
cooperatives in, 130, 131,
132, 134, 135, 136; debt
service, 164; economic
crisis in, 23; gross domestic
product, 5, 164, 165; growth
rate, 164; income distribution, 166; international debt
of, 163; opposition parties
in, 172; socioeconomic
indicators, 5; state intervention, 130, 164; war with
Honduras, 38
Emigration. See Migration
Employee stock option plans,
10, 109-111, 122-123
Empowerment: externalities, 63-
66; of workers, 10

Empresa Nacional de Algodón
(Nicaragua), 134
ESOPs. See Employee stock
option plans
Esquipulas Agreement, 32,
171, 172
European Coal and Steel
Community, 169
European Economic Commu-
nity, 106, 147, 153, 162,
168, 170, 185, 190
Exchange, foreign, 83
Exchange rates, 84, 85, 86, 87,
99n5, 106, 146; bias in, 46
Export(s): agricultural, 47,
134; competitive, 89; of
culture, 199; diversification
of, 48; earnings, 149;
labor-intensive, 51; non-
traditional, 8, 43, 46, 48,
83, 84, 93, 96, 194; policy,
6; promotion, 8, 30, 43, 46,
61, 69, 76, 85; quotas, 107;
subsidized, 46, 48; support
for, 97; tax, 106; tradi-
tional, 22, 79, 83, 84, 93,
97

Family Allotment Program
(Honduras), 85
FFDE. See Fiduciary Fund of
Foreign Debt
Fiduciary Fund of Foreign Debt,
185, 186, 187
Figueres, José, 17, 31

GATT. See General Agreement
on Tariffs and Trade
General Agreement on Tariffs
and Trade, 48, 144, 145,
189, 197, 199; Uruguay
Round, 153
Globalization, 181-200

Goldstein, Walter, 11, 143-159
González del Valle, Jorge, 11, 181-190
Granger movement, 69
Great Society, 32
Gross domestic product, 5, 44, 45; Costa Rican, 20, 22
Gross national product, 144, 147, 148, 163; Costa Rica, 47; Dominican Republic, 47; Jamaica, 47
Group of Seven, 144, 147, 154
Guatemala: cooperatives in, 131, 132, 134, 135, 136; debt service, 164; gross domestic product, 5, 164, 165; growth rate, 164; income distribution, 166; international debt of, 163; socioeconomic indicators, 5; state intervention, 165

Haiti, 44
Havana Treaty, 189
Helsinki Accords, 192
Homestead Act, 62, 66, 68, 74, 78n9
Honduran Corporation of Investments, 82
Honduran Forest Development Corporation, 81
Honduran Fund for Social Investment, 84, 85
Honduran Institute of Agricultural Marketing, 81
Honduras, 20; agrarian reform in, 72; Agricultural Modernization Law, 76; agriculture in, 8-9, 79-98; cooperatives in, 130, 131, 132, 133, 135, 136; debt service, 164; economic crisis, 82; economic expan-

sion, 80; exports, 80, 82, 96; external debt in, 182-183; gross domestic product, 5, 80, 164, 165; gross national product, 82; income distribution, 166; international debt of, 163; opposition parties in, 172; socioeconomic indicators, 5; state intervention, 164; structural adjustment in, 9, 79-98; United States' relations with, 39n1; war with El Salvador, 38
Hong Kong, 145
Housing, 24

IDB. See Interamerican Development Bank
IICA. See Central American Research Institute
IMF. See International Monetary Fund
Immigration. See Migration
Import(s), 44, 105; duties on, 48; financing of, 46; increasing, 182; of investment capital, 148; moratoria on, 182; price declines in, 52; quotas, 48; subsidization of, 106; tariff reduction on, 51; taxes on, 84
Income: distribution, 28, 31, 61, 71, 76, 77n3, 96, 165, 166, 195; farm-derived, 70; inequality, 6, 23; per capita, 4, 25-26, 156; redistribution, 97; rural-urban inequality, 24, 25, 28, 29
Indexation, 50
Industrial: bonds, 64; decision making, 104, 111-112; democracy, 9, 10, 103-123;

development, 21; economy,
46; labor, 103, 104; peace,
109; production, 10, 98,
107; protectionism, 85, 86,
87
Industrialization: import
substitution, 9, 20, 21, 46,
85, 86, 97, 149, 155;
undermining, 194; and
urban migration, 73
Industrial Revolution, 103,
124n2
Industry: community ownership
of, 108; cooperatives in,
109, 132, 135; job loss in,
105, 108; mass-production,
121-122; non-traditional, 47;
urban, 93; worker ownership
of, 108-111
Inflation, 22, 48, 50, 79, 83, 147
Infrastructure, 4

Initiative for the Americas, 193,
196, 197
Institute of Agrarian Development (Costa Rica), 94
Instituto Mixto de Ayuda
Social (Costa Rica), 134
Instituto Nacional del Café (El
Salvador), 134
Instituto Nacional de
Transformación Agraria
(Guatemala), 134
Insurgency, 13
Integration: complementarity
in, 162-166; economic, 5,
11, 192, 201-208; national,
10; political, 5, 11, 161-
176; regional, 10, 11, 12,
20, 21, 139, 162-176, 206;
role of sovereignty in, 167-
169; and socio-cultural
diversity, 169-173

Interamerican Development
Bank, 22-23, 24, 183, 185
International Monetary Fund,
30, 33, 43, 48, 165, 167,
182, 183, 184, 185, 189,
204; Special Drawing
Rights, 47
Interest rates, 10, 104, 106,
146, 147
International Organization of
Trade, 189
Investment: in agricultural
research, 65; capital, 148;
diversifying, 149; foreign,
48, 93, 106, 107; foreign
direct, 6, 11, 45, 46, 47, 143-
157; in free trade zones, 48;
gross domestic, 5, 45;
international, 10; Japanese,
106; public, 65; reduction in,
21
Isolationism, 194, 195; Costa
Rican, 20

Jamaica: gross national product, 47; labor costs, 50;
migration rates, 49; real
wages, 50; structural
adjustment in, 47-50
Jamestown Area Labor-Man-
agement Committee, 112-
113, 122
Japan, 10, 106-107
Johnson, Lyndon, 32
Junta Fundadora (Costa Rica),
30-31

Kelso, Louis O., 110
Kennedy, John F., 32

Labor: added-worker phenomenon, 52; costs, 48, 50;
division of, 18, 107, 148,

156; elasticity of demand
for, 57; family, 26, 27, 34, 53,
56, 57, 59n8; foreign, 113;
indentured, 74; industrial, 9,
103, 104; inelastic supply,
51; informal market, 24;
management cooperation,
111-113; marginalization
of, 58; market adjustments,
51-58; markets, 43, 44, 50;
migration, 68; mobility, 52;
movements, 35; organized,
9, 109. See also Unions,
trade; skilled, 46, 52;
underutilization, 50;
unskilled, 52; wage, 53, 56,
57, 58
Land: access to, 90, 94; banks,
94; debt, 64; distribution,
62, 63-66, 76, 77n1, 77n5,
93, 94; distribution inequities, 9; ordinances, 67;
public, 68; reconcentration,
72; reform, 63, 70, 71, 81;
social function, 93; tax, 88;
tenure, 61, 67, 69, 87, 88,
89, 90; titling, 72, 93,
100n24; transfer of, 64, 74;
use, 88, 89
Latin American Economic
System, 161
Latin American Free Trade
Area, 161
Law for Modernization and
Agricultural Development
(Honduras), 86, 89-95,
99n6
Law of Structural Regulation of
the Economy (Honduras),
83, 84, 85, 89
Letter of Rights and Economic
Obligations of States, 203-
204

Liberalization: commercial, 95;
economic, 8, 43, 48, 79,
83, 86; effects of, 51; of
land policies, 67; market,
61, 139; price, 85; sectoral
impact, 53-55; trade, 52,
91, 92
Loans: agricultural, 92; commercial, 182; from official
institutions, 182; private,
43; public, 92
Lomé Accords, 193, 195

Magid, Alvin, 3-12, 103-127
Maquiladoras, 145, 147
Marginalization, 11, 192, 193;
of labor force, 58
Market(s): access to, 87, 88,
95, 144, 154; competition
for, 193; credit, 146;
currency, 152; distortions,
98; domestic, 5, 30, 168, 192;
family labor, 34; foreign, 5,
30; global, 78n14; informal,
24, 26, 59n2; interdepen-
dence, 21; labor, 43, 44, 50,
51-55; liberalization, 61, 139;
local, 88, 149; mass, 149,
150; niche, 149; offshore,
144; protection of, 129;
regional, 21
Melmed-Sanjak, Jolyne, 3-12,
61-78
MERCOSUR, 161, 173, 177n23
Mexico: agrarian policies, 75-
76; debt crisis, 183;
structural adjustment in,
44, 71
Migration, 35, 37, 49, 55;
circular, 49, 55; external,
58; interregional, 81; labor,
68; place-to-place, 55; rural-
urban, 55; state promotion

of, 55; urban 73, 93
Military: abolition in Costa Rica,
    17, 19, 36; expenditures, 36;
    institutionalized, 29;
    regional, 168
Mill-Marshallian model, 62,
    65, 69, 76, 77n1
Ministerio de Agricultura y
    Ganaderia (Panama), 134
MNCs. See Corporations,
    multinational
Mondragón (Spain), coopera-
    tives in, 115-117, 118, 121,
    122, 123
Morrill Act, 62

NAFTA. See North American
    Free Trade Agreement
National Agrarian Bank, 92
National Agrarian Institute
    (Honduras), 81, 88
National Association of Women
    Peasants (Honduras), 94
National Bank for Agricultural
    Development (Honduras),
    99n1
National Bank for Development
    of the Agricultural Sector
    (Honduras), 88
National Bank of Public Works
    (Honduras), 81
National Economic Council
    (Honduras), 81
NATO. See North Atlantic
    Treaty Organization
Nicaragua, 19; civil war in, 3,
    30; cooperatives in, 130,
    131, 132, 133, 134, 135, 136;
    debt service, 164; economic
    crisis in, 23; external debt
    in, 181, 182; gross domestic
    product, 5, 164, 165; growth
    rate, 164; income distribu-

tion, 166; international debt
    of, 163; opposition parties
    in, 172; socioeconomic
    indicators, 5
Noé Pino, Hugo, 8-9, 79-101
North American Free Trade
    Agreement, 19, 124n1, 205
North Atlantic Treaty Organi-
    zation, 16

OAS. See Organization of
    American States
OECD. See Organization for
    Economic Cooperation and
    Development
Organization for Economic
    Cooperation and Develop-
    ment, 143, 156
Organization of American
    States, 205
Organization of Central Ameri-
    can States, 171, 177n18
Ortega, Daniel, 19

Panama, 3; cooperatives in,
    130, 131, 132, 135, 136; debt
    service, 164; gross domestic
    product, 5, 164, 165; growth
    rate, 164; income distribu-
    tion, 166; international debt
    of, 163; socioeconomic
    indicators, 5; state interven-
    tion, 164
Paris Club, 48, 186
Partido de Liberación Nacional
    (Costa Rica), 20
Partido Unidad Social Cristiana
    (Costa Rica). See Social
    Christian Unity Party
Paternalism, 31, 138
Peru, 44
PLN. See Partido de Liberación
    Nacional

PLN (Costa Rica), 31, 32
Policies: agrarian, 61-77, 82;
    economic reactivation, 83;
    export, 6; foreign, 29, 32,
    168; public, 33-35; restruc-
    turing, 9; socioeconomic
    development, 32; stabiliza-
    tion, 10, 83; wage, 28
Political systems: Costa Rican,
    30-32; multiparty, 30;
    opposition parties, 30, 172,
    177n22; participation in,
    30, 32, 36; "penetrated,"
    167; public support for, 29;
    two-party, 29, 32, 33, 34
Population: growth, 49; nutri-
    tional security of, 97; rural
    marginalization, 82
Populism, 16
Poverty, 6, 23, 24, 44, 74, 145
Presidential Declaration of
    Guadalajara, 197
Price: controls, 48; of credit,
    148; stabilization, 92;
    strategy, 150; structure, 87;
    systems, 98; volatility, 92
Privatization, 4, 43, 47, 129;
    agricultural, 70, 72, 73; of
    state enterprises, 83, 85,
    98, 165
Production: agricultural, 69;
    costs, 145, 148, 150;
    diversification of, 22;
    globalization of, 3, 11;
    household, 44, 58; incen-
    tives, 98; industrial, 98,
    107; internationalization of,
    148; market-oriented
    surplus, 69; per capita, 22
Productivity: agricultural, 69,
    77n3, 88; decline of, 10, 103;
    industrial, 10
Profit-seeking, 64-65, 73

Proposal for Latin America and
    the Caribbean of 1990, 184
Protectionism, 9, 38, 46, 107,
    144, 146, 149, 153, 192;
    domestic, 139; industrial,
    85, 86, 87
Pueblo Unido (Costa Rica), 32
Puerto Rico: economic growth,
    47; migration rates, 49;
    real wages, 50; structural
    adjustment in, 47-50;
    United States' relations
    with, 47

Quito Declaration of 1984, 184

Ramírez, Dante, 12, 201-208
Ranching, cattle, 9, 86, 99n14
Reagan, Ronald, 19, 105
Recession, 19, 33, 106, 153,
    183, 192
Reform: agrarian, 8, 9, 62, 64,
    65, 71, 75, 82, 87, 94, 95,
    99n2; banking, 47; demo-
    cratic, 3; failures, 32;
    institutional, 80; land, 63,
    70, 71, 81; policy, 6;
    pricing, 87; productive
    impact, 63; social, 20;
    state, 30; tax, 47; work-
    place, 104
Reindustrialization, 9, 103-
    123; and industrial democ-
    racy, 121-123
Religion, 34
Rent-seeking, 64-65, 70
Resources: access to, 98;
    allocation of, 63, 86, 97,
    98; conservation of, 89;
    depletion of, 6; distribution,
    66; exploitation of, 95;
    natural, 6; public, 46
Rights: civil, 31; human, 31;

property, 78n15
Rojas Viquez, Marielos, 9, 10,
    129-141

Santiago, Carlos, 3-12, 43-60
Sector, agrarian: Costa Rican,
    22; restructuring, 9
Sector, formal, 50; employment
    in, 54-55; wages in, 52
Sector, industrial, 22
Sector, informal, 26, 57; as
    employer of last resort, 56;
    growth of, 50; urban, 44,
    53, 59n4; wages in, 50, 52,
    59n2
Sector, private: in agriculture,
    73; Costa Rican, 31;
    emergency programs, 34;
    technology in, 94; wages,
    28
Sector, productive, 30
Sector, public, 89, 165; Costa
    Rican, 26, 28, 34; wages,
    28
Sector, urban, 34
SELA. See Economic Secre-
    tariat for Latin America
Singapore, 145
Sinking fund, 186-187
"Soccer War," 20
Social: benefits, 129; compen-
    sation, 85, 133; conflict,
    34, 138; consciousness, 12;
    debt, 30, 207; expenses, 33,
    84; inequality, 23; mobil-
    ity, 28, 29, 31; movements,
    31; peace, 8, 13, 32; prob-
    lems, 133; programs, 36;
    reform, 20; spending, 30;
    stability, 28; stratification,
    23; structure, 23; welfare,
    76; well-being, 26
Social Accounting Matrix, 53-

55, 59n4
Social Christian Unity Party,
    32, 35, 36
Socialism, 18
South Korea, 144, 145
Spain, 115-117
Stagnation, 3, 4, 13, 79, 193
Standard of living, 76; Costa
    Rican, 28, 33; decline in,
    3, 4; rural, 54, 70
State: economic role, 164;
    inability to promote em-
    ployment, 55; intervention,
    31, 33-34, 34-35, 48, 55,
    79, 81, 83, 86, 89, 97, 130,
    138; ownership of enter-
    prise, 48; reform, 30; role
    reduction, 129
Stone Container Agreement, 95
Structural adjustment, 8, 44-
    58, 75, 129, 133, 138, 139,
    181; in agriculture, 9, 63,
    70-73, 79-98; Costa Rican,
    14, 47-50; and debt re-
    scheduling, 183; Domini-
    can Republic, 44, 47-50;
    and external debt, 184,
    190; Honduran, 9; Jamai-
    can, 47-50; and land
    tenure, 61; Puerto Rican,
    47-50; social consequences
    of, 85
Structural resistance, 26-29
Subsidization, 84; agricultural,
    62, 70, 72
Sweden, 113-114

Taiwan, 144, 145
Tariffs, 153, 156; bias in, 46;
    policy coordination, 92;
    reduction in, 51, 52, 84, 89,
    92, 197; surcharges on, 84
Tavistock Work Research

Institute, 112
Tax: corporate, 48; on exports, 106; import, 84; land, 88; profit, 84; reform, 47; on tourism, 47
Taylorism, 103, 109, 117, 121
Technology, 21, 121; access to, 87, 139; acquisition of, 46; changing, 192; firm-specific, 148, 155; gap, 193; transfer of, 94, 199
Tourism, 47, 48
Trade: barriers, 149; blocs, 3, 12, 196, 201; deficits, 10, 104, 105-106, 153, 154; foreign, 44, 85, 91, 97, 183; free, 48, 50, 145, 146, 155, 171, 189; international, 10, 104, 105, 144-145; intra-firm, 145; liberalization, 52, 91, 92; managed, 146; North-South, 156; regional, 171; terms of, 22, 89, 163; theoretical model, 51; unions, 31, 59n3, 103, 111, 113; warfare, 145, 156; West-West, 144
Transnationalism, 12
Trifinio Plan, 177n20
Trist, Eric, 112
Tuxtla Gutiérrez Agreement, 196, 197

UNCTAD, 145, 156
Unemployment, 26, 27, 51, 55, 61, 79; Costa Rican, 22, 24; non-trivial, 51; queing, 51, 52; rural, 93
Unions, trade, 31, 59n3, 103, 111, 113
United Nations, 143, 145, 202; Fund for Economic Promotion, 204; reassessment of

structure, 12; reevaluation of, 204-205
United Provinces of Central America, 170
United States: agrarian policy, 61-70; Costa Rican relations with, 19, 33, 39n1; as debtor nation, 105-106, 147-148; Honduran relations with, 39n1; in international trade, 105; Japanese investment in, 106; Japanese relations with, 10, 106-107; Puerto Rican relations with, 47; and reindustrialization, 107-108; trade deficits, 153-154
United States Agency for International Development, 30, 33, 85, 87, 88
Urbanization, 54
Uruguay, 21
USAID. See United States Agency for International Development

Vega Carballo, José Luis, 7-8, 13-39

Wage(s), 103; declining, 51, 53; fixed, 59n3; floors, 59n3; minimum, 50, 51, 52; policies, 28; private sector, 28; public sector, 28; repression, 30, 43, 48, 57; reservation, 55; virtual, 59n7
Whyte, William Foote, 112
Women: in agriculture, 94; in cooperatives, 138; in labor market, 52
Workers: alienation of, 103, 111; cooperatives, 123,

124n2; empowerment of, 10;
family, 26, 27; industrial,
103, 104; participation of,
10, 110, 122; preferences,
122; salaried, 27
World Bank, 30, 33, 43, 47, 48,
88, 165, 167, 182, 183, 185,
89, 204

Yugoslavia, 117-120, 124n4-17

Contributors

CARLOS A. ASTIZ is professor with joint appointments in the Department of Political Science and the Department of Latin American and Caribbean Studies in the State University of New York at Albany.

ALVARO DE LA OSSA is president of the Fundación Centroamericana por la Integración in San José, Costa Rica. Formerly, he was an official of the United Nations Development Programme.

WALTER GOLDSTEIN is professor in the Department of Political Science in the State University of New York at Albany.

JORGE GONZÁLEZ DEL VALLE is an economist with Consultores Financieros de Guatemala in Guatemala City. Formerly, he was director of the Centro de Estudios Monetarios de América Latina in Mexico City.

ALVIN MAGID is professor with joint appointments in the Department of Political Science, the Department of Latin American and Caribbean Studies, and the Department of East Asian Studies in the State University of New York at Albany.

JOLYNE MELMED-SANJAK is assistant professor with joint appointments in the Department of Economics and the Department of Latin American and Caribbean Studies in the State University of New York at Albany.

HUGO NOÉ PINO is a professor of economics and director of the Postgrado Centroamericano en Economía y Planificación del Desarrollo in the National Autonomous University of Honduras at Tegucigalpa.

DANTE RAMÍREZ is an economist with the Permanent Secretariat of the General Treaty for Central American Economic Integration in Guatemala City.

MARIELOS ROJAS VIQUEZ is a professor in the Institute of Social Research in the University of Costa Rica at San José.

CARLOS E. SANTIAGO is associate professor with joint appointments in the Department of Economics and the Department of Latin American and Caribbean Studies in the State University of New York at Albany. He is also associate director of the Center for Latin America and the Caribbean in the University at Albany.

JOSÉ LUIS VEGA CARBALLO is a professor in the School of Political Science in the University of Costa Rica at San José.